www.standort-deutschland.com

Wirtschafts- und Wissenschaftsstandort Dresden

Chancen und Perspektiven einer Stadt

Opportunities and prospects of a city

EUROPÄISCHER WIRTSCHAFTS VERLAG
Landeshauptstadt Dresden
2001/2002

Vorwort/Foreword

Sehr geehrte Damen und Herren,

Weltweit konkurrieren die Städte heute um die Gunst von Investoren. Dabei wird es immer wichtiger, sich von anderen Wirtschaftsstandorten durch seine standorteigenen Vorteile positiv zu unterscheiden. Jeder Unternehmensstandort in Deutschland bietet spezielle Vorteile für die Ansiedlung von neuen Betrieben, nationalen und internationalen Investoren. In der Vielzahl von miteinander konkurrierenden Regionen liegt aber auch die Chance einer Stadt, durch besondere Qualifikationen die Entscheidung zur Standortwahl positiv für sich zu beeinflussen.

Die Landeshauptstadt Dresden gehört heute beim Wirtschaftswachstum zur europäischen Spitze, sie ist zu einem Magneten für die internationale Hightech-Industrie geworden. Hier investieren Welt-Unternehmen wie Infineon Technologies, AMD und VW. Für das Ziel Dresdens, einen Platz unter den Top 10 der deutschen Wirtschaft einzunehmen, gibt es realistische Chancen.

Der Name Dresden ist seit Jahrhunderten mit Innovationen verbunden. Porzellan, das weiße Gold, ist hier erfunden worden, die erste deutsche Dampflokomotive konstruierten und montierten Dresdner Ingenieure und Maschinenbauer, und Weltpremiere hatte hier an der Elbe auch die erste Kleinbild-Spiegelreflexkamera.

Mit der politischen Wende hat in der Stadt eine neue Gründerzeit begonnen. Mehr als 38.000 Gewerbe sind inzwischen angemeldet, 150 Hektar Gewerbeflächen, preiswert und verkehrsgünstig, stehen für weitere Neuansiedlungen zur Verfügung.

Dieses Buch will dem interessierten Leser die Region aus verschiedenen Perspektiven näher bringen. Es beleuchtet die wesentlichen wirtschaftlich relevanten Faktoren und portraitiert eine repräsentative Auswahl von in der Region ansässigen Unternehmen. Außerdem vermittelt es einen Einblick in Kultur, Kunst, Geschichte und Landschaft.

Zwinger, Semperoper, Gemäldegalerie, Grünes Gewölbe, Kreuzchor, Staatskapelle, Dixielandfestival, Filmnächte – nur wenig europäische Städte können ein so reichhaltiges Angebot vorweisen. Jeder Besucher – jährlich kommen immerhin sieben Millionen – ist von der berühmten Silhouette und dem unverwechselbaren Charme beeindruckt.

Dieses in Zusammenarbeit mit der Stadt Dresden entstandene Werk soll neben dem informativen und unterhaltenden Stellenwert auch eine praktische Aufgabe erfüllen. Es soll Koopera-

tionen und neue Geschäftskontakte mit den in diesem Buch präsentierten Firmen und Ihnen als Leser dieses Werkes fördern.
Das Buch ist ein wichtiger Bestandteil des bundesweiten Standardwerkes zu deutschen Wirtschaftsregionen und international auch im Internet unter der Adresse „www.standort-deutschland.com" präsent.
Möglicherweise ist Dresden ja auch Ihr „Unternehmensstandort der Zukunft"?!

Dear Reader

Today, cities are worldwide competing to be favoured by investors. In this respect, it is becoming increasingly important to distinguish oneself positively from other economic locations through one's own location advantages. Each company location in Germany offers special advantages for the settlement of new firms, national and international investors. But in the great number of regions competing with each other lies also the chance for a city to influence to its own benefit the decision of location selection through particular qualification.

Today, the state capital of Dresden in terms of economic growth is among the European top cities, it has become a magnet for the international high-tech industry. World corporations like Infineon Technologies, AMD and VW have invested here. Dresden's aim to be among the top 10 ranking places in the German economy has realistic chances.

Since centuries, the name of Dresden has been linked with innovations. Porcelain, the white gold, was invented here, the first steam locomotive was constructed and assembled by Dresden engineers and machine constructors, and also the first candid reflex camera had its world premiere here on the river Elbe.

A new business-floating boom has started in the city with the political change. More than 38,000 businesses are meanwhile registered, for further new settlements 150 ha. of industrial area, inexpensive and conveniently situated, are at disposal.

This book is designed to familiarize the interested reader with the region from different perspectives. It throws light on the essential economically relevant factors and portrays a representative selection of companies resident in the region. Furthermore, it conveys an insight into culture, art, history and landscape.

Zwinger, Semperopera, art galleries, Grünes Gewölbe (green vaults), Kreuz Choir, State Orchestra, Dixieland Festival, movie nights – only few European cities are able to boast such a rich provision. Each visitor – indeed 7 million come each year – is impressed by the famous silhouette and it's unmistakable charm.

This work, created in co-operation with the City of Dresden, is also intended to meet a practical task apart from its informative and entertaining value. It is designed to promote co-operations and new business contacts between the companies presented in this book and You as reader of this work. The book is an important component of the national standard work regarding German economic locations and internationally also present in the Internet under the address www.standort-deutschland.com.
Could it be that Dresden is also your "Company location of the future"?

Christian Kirk
Managing Director of
MEDIEN GRUPPE KIRK AG

Vorwort/Foreword

Sehr geehrte Damen und Herren,

Seit 1990 hat der Wirtschafts- und Wissenschaftsstandort Dresden eine atemberaubende Entwicklung vollzogen. Die Unternehmenslandschaft der Region hat an Breite, Vielfalt und Wettbewerbsfähigkeit erheblich gewonnen. Viele kleine Unternehmen, aber auch international agierende Konzerne haben sich in und um die sächsische Landeshauptstadt angesiedelt. Die Stadt ist auf dem besten Weg, an die große Tradition der Gründerjahre anzuknüpfen, in denen der Ballungsraum Dresden zu einem der bedeutendsten Zentren in Deutschland gehörte.

Die vorhandenen Wirtschaftspotenziale, und hier vor allem das erstklassige Wissen und Können der Menschen vor Ort, bilden hierfür die Grundlage und geben Dresden die Perspektive, die dynamische Entwicklung in den nächsten Jahren fortzusetzen. Die Region Dresden ist heute auch ein Tor der Europäischen Union zum Osten. Durch die Osterweiterung der Gemeinschaft verlagert sich ihr Gravitationspunkt weiter in Richtung Sachsen.

Auch gemessen an internationalen Maßstäben hat sich dieser Raum bereits heute zu einem bedeutenden Hightech-Standort entwickelt. Auf dem Gebiet der Mikroelektronik gehört der Standort Dresden zu Europas Metropolen. AMD und Infineon setzen Welt-Maßstäbe. Zugleich erhalten sächsische KMU's optimale Möglichkeiten, um in einem der am stärksten wachsenden Technologiemärkte einzusteigen. Durch die vorgesehene Errichtung eines Bio-Gentechnologiezentrums wird der Standort weiter aufgewertet. Aber auch der Maschinenbau, die Ernährungswirtschaft und zunehmend die produktionsnahen Dienstleistungen prägen die Wirtschaftsstruktur. Dresden setzt für die Zukunft sowohl auf traditionelle als auch auf neue Wirtschaftsfelder; entscheidend ist, die vorhandenen Potenziale im Wettbewerb erfolgreich einsetzen zu können.

Mehrere Netzwerke sind inzwischen im Raum Dresden entstanden. Größenbedingte Nachteile werden ausgeglichen, eine Verzahnung der Unternehmen mit anwendungsnahen Forschungs- und Entwicklungseinrichtungen erreicht und der Zugang zu ausländischen Märkten erleichtert. Dresden zählt heute zu den wachstumsstärksten Städten in Europa. In einer Prognose über das Wirtschaftswachstum im Zeitraum 1999-2003 liegt die Stadt Dresden mit einer erwarteten Zuwachsrate des Bruttoinlandproduktes von 2,7 % vor allen anderen deutschen Metropolen. Die Attraktivität der sächsischen

Landeshauptstadt wird zusätzlich dadurch erhöht, dass Dresden eine Kulturmetropole von europäischem Rang ist und eine reizvolle Landschaft besitzt.

Das vorliegende Buch soll Ihnen helfen, die Region Dresden noch besser kennenzulernen und mögliche Geschäftskontakte anzubahnen.

Dear Reader

Since 1990, the economic and science location Dresden has taken a breathtaking development. The landscape of enterprises in the region has considerably improved in terms of range, variety and competitiveness. Many small companies, but also internationally active corporations have settled in and around the regional capital of Saxony. The city is definitely on its way to continue in the great tradition of the German business floating-boom of the 1870s and 1880s, in which the congested area of Dresden was among one of the most important centres in Germany.

The existing economic potentials and above all the first-rate knowledge and expertise of local people form the basis for this and give Dresden the perspective required to maintain this dynamic development in the coming years. The region of Dresden today is also a gate to the East for the European Union. Through the Eastern Extension of the Community, its point of gravitation is shifting more to the direction of Saxony.

Also compared with international standards, this area has already evolved into one of the significant high-tech locations today. In the field of microelectronics the Dresden location is among the metropolitan cities of Europe. AMD and Infineon are setting world standards. At the same time, Saxon KMUs have ideal possibilities to enter into one of the fastest growing technology markets. The location will receive additional value through the intended establishment of a biogenetic technology centre. But also machine construction, the foodstuff industry and increasingly services near to production characterise the economic structure. For the future, Dresden is relying on both traditional and new fields of the economy; what is decisive however, is to be able to utilize the existing potentials in competition.

Several networks have meanwhile been created in the Dresden area. Disadvantages due to size are levelled out, interrelation between companies with application-oriented research and development institutions is achieved and access to foreign markets is facilitated. Today Dresden is among the fastest growing cities in Europe. A forecast about economic growth in the period 1999-2003 shows the City of Dresden with an expected growth rate of gross domestic income of 2.7 % in front of all other German metropolitan cities. In addition, the attractiveness of the Saxon regional capital is increased by the fact the Dresden is a cultural metropolis of European ranking and that it lies in a charming surrounding landscape.

The present book is designed to help you to familiarize yourself with the region of Dresden and to open up possible business contacts.

Dr. Kajo Schommer
State Minister
for Economy and Employment of Saxony

Inhalt/Contents

Wirtschafts- und Wissenschaftsstandort Dresden
Business- and Science Location Dresden

Christian Kirk Vorstandsvorsitzender der Medien Gruppe Kirk Holding AG	Vorwort Foreword	3
Dr. Kajo Schommer Sächsischer Staatsminister für Wirtschaft und Arbeit	Vorwort Foreword	5
Dr. Herbert Wagner Oberbürgermeister der Stadt Dresden	Dresden ist stark seit August Dresden has been strong since August	8
Rolf Wolgast Bürgermeister der Stadt Dresden, Beigeordneter für Wirtschaft und Verkehr der Landeshauptstadt Dresden	High- und „advanced" technologies: die attraktive und zukunftsorientierte Stadt High and advanced technologies: the attractive and future-oriented city	18
Dr. Werner Mankel Geschäftsführer des Bereichs Berufsbildung bei der IHK Dresden	Bedarfsgerechte Bildung als Standortfaktor Education suitable to the demand becomes a location factor	36
Dr. Peter Kücher Geschäftsführer der Infineon Technologies SC 300	Speicherchips und Logikbausteine, gefertigt mit modernster Technologie Memory chips and logic components produced with the most modern technology	48
Dr. Bertram Dressel Geschäftsführer der TechnologieZentrumDresden GmbH	TechnologieZentrumDresden – Brutstätte für Unternehmen und Ideen TechnologyCentreDresden – Place of procreation for enterprises and ideas	54
Alfred Post Kanzler der Technischen Universität Dresden	TU Dresden: Brückenschlag zwischen Wissenschaft und Wirtschaft TU Dresden: Building Bridges between science and the economic sector	66
Werner Ulrich Geschäftsführer der Automobilmanufaktur Dresden GmbH und Leitung der Markenplanung Volkswagen	Ein Juwel für Dresden und eine Krone für den Automobilbau in Deutschland A Jewel for Dresden and a crown for the automobile industry in Germany	76

Inhalt/Contents

Bernd Rendle Präsident der Handwerkskammer Dresden	Dresdner Handwerk im neuen Jahrtausend Dresden's skilled trades in the new millennium	86
Volkmar Stein Vorstand der Mitteldeutschen Flughafen AG	Flughafen Dresden – Tor zur Welt Dresden Airport – Gate to the world	94
Wolfgang Wirz Präsident des Landesverbandes der Mittel- und Großbetriebe des Einzelhandels in Sachsen, Vorsitzender des Vereins Citymanagement Dresden	Dresdens City – sehenswert, lebenswert, attraktiv Dresden's City – worth seeing, worth living in, attractive	104
Yvonne Kubitza Geschäftsführerin der Dresden-Werbung und Tourismus GmbH	Dresden wird eine der wichtigsten deutschen Tourismus-Destinationen Dresden is becoming one of the most important german destinations for tourism	116
Prof. Dr. rer. nat. Christian Wegerdt Ehem. Geschäftsführender Gesellschafter der IMA Materialforschung und Anwendungstechnik GmbH	Dresden, die Wiege vieler Innovationen – gestern, heute und in Zukunft Dresden, the cradle of many Innovations – yesterday, today and in future	124
	Verzeichnis der vorgestellten Unternehmen List of Companies	134
	Impressum Imprint	136

Einleitung

Dresden ist stark seit August

Dresden has been strong since August

In Dresden läuft der Film vorwärts. Die Stadt nutzt ihre Chancen im wieder vereinten Deutschland zum wirtschaftlichen Aufbruch – und sie erreicht dabei neue Ufer.

Dresden dringt nicht nur im Wirtschaftswachstum an die europäische Spitze vor, sondern entwickelt sich auch zunehmend zum Magneten für die Hightech-Industrie. Siemens, AMD, Motorola – die großen Investitionen weltweit agierender Unternehmen bringen hochmoderne Arbeitsplätze und wachsendes Vertrauen der Branche.

Woraus wächst dieses Vertrauen?

Das inzwischen hier angesiedelte Hightech-Potenzial, der stabile Branchenmix, der kräftige Mittelstand, die konzentrierten Forschungskapazitäten, dazu die Lage im Herzen Europas und die Funktion als Tor zum Osten, außerdem eine entwicklungsfähige Infrastruktur, eine kooperative öffentliche Verwaltung, motivierte und gut ausgebildete Fachkräfte und last, not least die besondere kulturelle Ausstrahlung – das ist die Mischung, die Investitionsfreude weckt und Leistungsfähigkeit fördert. Während der letzten zehn Jahre sind in Dresden über 100 Milliarden Mark in Gang gekommen, davon 55 Milliarden Mark allein in Industrie und Handwerk. Zuletzt sorgte der Volkswagen-Konzern in Dresden für Furore mit der Ansiedlung seiner Gläsernen Manufaktur, der weltweit ersten ihrer Art. VW möchte den Glanz seiner neuen Nobelkarosse mit dem Glanz der Kulturstadt Dresden verbinden. Das nützt VW – das nützt aber auch Dresden. Der Weltkonzern ist hier willkommen.

Immerhin, der erste Chip des Ostblocks kam in den achtziger Jahren aus Dresden, und das hier arbeitende Zentrum für Mikroelektronik (ZMD) und die Technische Universität bildeten die Basis für eine vor zehn Jahren noch ungeahnte Entwicklung. Inzwischen steht fest, der Wirtschaftsstandort Dresden wird auch in Zukunft vor allem

Dr. Herbert Wagner

Der Autor, 1948 in Neustrelitz/Mecklenburg geboren, studierte von 1969 bis 1973 Informationselektronik an der TU Dresden und war von 1973 bis 1990 als Entwicklungsingenieur in der Industrie tätig. Daneben absolvierte Herbert Wagner einen dreijährigen Fernkurs Theologie. 1985 promovierte er zum Dr.-Ing. Vor der politischen Wende parteilos, wurde er 1990 Vorsitzender der Basisdemokratischen Fraktion der Dresdner Stadtverordnetenversammlung und trat noch im selben Jahr in die CDU ein.

1990 wurde Dr. Herbert Wagner zum Oberbürgermeister von Dresden gewählt, 1994 erfolgte seine Wiederwahl.

The author, born 1948 in Neustrelitz/Mecklenburg, studied from 1969 until 1973 computer electronics at the TU Dresden and worked from 1973 until 1990 as development engineer in the industrial sector. Besides this, Herbert Wagner completed a three-year remote study course in theology. In 1985, he attained his PhD in engineering. Before the political change he was independent, in 1990 he became chairman of the democratic base of the fraction of the Dresden town council and in the same year he entered the CDU party (Christlich-Demokratische Union). In 1990, Dr. Herbert Wagner was elected Lord Mayor of Dresden, he was re-elected in 1994.

„Pizza à la Hightech". Auf Siliziumscheiben (Wafern) mit 300 Millimetern Durchmesser werden die Mikrochips der Zukunft gefertigt. Gegenüber heute gebräuchlichen 200-mm-Wafern ist dort Platz für die zweieinhalbfache Zahl von Chips. Dies führt zu einer Kostenersparnis von etwa 30 Prozent.

"Pizza à la High-tech". On wafers 300 mm in diameter the microchips of the future are produced. Compared with the 200-mm-wafers used today, there is space for two-and-a-half times the number of chips. This leads to cost savings of around 30 percent.

Hightech-Standort sein. Mit ZMD, der Siemens-Chipfabrik – die jetzt aus der Konzernfamilie ausgegliedert „Infineon Technologies" heißt – mit Advanced Micro Devices (AMD) und Motorola

Introduction

Einleitung

Das Infineon-Werk, in dem die neue 300-mm-Wafer-Technologie erstmals angewandt wird.
The Infineon works, which applies the new 300-mm-wafer technology for the first time.

hat Dresden es bereits geschafft, im europäischen Konzert der Mikroelektronikstädte mitzuspielen. Die Investitionen dieser Giganten bringen Dresden die Aufmerksamkeit der Branche und hochmoderne Arbeitsplätze.

Allein die Chipfabrik beschäftigt statt der ursprünglich zugesagten 1.400 nun schon 3.000 Fachkräfte. Sie ist der Kern einer so genannten Cluster-Struktur mit Werken in Frankreich, Amerika und Taiwan, die von Dresden aus gesteuert werden. Die jetzt neu entstehende Infineon-Fabrik, in der die mit Motorola entwickelte 300 mm-Wafer-Technologie zum Tragen kommt, wird einmal weitere 1.100 Mitarbeiter beschäftigen. Das Dresdner Werk setzt weltweit den Standard. Der Intel-Konkurrent AMD, der 1999 die Produktion des zurzeit weltweit schnellsten Prozessors „Athlon" in seinem Dresdner Werk aufnahm, beschäftigt bereits 1.200 Mitarbeiter. Insgesamt arbeiten in der Mikroelektronik und den darauf aufbauenden Bereichen der Informationstechnologien in Dresden und Umgebung rund 500 Unternehmen mit bald 20.000 Beschäftigten, die große Masse davon in mittelständischen Betrieben.

Die Technische Universität Dresden, mit mehr als 25.000 Studenten die größte Uni Sachsens und Dresdens wichtigste Fachkräfte-Schmiede, dazu die in Dresden ansässigen renommierten Institute der Fraunhofer-Gesellschaft, der Max-Planck-Gesellschaft und der Wissenschaftsgemeinschaft Gottfried-Wilhelm-Leibniz, außerdem das Forschungszentrum Rossendorf und das Von-Ardenne-Institut – sie alle zusammen machen Dresden zum leistungsfähigen Zentrum für Wissenschaft und Forschung.

Dresden ist offen für Zukunftstechnologien – zunehmend auch in der Biotechnologie. Dafür steht das neue Max-Planck-Institut für Molekulare Zellbiologie und Genetik. Demnächst entstehen ein Gründerzentrum für Bioinformation und ein Bioinnovationszentrum. Vielseitigkeit war, ist und bleibt ein Dresdner Trumpf! Trotz erheblicher Umstrukturierungen in der Wirtschaft und unvermeidlichem Abbau unrentabler Arbeitsplätze – die Mehrzahl der hier verwurzelten Branchen blieb erhalten. So wird mit den Unternehmen Sächsisches Serumwerk Dresden der Glaxo Smith Kline-Gruppe und Arzneimittelwerk Dresden der ASTA Medica AG die Geschichte der Dresdner Arzneimittelindustrie weiter geschrieben. Das Druckerei- und Verlagswesen lebt auf hohem Niveau fort, denn Gruner + Jahr errichtete in Dresden die modernste Illustrationsdruckerei Europas. Die für Dresden so typische Nahrungs- und Genussmittelindustrie hat mit Philip Morris ein neues Flaggschiff; schon jede zweite in Ostdeutschland gerauchte Zigarette kommt aus Dresden.

Der traditionsreiche Name Pentacon besteht weiter in der gleichnamigen Foto- und Feinwerktechnik GmbH. Der Flugzeugbau erlebt in Dresden neue Höhenflüge; hier testen Ingenieure den Rumpf des neuen Airbusses, des bislang größten.

Die Gründerzeit hält an. Die Zahl der angemeldeten Gewerbe steigt in der sächsischen Landeshauptstadt kontinuierlich und ist nun bei über 37.000 angelangt. Zum Vergleich: 1990 lag sie bei nicht einmal 13.000. Dies belegt, zahlreiche Dresdner warten nicht ab, sondern ergreifen ihre Chance, wagen den Schritt in die Selbstständigkeit und behaupten sich auch. Das vor dem Hintergrund jahrzehntelanger Zurückdrängung

Introduction

Abendstimmung vor der Semperoper.

Evening atmosphere infront of the Semperopera.

In Dresden, things are moving ahead. The city is using its chances for an economic change again in unified Germany – and in doing so is reaching new dimensions. Dresden is not only penetrating to the forefront of European to in economic growth, but is also increasingly becoming a magnet for the high-tech industry. Siemens, AMD, and Motorola – the large investments of worldwide active corporations bring about highly modern workplaces and growing confidence in the branch.

Where does this confidence arise?
The high-tech potential meanwhile settled here, stable mix of branches, strong middle-sized business sector, concentrated research capacities added to this a location in the heart of Europe and its function as gate to the East; furthermore an infrastructure capable of development, a co-operative public administration sector, motivated and well-trained expert workforce and last, not least the special cultural aura – this is the mix that stimulates investment and promotes efficiency. During the last ten years over 100 billion DM have be released in Dresden, of these 55 billion Marks alone in skilled trades and industry. Recently, the Volkswagen Group caused a sensation with the construction of their glass manufacturing halls, the first of their kind worldwide. VW wants to link the glamour of its new extravagant car with the glamour of the cultural city of Dresden. This benefits VW and also Dresden at the same time. The international corporation is welcome here. Indeed, the first chip of the Eastern Block came from Dresden in the eighties and the Centre for Microelectronics (ZMD) operating from here and the Technical University formed the basis for a development undreamt of ten years ago. Meanwhile it is clear that the economic location Dresden will continue to be above all a high-tech location also in future. With ZMD, the chip factory of Siemens – that is now called "Infineon Technologies" after having been outsourced from the group -, with Advanced Micro Devices (AMD) and Motorola, Dresden has achieved to play a part in the European concert of microelectronics cities. The investments of these giants have brought Dresden the attention of the branch and highly modern workplaces. The chip factory alone employs instead of the originally promised 1,400 now already 3,000 specialists. She is the core of a so-called cluster-structure with works in France, America and Taiwan that are being managed from Dresden. The now newly developing Infineon factory, which will implement the 300 mm-wafer technology developed together with Motorola, will finally employ further 1,100 staff members. The Dresden work is setting trends worldwide. The Intel-competitor AMD, that started producing the presently fastest processor worldwide called "Athlon" in its Dresden work, already employs more than 1,200 staff members. In total, around 500 companies with almost

Einleitung

Beschichtungsanlage für Architekturglas in der Von Ardenne Anlagentechnik GmbH Dresden.
Von Ardenne Anlagentechnik GmbH Dresden – coating plant for architectural glass.

dieser Bestrebungen! Handwerk und Mittelstand profitieren natürlich von den großen Neuansiedlungen in Dresden und gewinnen weiter an Boden. In Coschütz/Gittersee, im Gewerbepark Reick, im Technopark Nord und weiteren kommunalen Gewerbegebieten bietet die Stadt kleinen und mittelständischen Betrieben preiswerte und verkehrsgünstige Gewerbeflächen an – auf zusammen über 150 Hektar, von inzwischen über 1.000 Hektar Gewerbeflächen in Dresden insgesamt. Mit dem Gewerbe- und Gründerzentrum Löbtauer Straße fördert sie Handwerk und Mittelstand. Im TechnologieZentrum Dresden erhalten Erfinder und Existenzgründer ihre Chance. Das World Trade Center bietet moderne Arbeitsbedingungen mitten im Zentrum.

Wo sonst wäre die Entwicklung der letzten zehn Jahre so deutlich sichtbar, wenn nicht im Dresdner Stadtbild? Über der Silhouette von Elbflorenz rotierten zeitweise rund zweihundert Kräne, inzwischen sind es ein paar weniger. Kunstakademie, Residenzschloss, Taschenbergpalais, Katholische Hofkirche, Coselpalais – überall ist alter Glanz mit großem Aufwand aufpoliert worden.

Private und öffentliche Investitionen gehen Hand in Hand. Aber Dresden schließt auch noch offene Wunden, die wohl bekannteste mit der Dresdner Frauenkirche. Aus den Trümmern des Krieges ersteht die steinerne Kuppel neu. Die Frauenkirche als Symbol für die Überwindung von Krieg und Hass wiederaufzubauen, verbindet eine ständig wachsende internationale Fördergemeinschaft. Ein Fakt, der auch für den Bau der Synagoge zutrifft. Dafür ist Dresden dankbar, dafür wirbt Dresden weiter.

Dresden ist grün – nicht nur aus der Vogelperspektive! Mit 56 Prozent Grünfläche gehört die Stadt zu den grünsten Städten Europas. In fast acht Jahrhunderten wuchs hier eine Stadtlandschaft, die tatsächlich Stadt und Landschaft miteinander verbindet. Dresdner Heide, Großer Garten, Elbwiesen, Kleingärten – die grünen Inseln in der Stadt bringen Lebensqualität für ihre Bewohner.

Mit millionenschwerem Aufwand sanierte Dresden Gewerbebrachen und beseitigte Altlasten im Boden. Ehemals militärisch genutztes Gelände ist zurückgewonnen – für die Industrie wie bei Gruner + Jahr oder als Lebensraum wie in Nickern. Die Albertstadt beherbergt jetzt so bedeutende Einrichtungen wie die von Hannover nach Dresden verlegte Heeresoffizierschule, das MDR-Landesfunkhaus Sachsen und mit dem Neubau des Stadtarchivs das modernste Archiv Europas. Aufatmen konnten die Dresdner in einem ganz wörtlichen Sinne 1995 mit der Inbetriebnahme des neuen Gas- und Dampfturbinen-Heizkraftwerkes, das 97 % weniger Schadstoffe ausstößt als das alte Heizkraftwerk. Trotz insgesamt sinkender Kohlendioxidbilanz, der Anteil des Verkehrs an der Luftbelastung steigt noch immer.

Wie in den meisten deutschen Großstädten und in den ostdeutschen im Besonderen, so ist auch in Dresden der Verkehr ein Dauerthema mit Konfliktpotenzial und Problemstau. Bis heute trägt die Stadt Erblasten ab und stellt sich gleichzeitig neuen Aufgaben. Straßenbau, Nahverkehr, Flughafen – trotz schon erheblichen Aufwandes werden noch über Jahre Investitionen auf diesem Gebiet nötig sein. Wichtigste Projekte sind die Autobahn Dresden–Prag, die heute im Bau ist, und die Waldschlösschenbrücke, für die demnächst Baustart sein wird.

Introduction

20,000 employees work in microelectronics and the related fields of computer technologies in Dresden and its surrounding countryside, the largest part of it in mid-sized companies.

The Technical University of Dresden, with more than 25,000 students the largest university of Saxony and the most important producer of expert personnel, as well as the renowned institutes of the Fraunhofer-Society, the Max-Planck Society and of the Wissenschaftsgemeinsaft Gottfried-Wilhelm-Leibniz (Scientific Society G.-W.-Leibniz), furthermore the Rossendorf Research Centre and the Von-Ardenne Institute – they all together make Dresden the efficient centre for science and research that it is. Dresden is open for future technologies – increasingly also in biotechnology. The Max-Planck Institute for Molecular Cell Biology and Genetics proves this fact. Soon a founder centre for start-ups of bio-information and a bio innovation centre will be created. Diversity was, is and will remain trumps in Dresden! Despite of considerable restructurisation in the economic sector and the inevitable loss of uneconomic workplaces, the majority of branches rooted in this area were preserved. Thus, with the companies Sächsisches Serumwerk of the Glaxo Smith Kline Group and Arzneimittelwerk Dresden of ASTA Medica AG the history of Dresden's pharmaceutic industry will continue its chronology. The printing and publishing industry maintains its existence on very high level, because Gruner + Jahr established the most modern illustrating printers of Europe in Dresden. The food and tobacco industry typical for Dresden has a new flagship with Philip Morris; already every second cigarette smoked in East Germany is made in Dresden.

The name Pentacon, rich in tradition, still exists in the Foto- und Feinwerktechnik GmbH of the same name. The aviation industry is experiencing new heights; engineers are testing the hitherto largest fuselage of the new Airbus.

The business floating-boom continues. The number of registered businesses is constantly rising in the regional capital of Saxony and has now reached over 37,000. In comparison, by 1990 it was not even at 13,000. This proves that numerous citizens of Dresden are not waiting, but take their chance, risk the step into self-employment and also maintain their hold on the market. And this against the background of decades of oppression of these kinds of efforts! The skilled trades sector and middles-sized businesses of course benefit from the great new settlements in Dresden and keep on gaining ground. In Coschütz/Gittersee, in the Industrial Park Reick, in the Technopark North and other communal industrial areas the city offers inexpensive and conveniently situated industrial space to small and mid-sized companies – on an area of over 150 hectares, which is part of meanwhile totalling over 1,000 hectares of industrial areas in Dresden on the whole. The city promotes the skilled trades and mid-sized business sector with the Industrial and Founder Centre Löbtauer Strasse. In the Technology Centre Dresden, inventors and start-up business founders receive their chance. The World Trade Center offers modern working conditions in the middle of the city centre.

Where else could one see the development of the past ten years more clearly than in the Dresden cityscape? Above the silhouette of the "Florence on the Elbe" as it is called, at times around two

In der Produktion der Apogepha Arzneimittel GmbH Dresden, einem traditionellen, sehr erfolgreichen mittelständischen Unternehmen.

Apogepha Arzneimittel GmbH Dresden, a traditional, very successful mid-sized company.

Einleitung

Die Messe Dresden im Ostragehege setzt Akzente in der deutschen Messelandschaft.
The Dresden Fair in the Ostragehege is setting new trends in the fair landscape of Germany.

Wer Kunst und Kultur von europäischem Rang genießen will, sitzt in Dresden in der ersten Reihe. Elbflorenz hat davon reichlich zu bieten – eindrucksvolle Architektur, kostbare Kunstsammlungen, lebendige Musiktraditionen, verlockende Festivals, dazu bezaubernde Parkanlagen und landschaftlichen Liebreiz entlang der Elbe. Außerdem liegen nur einen Katzensprung entfernt so attraktive Ziele wie Moritzburg, Meißen, die Sächsische Schweiz oder das Erzgebirge.

Nach jahrzehntelanger Isolation hinter dem eisernen Vorhang verzeichnete Dresden mit der deutschen Wiedervereinigung eine sprunghaft wachsende Gästezahl. Jetzt ist sie bei jährlich über sieben Millionen angelangt – Tendenz weiter steigend. Touristen strömen in die Schatzkammern der Kurfürsten, Geschäftsreisende interessiert der wirtschaftliche Aufbruch. Anfangs waren nicht einmal genügend Hotelbetten da, doch das ist schnell aufgeholt worden. Inzwischen hat der Gast die Qual der Wahl, auch in der Gastronomie. Allein die Neustadt konzentriert über 16 Prozent des Dresdner Gastgewerbes. In Zukunft will Dresden noch mehr jüngere Touristen anlocken. Eine Attraktion ist das freitägliche Nacht-Skaten.

Mit der Messe im Ostragehege bietet Dresden einen Anziehungspunkt für Veranstalter von Messen und Ausstellungen – keine Konkurrenz zur Leipziger Messe, jedoch ein stimmungsvolles Ambiente für größere Regional- und Spezialmessen. Altes Erlweinsches Ensemble in Verbindung mit moderner Architektur setzen typisch Dresdner Akzente in der deutschen Messelandschaft. Für die wachsende Kongressnachfrage schafft Dresden nun die Voraussetzungen zum Bau eines größeren Kongresszentrums in traumhafter Lage am Elbufer, unmittelbar neben der historischen Altstadt.

Zwinger, Semperoper, Gemäldegalerie, Grünes Gewölbe, Porzellansammlung, Kreuzchor, Staatskapelle, Philharmonie, Dixielandfestival, Theaterkahn, Filmnächte, Elbhangfest ... Kunst und Kultur in Dresden – ein Thema ohne Ende. Kaum zu glauben für unsere Gäste, dass die Stadt nach den Bombardements vom Februar 1945 auf fünfzehn Quadratkilometern eingeäschert war. Obwohl vieles vom alten Dresden für immer verloren bleibt, ist die berühmte Silhouette wieder auferstanden, prägt sie mit unverwechselbarem Charme das Florenz an der Elbe. Bis heute leuchtet der Glanz der einstigen Residenz. Dresden ist stark seit August[1], und über Generationen gibt die Stadt Künstlern Inspiration.

[1] Friedrich August I., Kurfürst von Sachsen, genannt August der Starke, geboren 12.5.1670 Dresden, gestorben 1.2.1733 Warschau.

Kultur ist für Dresden einerseits Verpflichtung, andererseits Wirtschaftsfaktor. So gehört die Semperoper heute mit einer Auslastung von 98 % zu den wirtschaftlichsten Musiktheatern Deutschlands. Dresdner Ensembles wie die Staatskapelle oder der Kreuzchor sind feste Begriffe im internationalen Musikleben, werden aber auch zu Hause hoch verehrt. Die Anrechte der Philharmonie sind bei den Dresdnern gefragt wie eh. Neue Bühnen, wie die Komödie oder das Societätstheater, haben sich längst ihr Publikum erobert.

Stabilisierung der wirtschaftlichen Entwicklung, damit weiterer Abbau der Arbeitslosigkeit und der Schulden, schrittweise Investitionen – Dresden hat noch viel vor. Der Wiederaufbau geht weiter. Bis zur 800-Jahr-Feier im Jahre 2006 soll Dresden auch wirtschaftlich wieder zur Spitzengruppe der deutschen Städte gehören. ■

Introduction

hundred cranes were rotating, now there are less. The Art Academy, Residence Castle, Taschenberg Palace, Catholic Hofkirche, and Cosel Palace – everywhere the old glamour has been polished up with great effort. Private and public investments go hand in hand. But Dresden is also still closing open wounds, the most famous probably being the church called Dresdener Frauenkirche. From the ruins of the war, the stone dome is being created anew. The reconstruction of the Frauenkirche as a symbol of overcoming war and hate links together a permanently growing international group of sponsors. A fact that is also valid for the construction of the synagogue. Dresden appreciates this and continues to promote this.

Dresden is really green – not only from a bird's eye view! With 56 percent of green areas, the city is among the greenest cities of Europe. In almost eight centuries a city landscape has grown that indeed joins the city and landscape together. The Dresden Heath, Large Gardens, Elbe Meadows, and small gardens – the green islands of the city bring about quality of living for its inhabitants.

At an expense worth millions Dresden has redeveloped fallow industrial land and has removed residue from polluted grounds. Areas used by the military formerly have been reclaimed – for the industry like with Gruner + Jahr or as living space like in Nickern. The Albertstadt now houses such important institutions like the military school Heeresoffizierschule, the regional broadcasting station of the MDR-Landesfunkhaus Sachsen and with the new building of the city archives the most modern archive in Europe. Dresden citizens were able to take a deep breadth literally in 1995, when the new gas and steam turbine heating and power station started operations, since it emits 97 percentless harmful substances than the old heating and power station. In spite of the reduced balance of carbon dioxide, the share of the traffic in air pollution is still increasing. Like in most German cities and particularly in East German cities, traffic is also in Dresden the on-going subject, which carries potential for conflict and problems. Until today, the city is struggling to diminish inherited problems and is coping with new tasks at the same time. Road construction, local transport, the airport – despite considerable amounts of expenditure already many years of investments will be necessary in this field. The most important projects are the motorway Dresden-Prague, already under construction, and the Waldschlösschen Bridge, for which construction will start soon.

Whoever wants to enjoy art and culture of European ranking, is seated in the front row in Dresden. "Florence on the Elbe" has much to offer hereof – impressive architecture, valuable art collections, lively music traditions, attractive festivals, in addition charming parks and delightful landscapes along the Elbe. Furthermore, only a stone's throw away lay such attractive destinations as Moritzburg, Meißen, the Sächsische Schweiz (Switzerland of Saxony) or the Erzgebirge (Ore Mountains).

After years of isolation behind the Iron Curtain, Dresden has an enormously growing number of visitors after the German unification. It has now reached over seven million a year – with a still rising trend. Tourists pour into the treasuries of the electoral princes; business travellers are interested in the economic upsurge. In the beginning, there were not even enough hotel beds, but this has rapidly been adjusted. Meanwhile, guests are spoilt for choice, also with regard to restaurants. Over 16 percent of Dresden's catering and hotel trade is concentrated in the Neustadt, the new part of the city. In future, Dresden will attract far more young tourists. One attraction is the Friday night skating.

Die Bundesautobahn Dresden–Prag ist im Bau.

The federal motorway Dresden–Prague is under construction.

Einleitung

Introduction

The fair in the Ostragehege provides a further attraction for promoters of fairs and exhibitions – not in competition to the Leipzig fair, but a tremendous atmosphere for large regional and specialist fairs. The old Erlweinsche Ensemble combined with modern architecture set typical Dresden accents in the landscape of fairs in Germany. Due to the growing demand for conferences, Dresden is now creating the prerequisites for the construction of a larger congress centre in an enchanting location at the shores of the Elbe, directly next to the historic part of the city.

Zwinger, Semperoper, Galleries, Grünes Gewölbe (Green Vaults), porcelain collection, Kreuz Choir, State Orchestra, philharmonics, Dixieland Festival, Theatre, movie nights, Elbhang Festival … Art and culture in Dresden is a subject without an end. It must be unbelievable for our guests that the city was bombarded down to fifteen km² after the raids in February 1945. Although much of the old Dresden will remain lost forever, the famous silhouette has resurfaced; it is distinguishing with its unmistakable charms the Florence on the Elbe. Up to today, the glamour of the former residence city shines. Dresden is strong since August[1] and since generations the city inspires artists.

[1] Friedrich August I., Electoral Prince of Saxony, called August the Strong, born 12.05.1670 in Dresden, died 01.02.1733 in Warsaw.

Culture is an obligation to Dresden on the one hand, on the other an economic factor. Thus, the Semperopera is today with a full occupation rate of 98 percent among the most profitable musical theatres in Germany. Ensembles of Dresden like the State Orchestra or the Kreuz Choir are well-known names of the international music scene, but they are also honoured highly at home. The rights of the philharmonics are as popular with Dresden citizens as ever. New theatres like the Komödie or the Societätstheater have long conquered its public.

The stabilisation of economic developments, related to this the further reduction of unemployment and debts, step-by-step investments – Dresden has still much to accomplish. The reconstruction continues. Until the festivities of the 800-year-celebration in 2006, Dresden must be among the top cities of Germany again.

Die Elbbrücke „Blaues Wunder" und der Schaufelraddampfer „August der Starke".
The bridge across the river Elbe "Blaues Wunder" and the paddle steamer "August the Strong".

Standortvorteile

High- und „advanced" technologies: die attraktive und zukunftsorientierte Stadt

High and advanced technologies: the attractive and future-oriented city

Fast 300 Jahre ist es her, dass in Dresden das Geheimnis der Porzellanherstellung gelüftet wurde, wonach das „weiße Gold" auch in Europa produziert werden konnte. Die erste deutsche Dampflokomotive wurde vor ca. 150 Jahren hier gebaut, und im 20. Jahrhundert bereicherte Dresden die Hochtechnologie der Zeit u. a. mit der Weltpremiere der Kleinbild-Spiegelreflexkamera. Diese langen Traditionen als technologieorientierter Industrie-und Forschungsstandort und die für eine hochentwickelte Wirtschaft bedeutsamen Potenziale, die daraus entstanden, waren eine hervorragende Mitgift für die nach 1990 erforderliche Neuorientierung und Neuorganisation der Dresdner Wirtschaft und den Eintritt in eine durch rasante Entwicklung der Informations- und Kommunikationstechnologien und die Beschleunigung der Globalisierung geprägte Welt.

Die Dresdner Wirtschaftspolitik hat sich zu einem Zeitpunkt, als der Sprung Ostdeutschlands in das bis dahin nur durch Abschottungen hindurch wahrgenommene „Meer" der Weltwirtschaft für starke Turbulenzen in der ansässigen Wirtschaft sorgte, nicht nur auf die Bewahrung des wirtschaftlichen Bestandes in der Stadt konzentriert, sondern ist zugleich mit großer Energie, sekundiert durch eine gleichorientierte Technologiepolitik des Freistaates Sachsen, daran gegangen, einem erneuerten Hochtechnologiestandort Dresden erste Züge seines künftigen Profils zu verschaffen.

Heute kann ein „Neubau Dresdner Wirtschaft" besichtigt werden, der sich – wie der weltweit mit Aufmerksamkeit verfolgte Bau unserer Frauenkirche – bereits weit über „Grundmauern" und „Untergeschosse" hinaus erhebt. Fertig ist der „Bau" noch nicht; weiteres Wachstum ist vonnöten, aber – um im gewählten Bilde zu bleiben – auf „fertig", d. h. abgeschlossen und auf eine eng abgegrenzte Gestalt fixiert ist dieser „Bau" auch nicht angelegt. Die Dresdner Wirtschaft war nach den für sie maßgebenden Sektoren und Branchen immer vielseitig aufgebaut und damit für Entwicklungen und Umwälzungen stets offener als monostrukturierte Standorte. Dieser Vorzug wurde erhalten und so ist dieses „Gebäude Dresdner Wirtschaft" nicht als monolithischer Körper, sondern als Bau-Ensemble angelegt, geeignet, die einzelnen Teile in vielfältigste Beziehungen zueinander zu setzen und mit den künftigen Entwicklungen und sich daraus für den Standort ergebenden Chancen zu wachsen.

Dresden ist heute einer der bedeutendsten europäischen Standorte der Mikroelektronik und Informationstechnologie, ein Cluster, der Bauelemente- und Gerätehersteller, Ausrüstungs- und Materialzulieferer, Soft-

Rolf Wolgast

Der Autor wurde 1934 geboren. Nach Abitur und Studienabschluss als Diplom-Verwaltungswirt übte er verschiedene Tätigkeiten in Hamburg aus, zuletzt als Ortsamtsleiter.
Seit Ende Oktober 1990 ist Rolf Wolgast in der Stadtverwaltung Dresden tätig. Im April 1991 wurde er Beigeordneter für Wirtschaft, im Juni 1994 wurde er zum Stadtrat in Dresden gewählt und im September 1994 zum Beigeordneten für Wirtschaft und Wohnen.
Seit Juli 1999 ist Bürgermeister Rolf Wolgast Beigeordneter für Wirtschaft und Verkehr der Landeshauptstadt Dresden.

The author was born in 1934. After his A-levels and completing his studies as Certified Administration Officer, he worked in various positions in Hamburg, in the end as head of department of a registration office. Since the end of October 1990, Rolf Wolgast is working in the city administration of Dresden. In April 1991, he was appointed town councillor for economy; in June 1994, he was elected to the Town Council in Dresden and in September 1994 to town councillor for economy and housing. Since July 1999, Mayor Rolf Wolgast is town councillor for economy and transport of the regional capital Dresden.

warefirmen und andere unternehmensorientierte Dienstleister neben den universitären und außeruniversitären Forschungsinstituten integriert. 1996 wurde die Produktion von hochintegrierten Speicherschaltkreisen (DRAM) im Siemens-Halbleiterwerk – heute Infineon Technologies Dresden GmbH&Co.OHG – aufgenommen. Ca. 3.000 Menschen sind heute in diesem Unternehmen

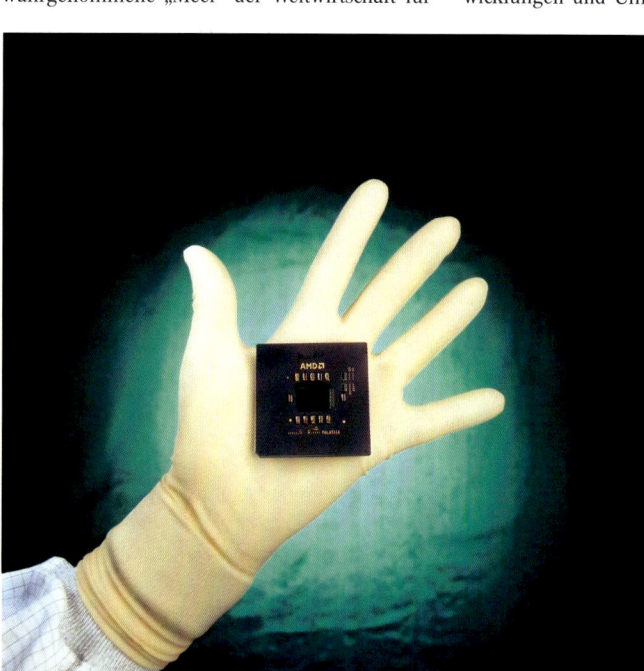

Der Athlon Prozessor von AMD, derzeit schnellster Mikroprozessor der Welt.

The Athlon processor of AMD, the presently fastest microprocessor of the world.

Location Advantages

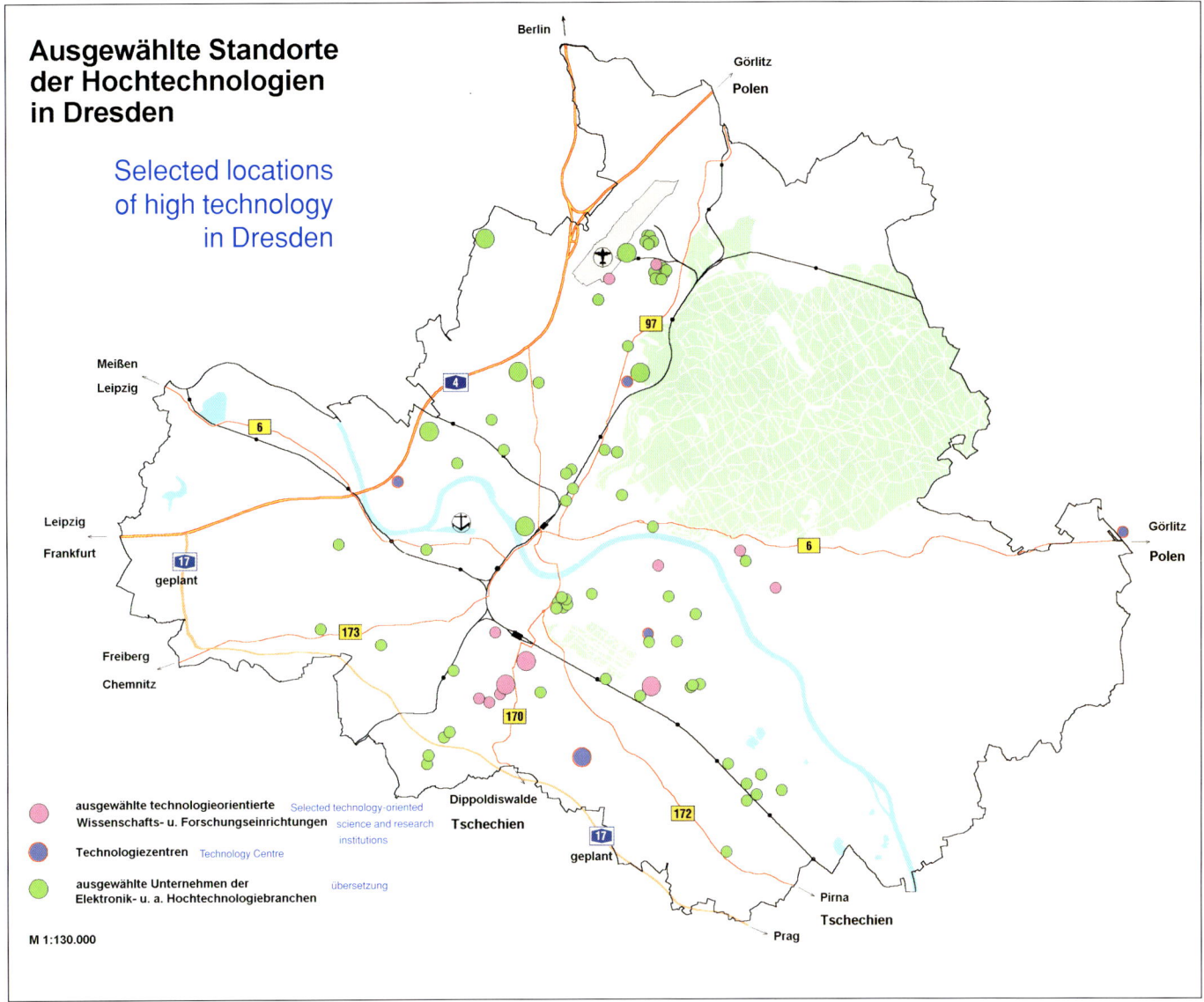

Ausgewählte Standorte der Hochtechnologien in Dresden

Selected locations of high technology in Dresden

- ausgewählte technologieorientierte Wissenschafts- u. Forschungseinrichtungen — Selected technology-oriented science and research institutions
- Technologiezentren — Technology Centre
- ausgewählte Unternehmen der Elektronik- u. a. Hochtechnologiebranchen — übersetzung

M 1:130.000

Almost 300 years ago in Dresden the secret of porcelain manufacturing was discovered and afterwards, the "white gold" could be produced also in Europe. The first German steam locomotive was constructed here around 150 years ago and in the 20th century, Dresden enriched the high technology of its time, for example, with the world premiere of the candid reflex camera. These long-standing traditions as a technology-oriented industrial and research location and the potential, which is important for a highly developed economy, that emerged from it have been an excellent dowry for the necessary new orientation and new organisation of the Dresden economy after 1990 and the entry into a world characterised by rapid developments of the computer and communications technologies and the acceleration of globalisation.

The economic policy of Dresden has not only concentrated on the maintenance of the economic assets of the city at a point, when the great leap of East Germany into the world market up to that point only perceived through barriers caused upheavals in the local economy, but also embarked with great energy, seconded by a similarly oriented technological policy of the Free State of Saxony, to give contours of its future profile to the renewed high-tech location of Dresden.

Today, the "New Building of the Dresden Economy" can be visited, which – like the worldwide attention given to the reconstruction of our Frauenkirche – is already rising far above "foundation" and "lower floors". The "construction" has not been completed yet; much more growth is necessary, but – in order to remain within the chosen picture -, this "construction" is not intended to be "completed", i. e. finished and limited to a narrow shape. The Dresden economy has always been structured variedly according to its decisive sectors and branches and thus always more open for developments and changes than mono-structured locations. This advantage was maintained and thus, this "Building of the Dresden Economy" has not been designed as monolithic body, but as construction ensemble, suitable for moving the single components into the most varied relationships to each other and for growing together with future developments and the chances arising from them for the location.

Dresden today is one of the most significant European locations of microelectronics and computer technology, a cluster of component and equipment producers, furnishers and material suppliers, software companies and other entrepreneurial service providers, all integrated besides the university and extra-university research institutes. In 1996, the production of highly integrated memory switch circuits (DRAM) was started in the Siemens semiconductor work, today Infineon Technologies Dresden GmbH & Co. oHG. Approx. 3,000 people are working today in the production of the latest generation (256 MbBit-SDRAM) of these components in this company.

Standortvorteile

mit der Fertigung der neuesten Generation (256 MBit-SDRAM) dieser Bauelemente beschäftigt. Und das Wachstum geht weiter – Bestätigung für die Vorzüge des Standortes Dresden ebenso wie für ein hervorragendes Unternehmensmanagement. Vorhandene qualifizierte Arbeitskräfte, das starke Forschungs- und Entwicklungspotenzial in der Stadt mit Schwerpunkten u. a. bei Werkstoffen, ihrer Entwicklung und ihrer Ver- und Bearbeitung, bei Elektronik, Informationstechnik wie auch bei der Fertigungstechnik, das außer von der Technischen Universität, der FH für Technik und Wirtschaft, den Instituten der Max-Planck-, der Fraunhofer-Gesellschaft und der Forschungsgemeinschaft „G.W. Leibniz" auch von auf bestimmte Gebiete spezialisierten mittelständischen F&E-Unternehmen repräsentiert wird, sind Stärken des Standortes.

Die Aufgabe für ein Entwicklungs-Joint venture von Siemens/Infineon und Motorola in Dresden, die beträchtlichen technologischen Probleme beim Übergang von einer Schaltkreisproduktion auf Wafern der bisherigen Standardgröße von 200 mm Durchmesser auf die der produktivitätssteigernden Größe von 300 mm zu bewältigen, wurde vorfristig gelöst und haben den Unternehmen eine Pionierposition in der Welt bei der Anwendung dieser Technologie verschafft. Aus Dresden, aus dem gegenwärtig in direkter Nachbarschaft des bestehenden Infineon-Werkes für ca. 2,2 Mrd. DM errichteten neuen Betrieb Infineon Technologies SC 300, werden auch die Produkte der Serienfertigung von Speicherchips auf der Basis der neuen Technologie kommen. Dass sich Dresden, bereits vor 1990 eine der „Hauptstädte" der Mikroelektronik und Informationstechnologie im ehemaligen COMECON, innerhalb weniger Jahre erneut einen weit über Deutschland hinausreichenden guten Ruf als bedeutender Standort dieser Branche erworben hat, hat die Entscheidung des US-amerikanischen Konzerns Advanced Micro Devices (AMD) bewiesen, hier seine erste Unternehmensansiedlung in Europa mit einer 3,4 Mrd.-DM-Investition durchzuführen. Aus einer kleinen „Arbeitsstelle für Mikroelektronik", der Keimzelle für eigenständige Mikroelektronikentwicklungen in Dresden in den 60er Jahren des 20. Jahrhunderts, wurde später das Unternehmen Zentrum Mikroelektronik Dresden (ZMD). Heute ist dieses Dresdner Traditionsunternehmen ein profilierter Spezialist für Mixed Signals ASIC's, insbesondere für die Autoelektronik, der dritte größere Vertreter der Halbleiterbranche in Dresden (ca. 450 Mitarbeiter derzeit und mit kräftigen Wachstumszielen). Mit einer Neuentwicklung, einem elektronischen Abgas-Mess- und Motorsteuerungssystem für Kfz, präsentierte sich dieses Unternehmen im übrigen auch auf der Weltausstellung „EXPO 2000".

Andere Facetten des Clusters „Mikroelektronik/-Informationstechnologie" werden gebildet von dem Teil des Forschungspotenzials in Dresden, das sich auf das Spektrum der diesem Cluster zugehörigen Themen orientiert und der großen Zahl mittelständischer Unternehmen, die mittels ihrer Produkte, Leistungen und Kundschaft engen Bezug zu diesen Hochtechnologien haben. Für die Standortqualität und die wirtschaftliche Entwicklung in Dresden sind sie von nicht geringerer Bedeutung als die großen Unternehmen der Halbleiterbranche.

Dresden hat sich auf den Weg zur Entwicklung der Biotechnologie als einem künftig strukturbedeutsamen Teil der Wirtschaft in der Stadt und der Region gemacht. Ein unter dem Namen „BioMeT" gebildetes Netzwerk von Forschungseinrichtungen, Unternehmen und Unterstützern aus dem Finanzbereich, aus Verwaltung und Politik beschreibt mit seinem Namen die Spannweite von Biotechnologie in Dresden: Biologie, Medizin, Technik. Stellvertretend für die Forschungseinrichtungen, die an BioMeT insgesamt beteiligt sind, seien hier das in 2000 angesiedelte Max-Planck-Institut für Molekulare Zellbiologie und Genetik, die TU Dresden mit mehreren ihrer 14 Fakultäten, das derzeit mit dem Neubau eines Laborkomplexes aufwartende interdisziplinäre Zentrum für Biomaterialien des Instituts für Polymerforschung und des Zentrums für molekularbiologische und medizintechnische Materialforschung der TU Dresden genannt. Für eine starke Säule „Technik" erweist sich die traditionsreiche Dresdner Technologiekompetenz als vorteilhafte Basis. „Bio-Technik" wird künftig sicherlich die Unternehmenslandschaft der Biotechnologie in Dresden, deren Ausbau mit Hilfe der engagierten Wirtschaftsförderung der Stadt und der Impulse aus Initiativen wie „BioMeT" vorangebracht werden soll, in starkem Maße mit prägen. Das in der Planungsphase befindliche Bio-Innovationszentrum, ein der Biotechnologie vorbehaltenes Technologiezentrum in der Nachbarschaft von

Bearbeitung von Siliziumscheiben für die Waferfertigung, Zentrum Mikroelektronik Dresden GmbH.

Processing of silicon discs for wafer production, Zentrum Mikroeelektronik Dresden GmbH.

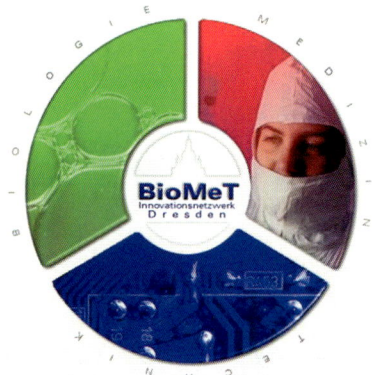

Signet des Dresdner Innovationsnetzwerkes BioMeT–Preisträger im InnoRegio-Wettbewerb.

Signature mark of the Dresden innovation network BioMeT award winner in the InnoRegio competition.

Location Advantages

And the growth goes on – A confirmation of the advantages of this city as well as of an excellent business management. The existing qualified labour force, strong research and development potentials in the city are the strengths of this location with focal points including materials, their development, processing and treatment, in electronics and computer technology as well as in production technologies, which apart from the Technical University, the FH of Technology and Economy, the Institutes of the Max-Planck Societies, the Fraunhofer Society and the Research Association "G.W. Leibniz" are also represented by specialised mid-sized R&D companies in certain fields.

The task of the joint-venture of Siemens/Infineon and Motorola in Dresden, to solve the considerable technological problems in the conversion of a switch circuit on wafers of the hitherto standard 200 mm diameter size to the productivity increasing 300 mm size was achieved before the scheduled time and has won the company a pioneering position in the world in the application of this technology. Also from Dresden, from the presently for around 2.2 billion DM newly built company of Infineon Technologies SC 300 in direct vicinity of the old existing Infineon work, will come the products for the serial production of memory chips on the basis of the new technologies. The fact that Dresden, even before 1990 one of the "capitals" of microelectronics and computer technology in the former COMECON, has acquired a good reputation reaching far beyond Germany as an important location of this branch within a few years, is proven by the decision of the US-concern Advanced Micro Devices (AMD) to carry out here its first company settlement in Europe with an investment of 3.4 billion DM. From a small "Arbeitsstelle für Mikroelektronik" (workplace for microelectronics), hub for independent microelectronic developments in the Dresden of the sixties in the 20th century, emerged later the Unternehmen Zentrum Mikroelektronik Dresden (ZMD). Today, this traditional company of Dresden is a profiled specialist of mixed signals ASIC's, particularly for car electronics, the third largest representative of the semiconductor branch in Dresden (approx. 450 employees at present, with strong growth aims). By the way, this company was also present at the EXPO 2000 with a new development, an electronic waste gas measuring and engine control system for cars.

Other facets of the cluster "Microelectronics/Computer Technology" are formed by the research potential in Dresden, which is oriented towards the range of topics underlying this cluster and the great number of mid-sized companies that have by means of their products, services and clients a close relationship to these high technologies. For the location quality and the economic development in Dresden they are by no means of less importance than the large corporations of the semiconductor branch.

Dresden has embarked on the path of the development of biotechnology as a structurally significant branch of the future economy for the city and the region. A network of research institutions, enterprises and supporters of the financial sector, from administration and politics called "BioMeT" stands for the spectrum of biotechnology in Dresden: biology, medicine, technology. In representation of the research institutions that are participating in BioMeT on the whole, there are to mention here the Max-Planck Institute for Molecular Cell Biology and Genetics settled in 2000, the TU Dresden with several of its 14 faculties, the presently boasting a new building of a laboratory complex interdisciplinary Center for Biomaterials of the Institute for Polymer Research and the Center for Molecular Biological and Medical Technology Material Research of the TU Dresden. Dresden's technological competence rich in tradition proves to be a valuable basis of for the strong pillar for the field of "technology". Surely, the field of "Bio Technology" will in future also influence to a great extent the landscape of biotech companies in Dresden, whose expansion will be advanced with the help of committed economic promotion of the city and impulses from initiatives like "BioMeT". The Bio-Innovation Center presently in its planning stage being a technology centre reserved for biotechnology located in the vicinity of Max-Planck Institute and University Hospital, will be providing after completion of its 1st construction phase planned for 2002, also to start-up founders and young entrepreneurs from technically oriented fields of biotechnology operational areas according to their needs.

Also nano technology in Dresden is receiving stimulation from biotechnology. Materials research at the TU Dresden and other Dresden institutes comprises also projects such as DNS-metallization for the production of electrical nano conductors, production of nano structured function coating by means of bacterial membrane proteins, of structured biopolymer coats, of bio molecular surfaces on medical metal implantates, which are designed to enable a growing together of implantates with living tissue and other non product developments.

With the name "BioParc", the Bio Computer Center planned by the Klaus-Tschira-Foundation will form a network node between bio and computer technologies. The interpretation of genotype data, development of mathematical models and of software building on it and similar work will be his focal points.

Modell BioParc (Klaus-Tschira-Stiftung) – Baustein für BioPolis Dresden.
BioParc Model (Klaus-Tschira-Foundation) – Component for BioPolis Dresden.

Standortvorteile

Die Dresdner Druck- und Verlagshaus GmbH & Co. KG – ein Unternehmen von Gruner+Jahr – ist die modernste Druckerei Europas.
The Dresden Druck- und Verlagshaus GmbH & Co. KG (printing and editorial house) a company of Gruner + Jahr, are the most modern printers of Europe.

Max-Planck-Institut und Universitätsklinikum, wird nach der bis 2002 geplanten Fertigstellung seines 1. Bauabschnittes auch Existenzgründern und jungen Unternehmen aus der „technik-orientierten" Biotechnologie deren Bedürfnissen entsprechende Betriebsflächen anbieten.

Auch die Nanotechnologie in Dresden erhält von der Biotechnologie Anregungen. Werkstoffforschung an der TU Dresden und anderen Dresdener Instituten umfasst dementsprechend auch Projekte wie z. B. DNS-Metallisierung zur Herstellung elektrischer „Nanoleitbahnen", die Erzeugung von nanostrukturierten Funktionsschichten mittels bakterieller Membranproteine, von strukturierten Biopolymerschichten, von biomolekularen Oberflächen auf medizinischen Metallimplantaten, die ein Verwachsen der Implantate mit dem lebenden Gewebe ermöglichen sollen, und andere Nanoprodukt-Entwicklungen.

Einen „Netzknoten" zwischen Bio- und Informationstechnologie wird das von der Klaus-Tschira-Stiftung in Dresden unter dem Namen „BioParc" geplante Bioinformatik-Zentrum bilden. Interpretation der Erbgutdaten, Entwicklung mathematischer Modelle und darauf aufbauender Software u. ä. werden Schwerpunkte seiner Arbeit sein.

Diese bisherige Entwicklungsdynamik auch zukünftig aufrechtzuerhalten ist eine der vorrangigsten Aufgaben für die Dresdner Wirtschafts- und Stadtentwicklungspolitik. 1990 stand die Stadt vor der gewaltigen Aufgabe, die Versäumnisse bei der Stadtentwicklung bis 1989 aus der Nachkriegs-Vergangenheit aufzuarbeiten und dabei auch wichtige materielle und administrative Voraussetzungen für den Erfolg ihrer Bemühungen um Bewahrung des Unternehmensbestandes und die Neuansiedlung von insbesondere Produktionsunternehmen und unternehmensnahen Dienstleistern mit einem breiten Branchen- und Betriebsgrößenspektrum und von lokaler bis internationaler Herkunft zu schaffen. Die Stadt hat auch unter den Bedingungen dieser Neuanfangsphase, als ein privater Immobilienmarkt noch nicht funktionierte, durch effektive Dienstleistungen dafür gesorgt, dass für ansiedlungsinteressierte Unternehmen kurzfristig geeignete Grundstücke verfügbar wurden und die Investoren Planungs- und Handlungssicherheit erhielten. Großansiedlungen wurden auch auf der „grünen Wiese" ermöglicht. Namhafte Konzerne, z. B. Gruner+Jahr, für seine modernste Illustrationsdruckerei, wie auch Infineon haben aber auch ehemalige Militärflächen in der Stadt als gute Standorte beurteilt und gezeigt, dass eine Konversion auch in der für ihre Investitionsvorhaben benötigten Kurzfristigkeit und Schnelligkeit erfolgreich möglich war. Die Stadt hat mit einem rationellen und wirksamen Projektmanagement bei den ihr obliegenden Planungs- und Genehmigungsverfahren eine optimale Organisation und Herstellung der erforderlichen Erschließungsmaßnahmen und Betreuung der Investoren – einschließlich der Vermittlung nichtkommunaler Grundstücke – gesichert und damit mit bis dahin in Deutschland ungewohnt kurzen Verfahrensfristen die Berechenbarkeit der Investitionen gewährleistet und die Investoren in die Lage versetzt, ihre eigenen, an den Bedingungen des Marktes orientierten Zeitpläne für die Realisierung ihrer Vorhaben uneingeschränkt umzusetzen.

Etwa 80 kleine und mittlere produzierende Unternehmen oder unternehmensnahe Dienstleister haben in den bisher von der Stadt durch Sanierung und Neuentwicklung von Industrie- oder Militärbranchen geschaffenen Gewerbegebieten mit einer Gesamtfläche von ca. 150 ha maßgeschneiderte, preisgünstige, gut erschlossene und sofort bebaubare Grundstücke für ihre Neuansiedlung oder Expansion gefunden. Mit dieser auf Fortsetzung ausgerichteten Gewerbeflächenpolitik ergänzt die Stadt den privaten Gewerbeimmobilienmarkt,

Kommunales Gründer- und Gewerbezentrum an der Löbtauer Straße.
Communal Founder and Industrial Centre at Löbtauer Street.

Location Advantages

To maintain also in future the present dynamism of developments is one of the foremost priorities for the economic and urban development policy of Dresden. In 1990, the city was confronted with the huge task to catch up with the omissions in urban development from the period after the war until 1989 and at the same time to create important material and administrative conditions to ensure the success of their efforts in preserving the existing stock of companies and acquiring new settlements especially of production companies and service providers close to companies with a broad range of branches and company sizes and of local and international origin. The city administration also took care, under the conditions of this phase of new beginning and when the private property market did not function yet, that suitable real estate was made available at short term for companies interested in settling here and that the investors received safety of planning and of action. Large settlements have also been enabled "on the green meadow" so to speak. Renowned corporations, like Gruner + Jahr for example, for its most modern illustration printers, as well as Infineon, have evaluated former military areas in the city as good locations and shown that a conversion has been successfully possible also in the short term and rapidity necessary for their investments. The city has ensured with a rational and effective project management of planning and permit procedures an optimal organisation and production of the required development measures and the support of investors – including the mediation of non-communal real estate – and thus guaranteed in short processing times, up to now very unusual in Germany, the feasibility of investments and thus enabled investors to implement completely their own time schedules for realizing their projects in orientation towards the conditions of the markets.

About 80 small and mid-sized manufacturing companies or service providers close to companies have found real estate for the new settlements or expansion in industrial areas created by the city through reconstruction and redevelopment of industrial or military fallow land of a total area of approx. 150 ha., tailor-made, inexpensive, well-developed and in a condition for immediate construction. The city complements the private industrial real estate market, which also offers areas for this usage, but mainly provides the

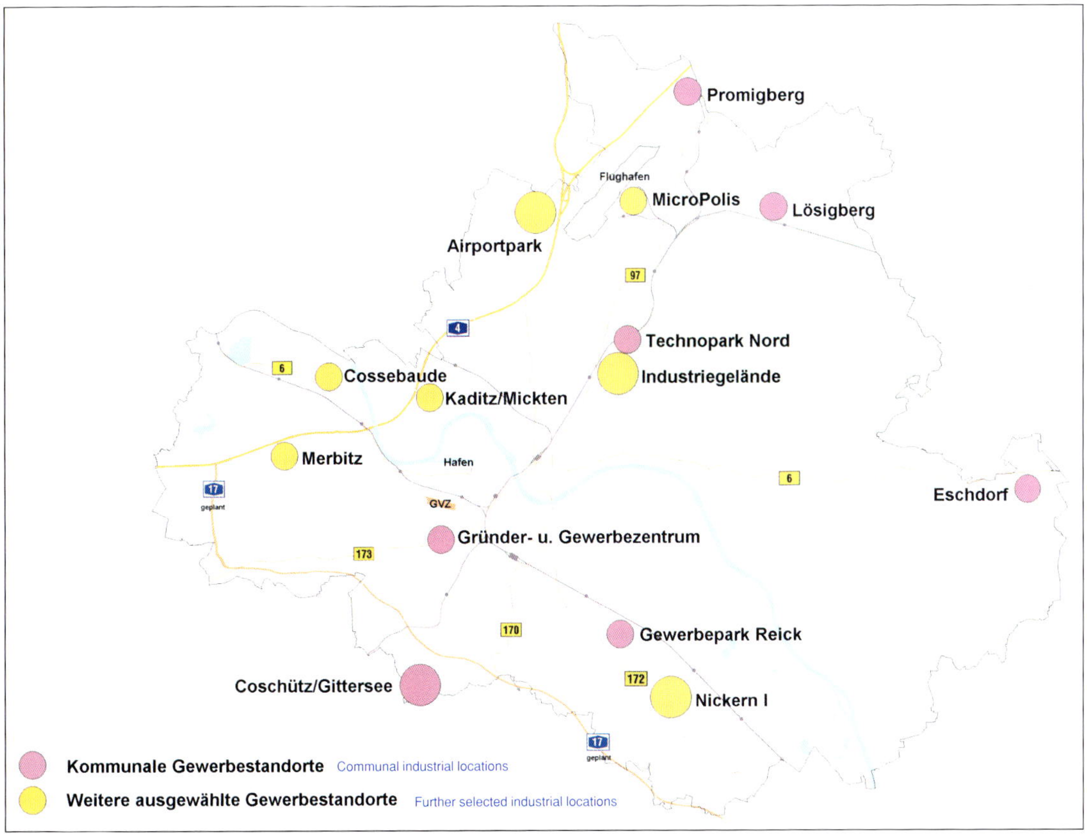

Technologiezentrum Dresden GmbH – Brutstätte und Sprungbrett für mittelständische Hightech-Unternehmen.

TechnologyCenterDresden GmbH – breeding place and springboard for mid-sized high-tech enterprises.

Ausgewählte Gewerbestandorte in Dresden.

Selected industrial locations in Dresden.

Standortvorteile

Autobahnabfahrt Dresden-Altstadt.

Motorway exit Dresden-Old Historic City.

der auch Flächen für diese Nutzungen anbietet, hauptsächlich aber die für konsum-, finanz- oder anderweitig büroorientierte Dienstleistungen benötigten Grundstücke bereitstellt.

Über 90 junge Technologieunternehmen haben sich in den Gebäuden der TechnologieZentrum Dresden GmbH, einem Gemeinschaftsunternehmen von u. a. Stadt und TU, eingemietet. Dank einer nachfragegerechten Investitions- und Dienstleistungspolitik und erfolgreicher Mieterakquisition hat sich das Technologiezentrum von allerbescheidensten Anfängen bei seiner Gründung 1991 zu einem der vier größten und anerkanntesten deutschen Technologiezentren entwickelt.

Handwerks-, Produktions- und Dienstleistungsunternehmen einer breiten Branchenpalette, die funktionsgerechte und kostengünstige Mietflächen für ihre Arbeit suchen, haben sie in dem ersten von der Dresdner Gewerbehofgesellschaft (DGH), ebenfalls ein Beteiligungsunternehmen der Stadt, fertiggestellten Gewerbehof so ihren Belangen entsprechend vorgefunden, dass dieses Objekt innerhalb kurzer Zeit vollständig vermietet werden konnte und die Gesellschaft sich schneller als geplant veranlasst sieht, weitere derartige Objekte zu entwickeln.

Seit dem Ende der staatlichen Abschottung gegenüber dem Westen und im Hinblick auf eine künftige EU-Mitgliedschaft mittel- und osteuropäischer (MEO) Staaten wächst der Standort Dresden weiter hinein in seine alte, neue Rolle als Keuzungspunkt west-östlicher und nord-südlicher Verkehrswege und als Drehscheibe für Geschäftsbeziehungen mit den benachbarten MEO-Ländern. Der dementsprechende Ausbau der erforderlichen Straßeninfrastruktur ist auf den überregionalen Verbindungen seit 1990 weit vorangekommen. Die Erneuerung und die Erweiterung der Bundesautobahnen 4 und 13 auf sechs Spuren ist im Bereich der Landeshauptstadt abgeschlossen. Der in 2000 erfolgte Lückenschluss zwischen den BAB 2 und 14 im Gebiet Halle/Magdeburg hat für Dresden neben den bestehenden Autobahn-Direktverbindungen nach Westen, Südwesten, Süden, Norden, Nordosten und Osten auch eine nach Nordwesten – über Leipzig in den Raum Hannover geschaffen. Im Bau ist die Südoststrecke (BAB 17), die, im Nordwesten Dresdens von der BAB 4 abzweigend, die Verbindung nach Südosten – über Prag, Brünn, Bratislava – herstellen wird und die Dresden nahe seiner Stadtgrenze von Nordwesten bis Südosten umgreifen wird, so eine hervorragende Anbindung der ihrer Revitalisierung harrenden ausgedehnten Gewerbeflächen im Südosten der Stadt schaffend. Neben der Europa-Straße entsteht damit gegenwärtig und in den nächsten Jahren auch eine vorzügliche City-Umgehung, die Autofahrern aus dem gesamten linkselbischen Dresden die Erreichbarkeit der überregionalen Verkehrswege und aller anderen Stadtgebiete beträchtlich erleichtern und die Innenstadt vom Durchgangsverkehr entlasten wird.

Bei der innerstädtischen Verkehrsinfrastruktur hat die Stadt zahlreiche aufwändige Bauvorhaben in Angriff genommen, die auch dem Wirtschaftsverkehr leistungsfähigere Trassen und auf die

Location Advantages

necessary real estate for consumer, financial or other office-oriented services, by means of this industrial area policy geared towards continuation.

More than 90 technology companies have rented spaces in the buildings of Technology Center GmbH, a joint venture of the City of Dresden and the TU, and others. Thanks to an investment and service policy suited to the demand and the successful acquisition of tenants, the Technology Center has developed into one of the four largest and most renowned German Technology Centres after it's most humble beginnings on foundation in 1991.

Skilled trade, production and service providing companies of a broad range of branches, which are looking for functional and inexpensive rental space for their work, have found it in this first by the Dresden Gewerbehofgesellschaft (DGH) – also a participating company of the city – completed industrial yard in such good conditions that suited exactly their needs and that have caused that this object has been completely occupied in a short time and the society has to plan faster than expected the development of further objects of this type.

Since the end of the state bulkhead against the West and in view of a future membership in the EU of the Middle and Eastern European States (MEO), the location of Dresden is growing further into it's old and new role as a crossing point of West-Eastern and North-Southern transport routes and as a turning wheel for business relations with neighbouring MEO-countries. The corresponding extension of necessary road infrastructure has been advanced considerably on the supraregional connections since 1990. The restoration and extension of federal motorways 4 and 13 on six lanes has been completed in the area of the regional capital. Closing the gap of the BAB 2 with 14 in the Halle/Magdeburg area in 2000 has created for Dresden, apart from the existing direct motorway connections to the West, South-West, South, North, North-East and East, also one to the Northwest across Leipzig into the Hanover area. The South-East stretch (BAB 17) is under construction, which – branching off in the North-West of Dresden from the BAB 4 – will create the connection to the South-East – via Prague, Brünn, Bratislava – and which will encircle Dresden near it's city limits from the North-West to the South-East, thus creating an excellent connection to the extensive industrial areas in the South-East of the city, which are waiting for their revitalization.

Thus, apart from the European Road there is presently and in the coming years being developed, an excellent city by-pass that will facilitate considerably access to supraregional transport routes and all other city districts for drivers of the whole of Dresden left-side of the river Elbe and will relieve the inner city from through traffic.

The city has embarked on numerous expensive construction projects for it's inner city transport infrastructure, which will also open up more efficient marked-out routes to the economic traffic and such routes that are related to the actual main

Eine der zahlreichen innerstädtischen Parkierungsanlagen: die Tiefgarage an der Semperoper.
One of the numerous inner-city parking provisions, here the underground car park at the Semperopera.

Innerstädtisches Flair in der Münzgasse, die direkt von der Brühlschen Terrasse zur Frauenkirche führt.
Inner-city flair in the Münzgasse, that leads directly from the Brühlsch Terrace to the Frauenkirche.

Standortvorteile

Modell der neuen Waldschlösschen-Brücke.
Model of the new Waldschlösschen Bridge.

heutigen Hauptstandorte der Wirtschaft im Stadtgebiet bezogene Routen eröffnen werden, darüberhinaus den historisch entstandenen Verkehrs-„Hauptknoten" Innenstadt weiter „entknoten" bzw. dem Einkaufs- und Tourismuszentrum Innenstadt einen Zugewinn an Aufenthaltsqualität und bei der Erreichbarkeit für den Zielverkehr bringen wird. Von den heute über 1.400 km Straßen im Stadtgebiet wurden seit 1990 ca. 200 km neu gebaut bzw. grundlegend erneuert.

Die neue Elbequerung („Waldschlösschen-Brücke") am östlichen City-Rand wird die direkteste Verbindung zwischen dem Dresdner Südosten und dem Norden mit den Hauptzentren der Mikroelektronik und Informationstechnologie, dem Flughafen, den BAB 4 und 13 herstellen. Im Ausbau befindet sich die Zufahrtsstraße zu dem unmittelbar am Stadtrand, mit Anschluss an die vorbeiführende BAB 4, gelegenen Flughafen, der im übrigen außer der Straße auch durch den Neubau einer S-Bahn mit dem Stadtzentrum verbunden ist. Die sogenannte „Nordtangente" nimmt die Bundesstraße 173 aus dem Bereich großer Wohngebiete heraus und schafft – insbesondere für Ziel- und Quellverkehre des rechtselbischen Dresdens, darunter vom und zum in diesem Stadtgebiet gelegenen Güterverteilzentrum und Elbehafen – einen weiteren günstigen Zugang zu den nördlichen und westlichen Teilen der Stadt und zum angrenzenden Umland sowie zur BAB 4. Abgeschlossen ist der Ausbau der B 172 zwischen dem Dresdner Osten und den südlichen und südwestlichen Stadtteilen.

Auch in den innerstädtischen Bereichen wurden und werden bedeutende Infrastrukturverbesserungen vorgenommen und weitere geplant. So wurde am Übergang vom Hauptbahnhof zum Stadtzentrum, wo in den nächsten Jahren einer der „Eingänge" zur Stadt baulich neu gestaltet wird, ein bisheriger Verkehrsknoten durch Neugestaltung wichtiger innerstädtischer Straßenführungen entflochten und der Verkehr um das unmittelbare Stadtzentrum herum erleichtert und beschleunigt. Mit der baulichen Stadtentwicklung verbunden ist das Ziel der Stadt, die Erreichbarkeit der City neben der sehr guten Erschließung durch die öffentlichen Verkehrsmittel auch für den Autoverkehr weiter zu verbessern. Die Herausnahme von Verkehr, dessen Ziel oder Quelle die Innenstadt nicht ist, durch das Angebot erneuerter City-Umgehungs-Trassen dient diesem Ziel. Die derzeitige Erneuerung und der Ausbau der S-Bahn-Trassen, die Dresden mit dem Umland verbinden, macht die bestehenden Alternativangebote zum eigenen Auto noch konkurrenzfähiger. Eine andere Maßnahme zur Verbesserung der Erreichbarkeit der City als Einkaufs-, Verwaltungs- und Kulturzentrum der Stadt ist die Schaffung von ausreichenden Anlagen des ruhenden Verkehrs, die in der City zwangsläufig ihren Platz auch unter der Erde finden müssen. Besuchern der historischen Altstadt mit ihren Sehenswürdigkeiten, Museen, Kunstgalerien, Theatern steht seit einiger Zeit eine große Tiefgarage am Landtag zur Verfügung. Mit der Ausschreibung des Altmarkt-Areals (der zentrale Platz in der Innenstadt) als Standort einer großen Tiefgarage hat die Stadt Ende 2000 weitere dementsprechende Entwicklungen angestoßen. Im Bau ist auch eine Tiefgarage am Hauptbahnhof/Wiener Platz, die zusammen mit der Altmarkt-Garage das bestehende Stellplatzangebot im Bereich der Prager Straße, einer der Hauptstandorte für den innerstädtischen Einzelhandel, beträchtlich erweitern wird.

Dresden ist ein interessanter, inspirierender, internationaler und innovativer Wirtschaftsstandort. Dafür legen Aussagen wie die des Vorstandsvorsitzenden der Silicon Vision AG, Hersteller von bisher weltweit einzigartigen Bildsensor-Chips, die sich 2000 hier ansiedelte, Zeugnis ab – mit dem Hinweis auf den Rang der Stadt als Technologiestandort: „Wenn man einen neuen Standort sucht, kommt man automatisch auf Dresden." ∎

Landeshauptstadt Dresden
Dezernat Wirtschaft und Verkehr
Postfach 12 00 20
D-01001 Dresden
Telefon: +49 (351) 488 23 46
Telefax: +49 (351) 495 23 30
Internet: www.dresden.de/wirtschaft

Location Advantages

locations of the economy in the city area. Furthermore, they will disengage the historically grown main junction of traffic in the inner city further and add to the staying quality in the shopping and tourist centres of the inner city as well as bring about accessibility for the destination traffic. Of the over 1,400 km of roads in the city area today, since 1990 approx. 200 km have been newly built or fundamentally renewed.

The new crossing over the river Elbe ("Waldschlösschen Bridge") on the Eastern city limits will create the most direct connection between the South-East of Dresden and the North with it's main centres of microelectronics and computer technology, the airport and the BAB 4 and 13. Presently under construction is the feeder road, with link onto the passing BAB 4, leading to the airport situated directly on the outskirts of the city, which by the way can also be reached in future by the newly built city railway linking it with the city centre. The so-called "North-Tangent" takes the federal highway 173 out of the great residential areas and creates – particularly for destination and source traffic in Dresden on the right-side of the Elbe river, including to and from freight distribution centre and the Elbe harbour located in this city district – further favourable access to the Northern and Western parts of the city and to the adjoining surrounding countryside as well as to the BAB 4. The extension of the B 172 between the East of Dresden and the Southern and Southwestern city districts has been completed.

Important improvements of infrastructure have been and are being made also in the inner-city areas and still further are being planned. Thus, at the crossing from main train station to the city centre, where in the next years one of the "entrances" to the city are redesigned in terms of construction, a till now existing traffic junction has been disengaged through the redesign of important inner-city street routings and traffic directly around the immediate city centre has been relieved and accelerated. Linked to the urban development is the aim of the city to improve further the accessibility of the inner city, besides the very good opening out through public transport also for car traffic. The removal of traffic, whose destination or source is not the inner city, through offering new city feeder routes serves exactly this aim. The present renewal and extension of the city railway routes, that connect Dresden with it's surrounding countryside, makes existing alternative offers even more competitive compared with one's own car. Another measure for the improvement of access to the city being the shopping, administration and cultural centre of the city, is the creation of sufficient spaces for still traffic, which must find in the city undoubtedly it's place also underneath the earth. Visitors to the historic old part of the city with it's places of interest for sightseeing, museums, art galleries, theatres have a large underground car park near the regional parliament to their disposal for some time now. With the tender for the Old Market area (the central square in the inner-city) as a location for a large underground car park, the city has brought about further corresponding developments at the of the year 2000. There is also an underground car park under construction at the main train station/Wiener Platz, which together with the Old Market garage will considerably extend the provision of parking places in the area of Prague-Street, one of the main locations of inner-city retail trade.

Dresden is an interesting, inspiring, international and innovative economic location. To this bear witness expressions like the one of the Chairman of the Board of Silicon Vision AG, producer of the till now unique picture-sensory-chip that settled here in 2000, pointing to the rank of the city as a technology location: "If one is looking for a new location, one automatically finds Dresden." ∎

Blick von der Brühlschen Terrasse auf Hofkirche und Semperoper.
View from the Brühlsch Terrace on the Hofkirche and Semperopera.

Innovativ und kompetent – DREWAG bietet überzeugendes Leistungspaket

Competent and Innovative – DREWAG offers convincing service package

Die sächsische Landeshauptstadt Dresden ist berühmt für ihre wertvollen Kunstsammlungen, ihre beeindruckende Geschichte und natürlich für ihre freundlichen Bürger. In den letzten Jahren ist ein weiterer Begriff hinzugekommen, der die Elbestadt weit über die Landesgrenzen bekannt gemacht hat: die Mikroelektronik. Deutsche und amerikanische Chiphersteller haben modernste Werke errichtet, die sich erfolgreich auf dem Weltmakt behaupten. Basis für solch funktionierende Wirtschaft ist nicht zuletzt eine moderne Versorgungsstruktur, wie sie die DREWAG - Stadtwerke Dresden GmbH in den zurückliegenden Jahren aufgebaut hat. Und natürlich Leistungsangebote, die - sowohl einzeln als auch im Paket - dem Kunden maximalen Nutzen bieten.

Zum Beispiel: Facility-Management
Hier kann der Kunde frühzeitig die Erfahrung und das Potenzial der DREWAG nutzen und die günstigsten Versorgungs- und Finanzierungsmöglichkeiten ermitteln. Die DREWAG übernimmt Projektierungs-, Bau- und Montageleistungen und gewährleistet nach der Inbetriebnahme die laufende Versorgung, Abrechnung sowie den technischen Rundum-Service. Auch für die Realisierung ganz neuer technischer und wirtschaftlicher Projekte ist sie die erste Adresse. Natürlich arbeitet das Versorgungsunternehmen nicht immer allein, sondern sucht sich kompetente Partner für Spezialaufgaben.

Zum Beispiel:
Wohn- und Geschäftsanlagen, Wohngebiete
Es muss nicht sein, dass die Zusammenarbeit mit der DREWAG an der Übergabestation endet. Sie können auch die komplette Planung, Installation, Lieferung, Service und detaillierte Abrechnung aus einer Hand erhalten. Und zwar für alle Basismedien: Strom, Wasser, Wärme und Klimakälte. Und natürlich können Sie über die Konditionen mit uns verhandeln.

Zum Beispiel: Industrie und Gewerbeprojekte
Dass sie große, auch komplizierte Versorgungsprojekte bestens bewältigen kann, hat die DREWAG längst bewiesen - nicht zuletzt im eigenen Haus mit dem Bau des modernen Gasturbinen-Heizkraftwerkes. Auch hier ging es darum, die wirtschaftlich beste, technisch sicherste und umweltschonendste Variante für viele Prozesse zu finden, zu verhandeln, kurzfristig Genehmigungen zu bekommen und gemeinsam mit erfahrenen Partnern in die Tat umzusetzen. Auch in der Folge ermittelt sie Energie-Einsparpotenziale für den Kunden, beschafft Verschleiß- und Ersatzmaterialien zu guten regionalen Einkaufskonditionen.

Zum Beispiel: Spezialprojekte mit Partnern
In weniger als einem Jahr realisierte die DREWAG gemeinsam mit AIR LIQUIDE Düsseldorf (Weltmarktführer im Bereich Industriegase) und mit dem Reinraumspezialisten M+W Zander Stuttgart (als Generalunternehmer) ein beispielloses Projekt: das Energieversorgungscenter Dresden Wilschdorf, ein 70 Millionen Mark teures Heizkraftwerk für das sächsische Unternehmen des amerikanischen Mikrochip-Herstellers AMD.
Über einen Zeitraum von 15 Jahren wird AMD von der DREWAG Strom, Wärme und Klimakälte im Wert von ca. einer halben Milliarde DM beziehen. Die technischen Anforderungen sind hoch. Für die Lieferung von Strom, Wärme und Kälte gelten strenge Toleranz-Vorgaben. Die Luft wird in einem aufwendigen Sterilisations-Verfahren „saubergekühlt".

Zum Beispiel: Unsere „Förderwege Heizung"
Für die Eigentümer von Mehrfamilienhäusern mit drei und mehr Wohneinheiten bietet die DREWAG in ihrem Versorgungsgebiet Fördermittel für den Ersatz von Kohleheizungen durch leitungsgebundene Energieträger – Fernwärme oder Erdgas – an. In der Regel werden Fördermittel für ein Gebäude je Eigentümer bereitgestellt. Die Förderung ist einmalig und erfolgt über einen Zuschuss, der mit der Inbetriebnahme gezahlt wird. Nimmt man die Wärmeservicemodelle der DREWAG in Anspruch, erhöht sich der Förderumfang um 20 Prozent. ■

DREWAG: Modernstes Equipment für Strom, Wärme, Erdgas und Wasser

Mit modernstem Equipment garantiert die DREWAG die zuverlässige Versorgung mit Strom, Wärme (Fernwärme und Erdgas) und Wasser. Das Heizkraftwerk an der Nossener Brücke produziert Qualitätsstrom und Fernwärme auf umweltfreundlicher Erdgasbasis und gehört zu den modernsten Gasturbinen-Heizkraftwerken Europas.
Fast 285.000 Tarifkunden und 2.200 Sonderkunden werden von der DREWAG mit Strom beliefert. Für die sichere Versorgung mit Trink- und Brauchwasser betreibt die DREWAG eigene Wasserwerke. Die Qualität des Wassers wird von einem zertifizierten Labor ständig überwacht.

Energieversorgungscenter Dresden-Wilschdorf.
The energy supply centre Dresden-Wilschdorf.

Company Profile

The Saxon regional capital Dresden is famous for it's valuable art collections, it's impressive history and, of course, for its friendly citizens. In the past years, a further term has been added, which has made the city on the river Elbe known way beyond it's regional limits: microelectronics. German and American chip producers have established the most modern works that can successfully maintain their hold on the world market. The basis for such a well-functioning economic situation is also the result of a modern supply structure as the DREWAG – Stadtwerke Dresden GmbH –; the city amenities of Dresden have built up in the recent years. And of course the service provision – either individually or as a package – that offers maximum effectiveness to the customers.

DREWAG: The most modern equipment for electricity, heating, natural gas and water.

With the most modern equipment, DREWAG guarantees the reliable supply of electricity, heating (district heating and natural gas) and water. The combined heating and power station at Nossener Brücke produces quality electricity and district heating on the basis of non-polluting natural gas and is among the most modern gas-turbine heating and power stations of Europe.
Almost 285,000 tariff customers and 2,200 special customers are supplied by DREWAG with electricity. For the safe supply of drinking and usage water DREWAG operates its own waterworks. A certified laboratory constantly controls the quality of the water.

For example: Facility Management
Here, the customer can use early the experience and potential of DREWAG and find out the most favourable supply and financing possibilities. DREWAG takes on project, construction and assembly services and guarantees after implementation, the continuous supply, invoicing as well as the technical all-round service. It is also a first address for the realization of completely new and economic projects. Naturally, the supply company does not always work alone, but co-operates with competent partners for special tasks.

For example: Housing and business facilities, residential areas
It must not necessarily be the rule that co-operation with DREWAG ends at the stage of handing over. You can also receive the complete planning, installation, supply, service and detailed invoice from one provider only. And this goes for all basic media: electricity, water, heating and air conditioning or cooling. And, of course you can negotiate the conditions with us.

For example: industrial and trade projects
DREWAG has long proven that it is well capable of managing also complicated supply projects – not least in its own house with the construction of the modern gas turbine heating and power station. Here, it was also an issue to find the best economic, technically safest and most non-polluting alternative for many processes, to negotiate and receive short-term permits and to actually realize this project together with experienced partners. In following-up services, it calculates energy saving potentials for customers and procures wearing and spare part materials at good regional purchasing conditions.

For example: Special Projects with Partners
In less than one year, DREWAG realised together with AIR LIQUIDE Düsseldorf (world market leader in the field of industrial gases) and with the clean room specialist M+W Zander Stuttgart (as Main Contractor) a unique project: the energy supply centre Dresden Wilschdorf, a heating and power station worth 70 million DM for the Saxon company of the American microchip producer AMD. Over a period of 15 years, AMD will receive electricity, heating and air conditioning worth approx. half a billion DM. The technical requirements are of a high standard. For the supply of electricity, heating and air conditioning or cooling there exist strict tolerance limits. The air is "clean-conditioned" in a complex sterilisation process.

For example: Our "Ways for Subsidised Heating"
For owners of multiple storey houses with three or more flats, DREWAG provides within its supply area promotional financial means for the replacement of coal heaters with pipeline conducted energy sources – district heating or natural gas. This is a one-time promotion in form of a subsidy that is paid at implementation. If the models of heating services of DREWAG are utilized the value of promotional aid increases by 20 percent. ■

DREWAG – Stadtwerke Dresden GmbH

Geschäftsführer/Managing Director:
Dr. rer. pol. Wolf-Rüdiger Frank (Sprecher)
Techn. Dipl.-Volkswirt Peter Bossert

Gesellschafter/Corporate member:
Technische Werke Dresden GmbH
Dresden
55 Prozent/55 percent

GESO Beteiligungs- und Beratungs-AG
Dresden
35 Prozent/35 percent

Ruhrgas Energie Beteiligungs-AG
Essen
10 Prozent/10 percent

Mitarbeiter/Employees:
1.700

Umsatz/Turnover:
rund 800 Mio. DM

Anschrift/Address:
Rosenstraße 32
D-01067 Dresden
Telefon +49 (351) 860-0
Telefax +49 (351) 860-45 45
Internet www.drewag.de

Gasturbinenheizkraftwerk der DREWAG.
The DREWAG gas turbine heating and power station.

VAKUUMTECHNIK DRESDEN · GmbH

Geschäftsführer/Manager:
Rüdiger Wilberg
Klaus-Dieter Steinborn
Wolfgang Steeg

Gründungsjahr/Year of Foundation:
1991

Mitarbeiter/Employees:
65

Geschäftstätigkeit/Business Activity:
VTD ist Entwickler, Hersteller und Exporteur von Vakuum- Beschichtungsanlagen
- für funktionale und dekorative PVD-Hartstoffbeschichtungen
- für die Metallisierung von Kunststoff, Glas, Keramik und Metall
- für vakuumtechnische Sonderaufgaben

Zum Angebotsprofil gehören Vakuumtechnologien, Lizenzen und Know-how.

VTD is a developer, producer and exporter of vacuum coating plants in the fields of
- functional and decorative PVD hard material coatings
- metallization of plastics, glass, ceramics and metals
- vacuum-engineering special jobs

Transfer of vacuum technologies, licences and know-how complete the scope.

Anschrift/Address:
Bismarckstraße 66
D-01257 Dresden
Telefon   +49 (351) 28 05-0
Telefax   +49 (351) 28 05 240
E-Mail   info@vtd.de
Internet www.vtd.de

Unternehmenssitz in Dresden.
Company head office in Dresden.

Company Profile

Anlagen und Technologien für Top-Oberflächen

Systems and Technologies for High-quality Surfaces

Montage einer Metallisierungsanlage.
Assembling of Metallization plant.

VTD spezialisierte sein Entwicklungs- und Produktionsprofil auf technologie- und kundenspezifische Hochvakuum-Beschichtungsanlagen.

Die PVD-Hartstoffbeschichtungs-, Metallisierungs-, Optik- und Sonderanlagen sind in allen Bereichen der Wirtschaft einsetzbar.

Die Grundausrüstungen können Vakuumkammern von 250 mm bis 2.800 mm Durchmesser umfassen.

Zum Leistungspaket zählen die garantierten technischen und technologischen Spitzenwerte, hohe Produktivität und Zuverlässigkeit der Anlagen sowie ein schneller und guter Service.

In der eigenen Forschungs- und Entwicklungsabteilung von VTD beschäftigt sich ein Team hervorragend ausgebildeter Wissenschaftler mit der ständigen Neu- und Weiterentwicklung von vakuumtechnischen Erzeugnissen.

VTD liefert Anlagen in fast alle Erdteile, wobei Europa der Hauptabsatzmarkt ist. ∎

VTD has specialized its development and production profile on technology and customer-specific high-vacuum coating plants.

Our PVD hard material coating, metallization, optical and special vacuum plants can be used in all branches of the economy.

The basic equipment can comprise vacuum chambers of diameters from 250 to 2,800 mm.

Our performance package also includes approved technical and technological peak values, a high productivity and reliability of the plants and a fast and good service.

In our own research and development department a team of excellently educated scientists is permanently occupied with new and further developments of vacuum-engineering products.

We deliver our plants to nearly all continents with Europe being the main market. ∎

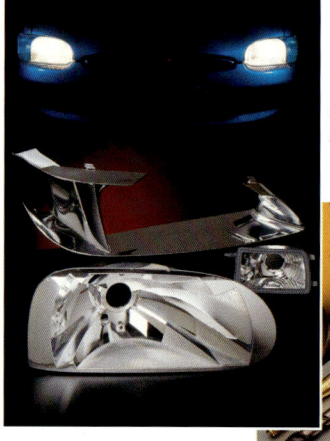

Metallische Schichten auf Kunststoff und Metall.

Metallic coatings on plastic and metal.

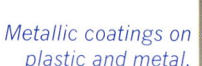

Company Profile

Werte schaffen mit Substanz und Service

Creating Value with Substance and Service

MicroPolis
Die IVG High-Tech-Area
in Dresden-Klotzsche

Anschrift/Address:
c/o IVG Immobilien GmbH
Christiane Hannemann
D-01109 Dresden
Telefon   +49 (351) 88 557-0
Telefax   +49 (351) 88 557-19
E-Mail   contact@micropolis.de
Internet www.micropolis.de

member of
it-parcs
Ein Technologiepark der IVG

IVG Holding AG

Vorstand/Executive Board:
Dr. Eckert John von Freyend (Vorsitzender/Chairman)
Dr. Dirk Matthey (Finanzvorstand/Executive Board Member for Finance)

IVG Immobilien GmbH Geschäftsführer/
IVG Immobilien GmbH Manager:
Dr. Bernd Kottmann (Vorsitzender/Chairman)
Manfred Thomas

Mitarbeiter/Employees (1999): 2.243

Umsatz/Turnover (1999): 423.6 Mio Euro

Immobilienverkehrswert/
Value of property portfolio: 3 Mrd. Euro

Geschäftstätigkeit/Business Activity:
Dienstleistungen rund um die Immobilie. Die IVG plant, finanziert, errichtet und vermietet Büro-, Gewerbe- und Spezialimmobilien in Europa.
All Services relating to real estate. IVG plans, finances, builds and rents office and commercial permises and specialty real estate in Europe.

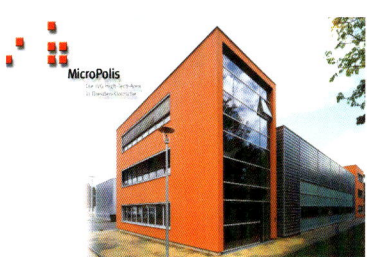

Im Dresdner Norden, dem Herzen der sächsischen Chip-Industrie, befindet sich Micropolis, ein Technologiepark der IVG. Geschaffen für Firmen der Mikroelektronik, Informations- und Kommunikationstechnik, Forschung und Dienstleistung, setzt der Park neue Maßstäbe bei der Raum- und Platzgestaltung durch die einzigartige Kombination von Produktionshallen, Serviceflächen und Büros. Micropolis bietet seinen Mietern eine flexibel gestaltbare Flächenaufteilung sowie eine funktionale Ausstattung, die sich jederzeit an die individuellen Bedürfnisse anpassen lässt. Nur wenige Minuten zum Flughafen und zur Autobahn garantieren erstklassige Verkehrsanbindung. Ebenso schnell ist der Standort mit dem ÖPNV zu erreichen. Schon heute findet man im Micopolis Namhafte Technologieunternehmen, die sich die Vorteile dieses Hightech-Standortes zu Nutzen machen.

it-parcs – eine Qualitätsmarke der IVG
it-parcs bietet innovativen Unternehmen in modernen Technologieparks inklusive umfassender Serviceleistungen. Von der IT- und TK-Ausstattung und dem Angebot von Sicherheitsdiensten über attraktive Konditionen beim Energiebezug oder der Beschaffung von Büroausstattungen bis zur Fördermittel- und Finanzierungsberatung oder dem Zugang zu Venture Capital vermittelt it-parcs Leistungen rund um Ihr Kerngeschäft. Eingebettet in ein internationales internet-gestütztes Kommunikationsnetzwerk können Ihre Ideen mit it-parcs um die Welt gehen. Heute sind unsere Netzwerk-Technologieparks bereits in Hamburg, Dresden, Düsseldorf, Nürnberg, München und Budapest zu finden, weitere Standorte sind in Vorbereitung.

IVG
IVG gehört mit einem Immobilienvermögen von 3 Mrd. Euro und einer Gebäudenutzfläche von 1,6 Mio. Quadratmetern zu den 10 bedeutenden börsennotierten Immobiliengesellschaften in Europa. IVG versteht sich als Immobilienpartner moderner innovativer Unternehmen, die sie immobilienseitig in ihrem Wachstumsprozeß begleitet. Die Investitionen von IVG konzentrieren sich auf Büroimmobilien und Technologieparks. ■

Located in the North of Dresden, the heart of the Saxon chip industry is Micropolis, a technology park of the IVG. Having been created for companies of the microelectronic, information and communication technology, research and service sectors the park sets new standards in the design of space and room through a unique combination of production halls, service areas and offices. Micropolis offers its tenants the possibility to apportion areas in a flexible manner as well as to equip these in such a functional way that it can be adjusted to individual requirements at any time. Since only a few minutes away from the airport and motorways, first-class transport connections are guaranteed. Just as fast, the location can be reached by public transport with the ÖPNV. Even today, one can find in Micropolis renowned technology enterprises that use the advantages of this high-tech location.

it-parcs – a quality brand name of IVG
it-parcs offers a comprehensive service provision to innovative companies in modern technology parks. Ranging from IT, TK equipment, and the provision of security services across attractive conditions in energy supply or the procurement of office equipment up to the consulting regarding promotional funds and financing or the access to venture capital it-parcs mediates services covering your core business. Imbedded in an international Internet supported communication network your ideas can go around the world with it-parcs. Today, our network technology parks can already be found in Hamburg, Dresden, Düsseldorf, Nürnberg, München and Budapest, further locations are being prepared.

IVG
IVG is among the 10 most important stock exchange registered real estate companies in Europe with real estate assets of 3 billion Euros and used area in buildings of 1,6 million m². IVG sees itself as real estate partner of modern and innovative companies that it accompanies in their growth in terms of real estate. IVG concentrates mainly on investments in office buildings and technology parks. ■

Zahlreiche namhafte Unternehmen haben sich bereits im Micropolis angesiedelt.

Numerous renowned enterprises have already settled in Micropolis.

Die Landeshauptstadt Dresden in Zahlen

Dresden, a state capital by numbers

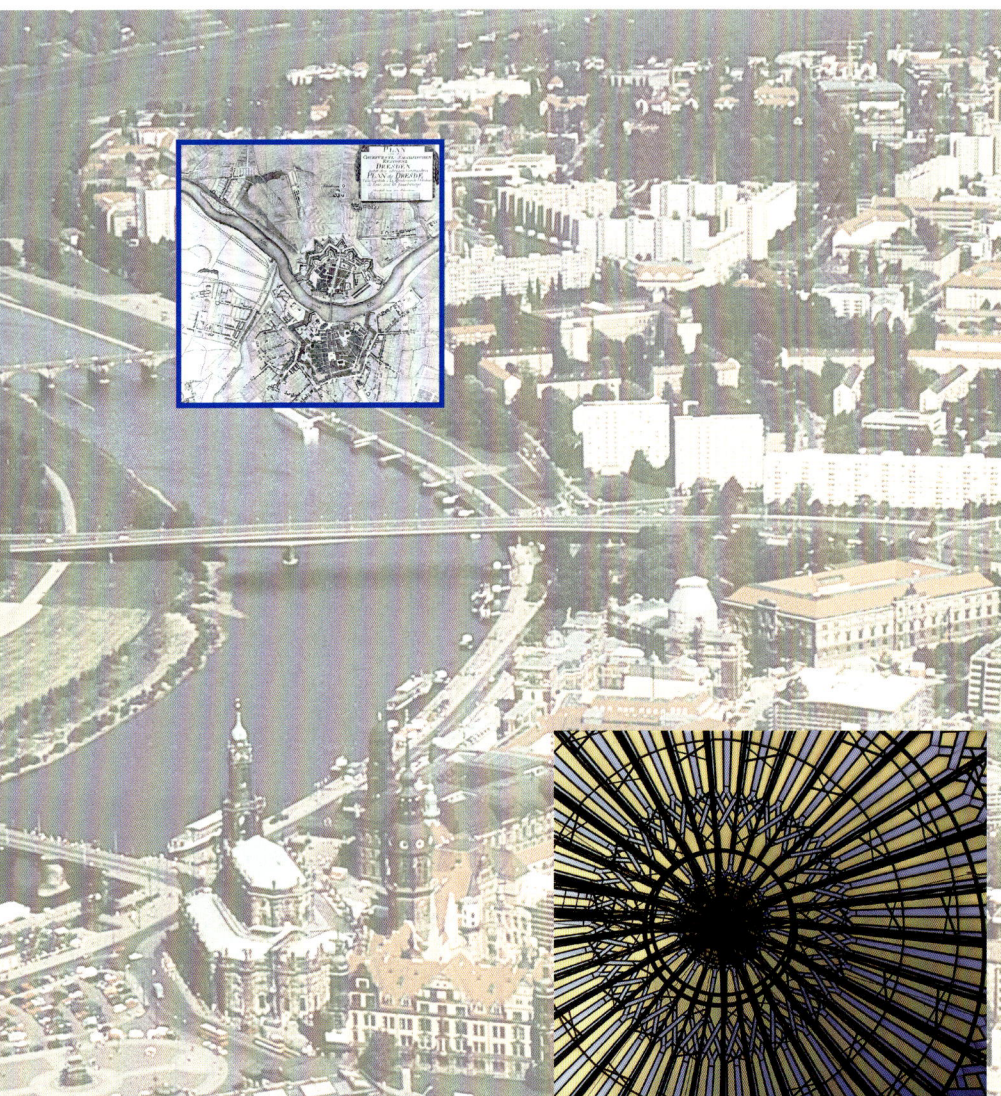

Landeshauptstadt Dresden

Im Bevölkerungsvergleich bundesdeutscher Städte steht Dresden an 15. Stelle.

Einwohner:	507.691
davon	245.623 Frauen (52 %)
	226.727 Männer (48 %)
darunter	13.363 Ausländer (3 %)
1206	Erste urkundliche Erwähnung
1216	Erstmalige Bezeichnung als Stadt
Partnerstädte:	Brazzaville (Kongo)
	Breslau
	Columbus (Ohio/USA)
	Coventry
	Florenz
	Hamburg
	Ostrava
	Salzburg
	Skopje
	St. Petersburg
	Straßburg
	Rotterdam
Gäste:	etwa 7,1 Millionen jährlich, davon 15 Prozent aus dem Ausland
Unterkünfte:	92 Hotels
	44 Pensionen
	5 Jugendherbergen
	4 Campingplätze

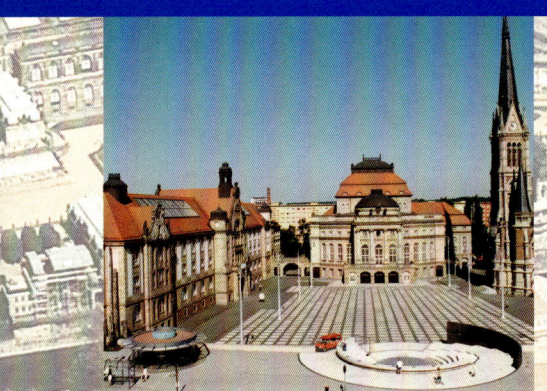

Statistics

Übersichtsbild aus dem Jahre 1852.

General map from 1852.

Dresden, a state capital

In comparison with other german cities, Dresden ranks at 15th position as to the population density.

Inhabitants:	507.691
	245.623 Women (52 %)
	226.727 Men (48 %)
among them	13.363 Foreigners (3 %)
1206	First documentary mention
1216	First denomination as a city
Twin-towns:	Brazzaville (Kongo)
	Breslau
	Columbus (Ohio/USA)
	Coventry
	Florenz
	Hamburg
	Ostrava
	Salzburg
	Skopje
	St. Petersburg
	Straßburg
	Rotterdam
Visitors:	about 7.1 million anually, among them 15 per cent from abroad
Accomodation:	92 Hotels
	44 Guest houses
	5 Youth hostels
	4 Camp sites

Company Profile

Dresdner Bank
Die Beraterbank

Dresdner Bank AG Region Ost

Geschäftsführung/Manager:
Hans-Jürgen Bartsch (Berlin)
Peter Becker (Berlin)
Dr. Holger Hatje (Berlin)
Paul Heimann (Dresden/Leipzig)
Hans-Kornel Krings (Berlin)
Dieter Schulte (Leipzig)
Jürgen Simon (Dresden/Leipzig)
Patrick Tessmann (Dresden/Leipzig)
Dieter Thomas (Berlin)
Eckhard Warnecke (Berlin)

Gründungsjahr/Year of Foundation:
1872

Mitarbeiter/Employees:
5.600

Anschrift/Address:
Dresdner Bank AG in Dresden
Ostra-Allee 9
D-01067 Dresden
Telefon +49 (351) 489-0

Dresdner Bank AG in Leipzig
Goethestraße 3-5
D-04093 Leipzig
Telefon +49 (341) 124-0

Dresdner Bank AG in Berlin
Pariser Platz 6
D-10877 Berlin
Telefon +49 (30) 31 53-0
Internet www.Dresdner-Bank.de

Das Hauptgebäude der Dresdner Bank in Dresden.
Main building of Dresdner Bank in Dresden.

Weltweites Unternehmen mit sächsischem Ursprung
Worldwide Corporation of Saxon Origin

Die Geschäftsstelle am Dr.-Külz-Ring.
Branch at the Dr.-Külz-Ring.

Es war ein 32-jähriger, der die Anregung zur Gründung der Dresdner Bank gab: Eugen Gutmann bewog 1872 die Inhaber des in Dresden alteingesessenen Bankhauses Michael Kaskel zur Umwandlung ihres Geschäftes in eine Aktienbank. Dieses Stammhaus arbeitete damals bereits 100 Jahre in Dresden. Sichtbar dokumentiert sich die Verbundenheit der Bank zu ihrem Herkunftsland Sachsen nach wie vor in Grün/Weiß, den Farben des Königreiches Sachsen.
Der Anschluss an das große Finanzierungsgeschäft und an die internationalen Anleihetransaktionen war aber nur von der Reichshauptstadt aus zu gewinnen. 1881 wurde deshalb eine Niederlassung in Berlin eröffnet und 1884 auch die Zentraldirektion nach Berlin verlegt.
Nachdem das Stammhaus in Dresden durch die Bombenangriffe im Februar 1945 zerstört worden war, verschärfte sich die Einschränkung der Geschäftstätigkeit durch den Einmarsch sowjetischer Truppen. Im August 1945 wurden alle Kreditinstitute geschlossen.
Nach der Öffnung der innerdeutschen Grenze beginnt eine neue Epoche für die Dresdner Bank. Bereits im Dezember 1989 ruft sie eine mit 20 Millionen DM ausgestattete Stiftung für ihre Geburtsstadt ins Leben, die Kulturstiftung Dresden der Dresdner Bank.
Heute sind mit Leipzig und Dresden gleich zwei Sitze der Geschäftsleitung der Dresdner Bank AG Region Ost in Sachsen etabliert. Von hier aus wird das Geschäft in den Bundesländern Sachsen, Sachsen-Anhalt und Thüringen gesteuert. Repräsentanzen und Filialen der Dresdner Bank gibt es in über 60 Ländern – der Name „Dresden" leuchtet somit in Santiago de Chile ebenso wie in Johannesburg, Baku, Shanghai oder Tokio. ■

A 32-year old provided the inspiration for the foundation of Dresdner Bank: In 1872, Eugen Gutmann persuaded the proprietors of the traditional local bank Michael Kaskel to change his business to that of a joint-stock bank. This parent bank had already been operating for 100 years in Dresden. In the colours green/white, the colours of the Kingdom of Saxony, the closeness of the bank to its country of origin Saxony is still visibly documented.
But only from the capital of the former German Reich, it was possible to penetrate into major financing business and to international bond transactions. For this reason, a branch was opened in Berlin in 1881 and in 1884, also the Central Directorate was relocated to Berlin.
After the parent house in Dresden was completely destroyed by bomb raids in February 1945, business activities were increasingly limited through the invasion of Soviet troops. In August 1945, all credit institutes were closed down.
After the opening of the inner-German border, a new era began for the Dresdner Bank. As early as 1989, it creates a foundation for its city of birth worth 20 million DM, the Kulturstiftung Dresden der Dresdner Bank (Cultural Foundation Dresden of Dresdner Bank).
Today, two locations of the Management of Dresdner Bank AG Region East are established in Saxony, in Leipzig and Dresden. Business in the regional states of Saxony, Sachsen-Anhalt and Thüringen is control from here. Representative offices and branches of Dresdner Bank exist in over 60 countries – the name "Dresden" thus shines in Santiago de Chile just as in Johannesburg, Baku, Shanghai or Tokyo. ■

Zugang zum Tresorraum Dr.-Külz-Ring.
Access to the vault at Dr.-Külz-Ring.

Company Profile

Kompetenz für Systeme mit Hochleistungskeramiken

Competence for systems with high-performance ceramics

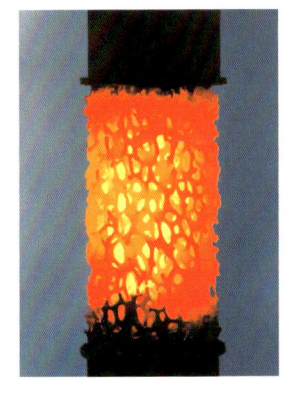

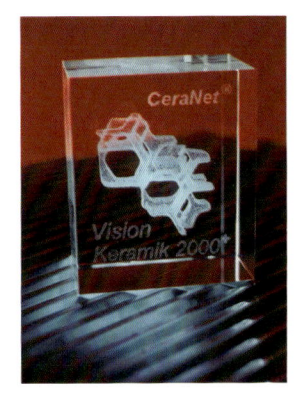

Fraunhofer Institut
Keramische Technologien
und Sinterwerkstoffe

Fraunhofer-Institut
Keramische Technologien
und Sinterwerkstoffe IKTS

Institutsleiter/Head of Institute:
Prof. Dr. rer. nat. habil. Waldemar Hermel

Gründungsjahr/Year of Foundation: 1992

Mitarbeiter/Employees: ca./approx. 130

Umsatz/Turnover: ca./approx. 8 Mio. Euro

Geschäftstätigkeit/Business Activity:
- Keramische Struktur- und Sonderwerkstoffe
  Dr. rer. nat. Christian Schubert
- Ceramic Structural and Special Materials
  Dr. Christian Schubert, PhD.

- Funktionskeramik und Systeme
  Dr. rer. nat. habil. Peter Otschik
  Dr. rer. nat. Andreas Schönecker
- Functional Ceramics and Systems
  Dr. Peter Otschik, PhD.
  Dr. Andreas Schönecker, PhD.

- Umweltverfahrenstechnik/Charakterisierung
  PD Dr. rer. nat. habil. Udo Gerlach
- Environmental Processing Technology/ Characterization
  PD Dr. Udo Gerlach, PhD.

Anschrift/Address:
Fraunhofer-Institut
Keramische Technologien
und Sinterwerkstoffe IKTS
Winterbergstraße 28
D-01277 Dresden
Telefon   +49 (351) 25 53-519
Telefax   +49 (351) 25 53-600
E-Mail   info@ikts.fhg.de
Internet   www.ikts.fhg.de

Das IKTS bietet industriellen Anwendern innovative Werkstofflösungen, vielfältige produktionsrelevante Prozesstechnologien und prototypische Erzeugnismuster auf dem Gebiet anorganisch-nichtmetallischer Hochleistungssysteme.

Auf der Basis angewandter Grundlagenforschung werden moderne werkstoffwissenschaftliche Konzepte in der Kette Herstellung – Struktur – Eigenschaften – Systemintegration applikationsorientiert und kundenspezifisch umgesetzt.

Das IKTS entwickelt neue funktionelle Verbünde, keramische Sonder- und Nanowerkstoffe, dielek- trische Komponenten der Sensorik und Aktorik, Lösungen der Mikrosystemtechnik (Dickschicht, LTCC), Energietechnik (SOFC) und Lösungen in der Umweltverfahrenstechnik (Filter, Ultraschalldesintegration von Klärschlämmen) sowie der qualifizierten Prozess- und Werkstoffanalytik.

In zunehmendem Maße werden applikationsorientierte Forschungsergebnisse bis zur Systemintegration und Pilotproduktion geführt.

Mehr als 5.000 m² Technika, Büros und Labors modernster Ausrüstung stehen hier für Forschungsaufträge zur Verfügung. ∎

The Fraunhofer-Institut for Ceramic Technologies and Sintered Materials IKTS provides industrial users with innovative solutions for materials, varied production-relevant processing technologies and prototypes of product samples in the field of inorganic non-metallic high-performance systems.

On the basis of the findings of applied scientific research, modern materials-relevant concepts are realized application-oriented and specific to customer requirements within the chain of: production – structure – properties – system integration.

The IKTS develops new functional combinations, ceramic speciality and nanomaterials, dielectric components of sensor and actuator technology, solutions in the areas of microsystem (thickness coating, LTCC), energy (SOFC) and ecological process technology (filter, ultrasound disintegration of sewage sludge) as well as the qualified process and materials analysis.

To a growing extent, application-oriented research findings are carried out up to the stage of system integration and pilot production.

More than 5,000 m² of technology, office and laboratory space furnished with the most modern equipment are available here for the execution of industrial research contracts. ∎

20 Ebenen SOFC stack für Hochtemperaturbrennstoffzellen.
20 levels SOFC stack for high-temperature fuel cells.

Berufsbildung

Bedarfsgerechte Bildung als Standortfaktor

Education suitable to the demand becomes a location factor

Die zunehmende Globalisierung der Märkte und die damit einhergehende durchgreifende Auswirkung auf die Wettbewerbssituation der Länder und Regionen führen zu Umbrüchen in den Wirtschaftsstrukturen, wie wir sie in Ostdeutschland durch den Prozess des Übergangs von der zentralen Staatswirtschaft zur Marktwirtschaft beispielhaft sozusagen im Zeitraffertempo gestaltet haben, mit Auswirkungen, die bei weitem noch nicht abgeschlossen sind.

Wichtigstes Moment dieses Strukturwandels ist das Qualifikations- und Bildungspotenzial der Fach- und Führungskräfte der Wirtschaft. Strukturwandel erfolgreich zu bewältigen, heißt Bildungsvorlauf zu schaffen als hinreichende Voraussetzung für diese Herausforderung sowohl für die Führungskräfte als auch für das benötigte, in den Anforderungen immer höherqualifiziert erforderliche Facharbeiterpotenzial besonders unter dem Aspekt des Dresdner Wirtschaftsraumes als Technologie- und Innovationsstandort.

Wirtschaftliches Wachstum wird in steigendem Umfange durch Innovationen getragen. Neue Produkte und Verfahren, neue Organisationslösungen und soziale Veränderungen sind jedoch unter den Bedingungen der zunehmenden Globalisierung nur dann erfolgreich, wenn sie zu einer Erhöhung der internationalen Wettbewerbsfähigkeit der Unternehmen führen. Um zur Lösung der wirtschaftlichen Probleme – speziell im Freistaat Sachsen und in den anderen neuen Bundesländern – beizutragen, müssen Innovationen zu neuen attraktiven hoch qualifizierten Arbeitsplätzen führen. Neue Beschäftigungsmöglichkeiten aus Innovationen ergeben sich jedoch nicht nur im Bereich von Forschung und Entwicklung, sondern auch im Marketing, in der Fertigung und im Management. Die Verstärkung der Innovationstätigkeit erfordert ferner in einem breiteren Umfange die Gründung neuer Unternehmen in der Industrie und im Dienstleistungsbereich, insbesondere die Gründung von technologieorientierten Unternehmen.

Aus den dargestellten Aufgaben resultieren hohe Anforderungen an die Qualifikation der Führungskräfte und Mitarbeiter in den existierenden und in den künftigen Unternehmen, an ihr Wissen, ihre Fähigkeiten und Fertigkeiten. Insbesondere kommt es darauf an, sich mit hoher Flexibilität und Mobilität den ständig neuen Herausforderungen des Marktes und der technologischen Entwicklung zu

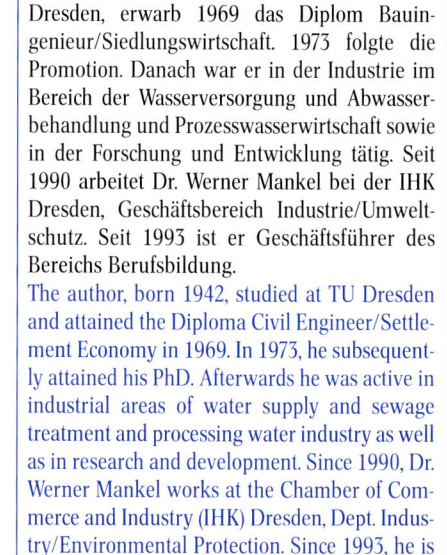

Dr. Werner Mankel

Der Autor, Jahrgang 1942, studierte an der TU Dresden, erwarb 1969 das Diplom Bauingenieur/Siedlungswirtschaft. 1973 folgte die Promotion. Danach war er in der Industrie im Bereich der Wasserversorgung und Abwasserbehandlung und Prozesswasserwirtschaft sowie in der Forschung und Entwicklung tätig. Seit 1990 arbeitet Dr. Werner Mankel bei der IHK Dresden, Geschäftsbereich Industrie/Umweltschutz. Seit 1993 ist er Geschäftsführer des Bereichs Berufsbildung.

The author, born 1942, studied at TU Dresden and attained the Diploma Civil Engineer/Settlement Economy in 1969. In 1973, he subsequently attained his PhD. Afterwards he was active in industrial areas of water supply and sewage treatment and processing water industry as well as in research and development. Since 1990, Dr. Werner Mankel works at the Chamber of Commerce and Industry (IHK) Dresden, Dept. Industry/Environmental Protection. Since 1993, he is Managing Director of the Department Vocation Education. The increasing complexity of work processes requires a constantly growing level of education of employees.

Die zunehmende Komplexität von Arbeitsprozessen erfordert einen ständig steigenden Bildungsstand der Mitarbeiter.

The increasing complexity of work processes requires a constantly growing level of education of employees.

stellen. Neue Aufgabenkomplexe entstehen im Innovationswettbewerb, die komplexes Wissen, strategische Fähigkeiten, kreative Arbeitsweisen, interdisziplinäre Teamfähigkeit, konsequente Marktorientierung und andere Eigenschaften der Beschäftigten verlangen. Diesen Anforderungen wird die bisherige Ausbildung in den Universitäten und Hochschulen nur bedingt gerecht. Die Wirtschaft bietet Bildung und Training an, die diese Voraussetzungen in der beruflichen Bildung erfüllen.

Zunehmende Innovationstätigkeit und Gründung neuer Unternehmen verlangen neue Wege und

Vocational Education

Increasing globalisation of the markets and the lasting effect connected with it on the competition between provinces and regions lead to changes in the economic structure as we have shaped it in East Germany exemplary through the process of transition from central state economy to free market economy so to speak in time-lapse speed, bearing impacts that are by no means completed yet.

The most important force of this structural change is the potential for qualification and education of expert and management personnel for the economy. To successfully manage the structural change means to create an educational lead as a sufficient prerequisite for this challenge both for management personnel and for the necessary expert workforce with ever higher required qualifications, especially considering the aspect of the economic region of Dresden as a location of technology and innovation.

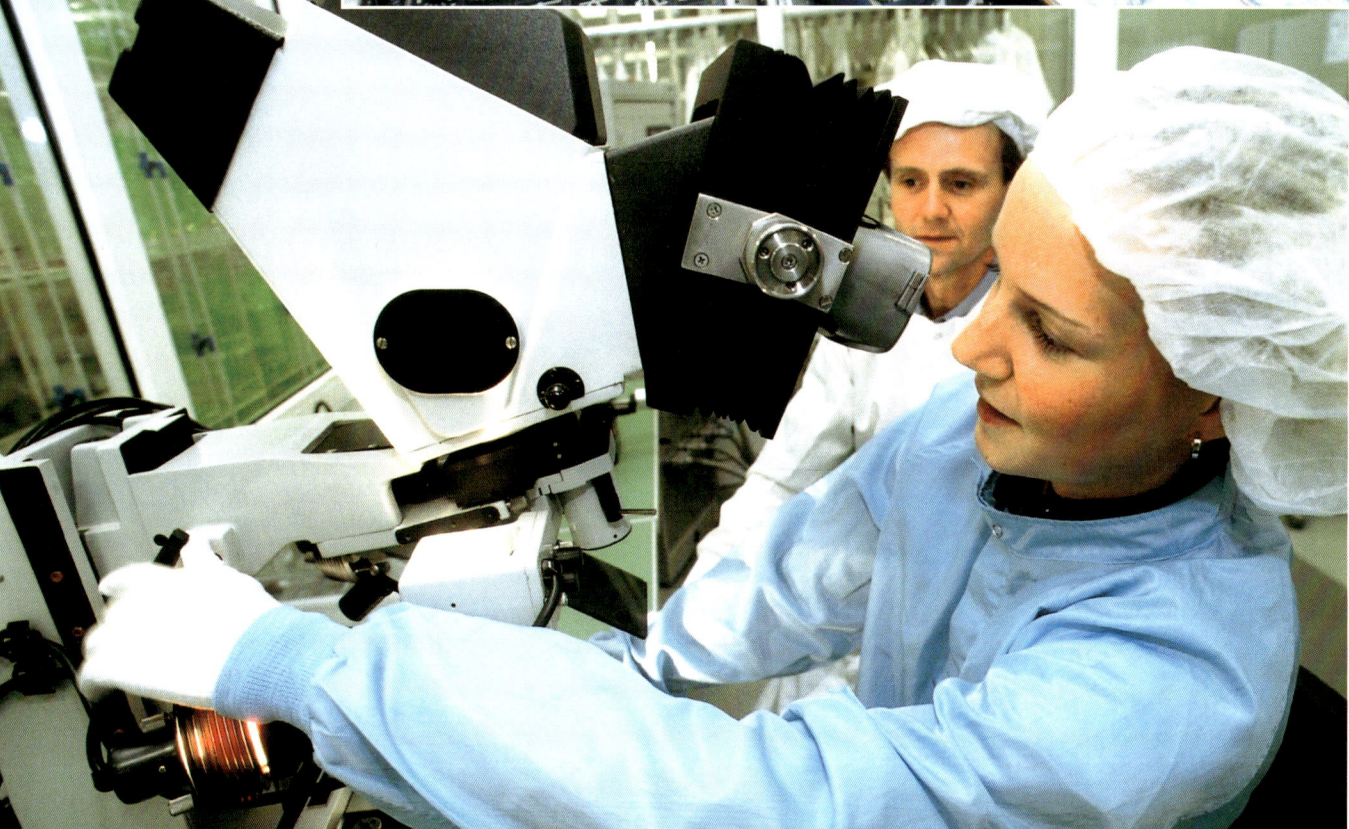

Von herausragender Bedeutung für den Großraum Dresden ist die Fachkräftesicherung der Wachstumsbranchen der Zukunft, wie Biotechnologie und Nanotechnologie.

Of marked significance for the greater area of Dresden is the securing of a specialist workforce in future growth branches like biotechnology and nanotechnology.

Berufsbildung

Inhalte in der beruflichen Bildung und Qualifizierung insgesamt sowie in besonderem Maße in der Hochschulbildung. Nach unseren Erfahrungen stehen dabei vor allem folgende Aufgaben im Vordergrund:

a) Vermittlung der für eine marktorientierte, wettbewerbsfähige Innovationstätigkeit der Unternehmen und für die Gründung neuer Unternehmen notwendigen Kenntnisse, Entwicklung und Training der entsprechenden Fähigkeiten und Fertigkeiten. Das betrifft Innovations- und Projektmanagement, Kreativitätstechniken, strategische Unternehmensplanung, Marketing, Mitarbeiterführung sowie Personalentwicklung.

b) Entwicklung der Teamfähigkeit und interdisziplinären Arbeitsweise.

c) Intensive Verknüpfung von Ausbildung – Forschung - Praxis, um die künftigen Hochschulabsolventen umfassend mit den Anforderungen ihrer späteren Berufstätigkeit zu konfrontieren. Daraus sollte auch eine stärkere Motivation für innovative Lösungen und für die Gründung neuer Unternehmen entstehen.

Die konsequente Orientierung der Innovationstätigkeit – angefangen bei der Ideenfindung und Projektplanung bis zur Produktions- und Markteinführung der neuen technischen Lösungen – ist ein Kernproblem für die erfolgreiche Entwicklung der Unternehmen. Diese Feststellung gilt für alle Industrie- und Dienstleistungsfirmen und trifft im besonderen Maße für Unternehmen in den neuen Bundesländern zu, die in der Regel noch nicht über langjährige internationale Markterfahrungen verfügen.

Systematische Beachtung der Bedürfnisse und Erwartungen der Kunden sowie möglichst frühzeitige Einbindung der Kunden in die Entwicklung und Vermarktung neuer Problemlösungen, Berücksichtigung der jeweils spezifischen Wettbewerbssituation für den Absatz neuer Produkte und Streben nach komparativen Wettbewerbsvorteilen, umfassende Vermarktung technischer Neuerungen, u. a. in Verbindung mit aktiver Schutzrechtstätigkeit und Lizenzpolitik des Unternehmens, langfristige Vorbereitung und effiziente Gestaltung der Markteinführung neuer Produkte und Verfahren sind grundsätzlich zu fordern.

Die Diskussion um die Perspektiven unseres Wirtschaftsstandortes tangieren in erheblichem Maße Fragen zur Personalentwicklung im Allgemeinen. Wie zur beruflichen Erstausbildung im Besonderen. Dementsprechend steht das duale Berufsausbildungssystem gegenwärtig in einem hohen öffentlichen Interesse und beherrscht mittlerweile die Medien als Dauerthema.

Es ist unstrittig, dass Unternehmen in unserem Hochlohnland nur bestehen können, wenn modernere Produkte in kürzeren Zyklen mit größerer Wirtschaftlichkeit hergestellt werden können. Sachsens Wirtschaft muss sich im europäischen und weltweiten Wirtschaftsraum bewähren und sich den Bedingungen eines ständig stärkeren Wettbewerbes stellen. Dazu fähig wird sie nur sein, wenn die richtig qualifizierten Mitarbeiter vorhanden sind, denn leistungsfähige, motivierte Mitarbeiter sind unverzichtbar für den unternehmerischen Erfolg. Die Frage kann daher nicht lauten, ob Ausbildung im Betrieb und in unternehmerischer Verantwortung Zukunft hat, sondern allenfalls, wie die Ausbildung in der Zukunft ausgestaltet ist.

Völlig unbestritten in allen gesellschaftspolitischen Auseinandersetzungen gilt Bildung als ein wichtiges Instrument zur Lösung der Arbeitsmarktprobleme. Je höher das Qualifikationspotenzial in den Unternehmen ist, desto größer ist

Den Unternehmen sind breit qualifizierende Ausbildungsberufe zu offerieren, die die klassische Unterscheidung zwischen technischen und kaufmännischen Qualifikationsprofilen aufheben.
The companies must be offered training professions with broad qualifications that eliminate the classical differentiation between technical and commercial qualification profiles.

Der Beruf der Floristin gehört zu den gefragten Dienstleistungsberufen.
The profession of florist is among the popular service professions.

Vocational Education

Von großer Bedeutung für die wirtschaftliche Perspektive sind die neuen Zukunftsberufe im Bereich der Informations- und Kommunikationstechnologien.

Of great significance for the economic perspective are the new professions of the future in the field of information and communications technologies.

Economic growth is founded to an increasingly extent on innovations. New products and procedures, new organisational solutions and social changes can however only be successful under the conditions of growing globalisation, if they lead to a development of international competition between companies. In order to contribute to a solution of economic problems – especially in the Free State of Saxony and in the other new Federal States – innovations must lead to new attractive high-qualified workplaces. New possibilities for employment do not only result from innovations in the field of Research and development however, but also in marketing, in production and in management. Intensification in the activities of innovation also require to a wider extent the foundation of new companies in industry and in the service sector, particularly the foundation technology-oriented companies.

The tasks presented above call for high requirements of the qualifications of management and staff in existing and in future companies in their knowledge, their capacities and skills. Particularly, it is important to confront the constantly new challenges of the market and technological development with a high degree of flexibility and mobility. New structures of responsibility emerge through the competition between innovations, which require complex expertise, strategic capacities, creative working methods, interdisciplinary ability to work in a team, a consequent orientation towards the market and other characteristics of the employees. These requirements are only met to a limited extent through the education provided by universities and polytechnics. The economic sector offers education and training that fulfils these conditions in vocational education.

Increasing activities of innovation and the founding of new companies necessitates new approaches and contents in vocational education and qualification as a whole as well as principally in higher education. According to our experiences, the following tasks are of main importance in this respect:

a) Imparting the knowledge, development and training of corresponding capacities and skills necessary for a market-oriented, competitive activity of innovation in companies and for the establishment of new companies. This relates to innovation and project management, techniques of creativity, strategic company planning, marketing, staff management as well as personnel development.

b) Development of the ability to work in a team and interdisciplinary working methods.

c) Intensively linking education – research – practical work, in order to confront the future university graduates comprehensively with the requirements of their later professional life. This should also result in a stronger motivation to find innovative solutions and to establish new companies.

The consistent orientation of activities of innovation – starting with finding ideas and project planning up to the production and introduction into markets of new technical solutions – is a core problem for the successful development of the companies. This fact is equally valid for all companies in the industrial and service sectors and is particularly applicable to companies in the new Federal States, which generally do not possess long-standing international market experience.

A systematic consideration of requirements and expectations of clients as well as the most early possible participation of clients in developments

Die Nachfrage nach Ausbildungsplätzen in den Zukunftsberufen ist noch größer als das Angebot.
The demand for training places in the professions of the future is far greater than the supply.

Berufsbildung

auch der Arbeitsplatzzuwachs. Das gilt in besonderem Maße für den eigenen Arbeitsplatz im eigenen neu gegründeten Unternehmen.

Die moderne Arbeitswelt verlangt zwingend nach einem Verbundsystem aus Wissen und Können, Fertigkeiten und Fähigkeiten, sozialen Kompetenzen und Handlungsorientierungen. Das Miteinander von Fach- und Schlüsselqualifikationen – also jenen wichtigen überfachlichen Fähigkeiten zu logischem Denken, zu kooperativem Verhalten und zur Teamarbeit, zu Verstehen und Verarbeiten von Informationen, zu Kreativität und Innovation, zu Veränderung und Neugestaltung – macht das heute besonders benötigte Qualifikationspotenzial aus.

Es gehört zu den großen Vorteilen des dualen Systems der beruflichen Bildung, diese umfassende fachliche und methodische, personale und soziale Kompetenzstruktur zu schaffen, die mit einer bloßen Aneinanderreihung von einzeln vermittelten Qualifikationsbausteinen niemals erreichbar wäre.

Das Berufsprinzip, das für Breite und Solidität der Ausbildung sorgt, ist angesichts der gegenwärtigen Entwicklungstendenzen hin zu ganzheitlich arbeitenden dezentralen Teams, zu mehr Selbstständigkeit und Eigenverantwortung, so wichtig wie eh und je.

Vielfältige Betriebsuntersuchungen seitens der Industrie- und Handelskammer Dresden zeigen, dass den Unternehmen breit qualifizierende Ausbildungsberufe besonders wichtig sind, die die klassische Unterscheidung zwischen technischen und kaufmännischen Qualifikationsprofilen aufheben. Gründe dafür sind einerseits die zunehmende Verschmelzung von Produktion und Dienstleistungens sowie andererseits die generell wachsende Bedeutung von Service-Tätigkeiten in hochtechnologisierten Produktionsprozessen.

Tradition und Moderne faszinieren beim Erlernen der Herstellung kostbarer Porzellangegenstände.
The fascination of tradition and modernism when acquiring knowledge of the production of valuable porcelain objects.

Von großer Bedeutung für die wirtschaftliche Zukunft unseres Landes sind die neuen „Zukunftsberufe" im Bereich der Informations- und Kommunikationstechnologien. Dennoch müssen große weitere Anstrengungen erfolgen: Vor allem im wachsenden tertiären-Sektor fehlen noch moderne Berufsbilder, die zu einem Plus an Ausbildungsstellen und Beschäftigung beitragen können.

Der gesamte Bereich der Dienstleistungen entwickelt sich enorm. Sowohl in der personenbezogenen Dienstleistung wird es eine rasante Entwicklung geben, als auch im Bereich der Sachdienstleistungen durch verschiedene Outsourcings. Vor allen Dingen werden sich durch das Etablieren von E-Commerce neue Entwicklungen auftun.

Von herausragender Bedeutung für den Großraum Dresden ist die Fachkräftesicherung der Wachstumsbrachen der Zukunft wie Biotechnologie und Nanotechnologie. Dresden ist auf dem Wege, der Standort der Zukunftstechnologien zu werden. In den sich entwickelnden Unternehmen und Institutionen werden im Prognosezeitraum Fachkräfte benötigt, die heute weder von der Qualität noch von der Quantität her genau beschreibbar sind. Auch hierfür muss gemeinsam gehandelt werden, um vorbeugend einem Fachkräftemangel entgegen zu wirken.

Nach wie vor ist aber das einzelne Unternehmen, das einzelne Institut verantwortlich für die dort benötigten Fachkräfte, wobei eine individuelle Verantwortung des Einzelnen für seine Qualifizierung und vor allem für sein lebenslanges Lernen genauso besteht.

Im Bereich des computerunterstützten Lernens hat die Berufsbildung eine Pionierrolle übernommen. Multimedia mit den Verknüpfungsmöglichkeiten von verschiedenen Techniken und Instrumenten, Datenbanken und Lernprogrammen, Kommunikations- und Informationsformen haben einen festen Platz in der Bildungsarbeit gefunden. Die Zukunft der Berufsbildung liegt in ihrer Erneuerungskraft, in der Fähigkeit, sich ständig an neue Anforderungen anpassen zu können.

Auch in der Gastronomie und im Einzelhandel werden die Chancen für gut ausgebildete Fachleute weiter wachsen.
Also, in the restaurant business and in the retail sector the chances for thoroughly trained experts will continue to grow.

Vocational Education

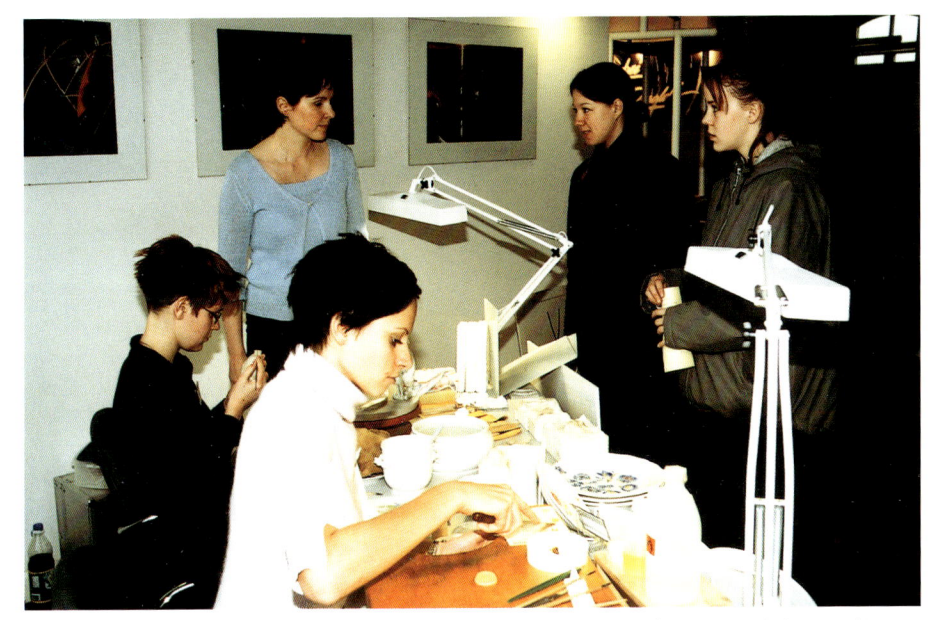

Der Ausbildungsbetrieb, aber auch der Auszubildende sollten mehr Gestaltungsfreiräume für Bedarf und Neigung haben.

Room that is more creative should be left to the company training apprentices as well as to the apprentice himself for the existing demand and for talents.

and marketing of new solutions, concern for the specific individual situation of competition for the sale of new products and an engagement for comparative competition advantages, integral marketing of technical innovations, including a combination of active legal protection and licensing policies of the companies, long-term preparation and efficient design of market introduction or new products and methods must be required primarily.

Discussions about the perspectives of our economic location tend to deal considerably with issues of personnel development in general and of vocational initial training in particular. Correspondingly, the dual vocational education system is presently of high public interest and dominates the media now as a permanent topic.

Indisputably, the companies in our high-wage country can only survive if products that are more modern can be produced in shorter cycles with greater profitability. The economy of Saxony must prove itself in a European and worldwide context and confront the conditions of a continuously increasing competition. It will only be capable to do so, if adequately qualified staff is available, because efficient, motivated employees are inevitably necessary for entrepreneurial success. The question must therefore not be, whether training within a company and in the responsibility of the company has a future, but if at all, how training is to be structured in future.

Undeniably, training and education is considered in all socio-political debates as an important instrument for the solution of the problems of the labour market. The higher the potential for qualification within the companies, the larger therefore is the increase of workplaces. This can be said especially for the own workplace in a self-owned new established company.

The modern world of work urgently needs a joint system of knowledge and expertise, capacities and skills, social competences and directions for actions. The combination of specialist and key qualifications – that is those important capacities above expertise for thinking logically, for cooperative behaviour and for team work, for understanding and processing information, for creativity and innovation, for the courage to change and create new structures – this is what characterises today especially the required potential for qualification.

One of the great advantages of the dual system of vocational education is to be able to create this comprehensive specialist and methodical, personal and social structure of competence, which it would be impossible to achieve by merely joining together individually imparted qualification modules.

The principle of professional qualification that takes care of a broad scope and thoroughness in training is as important as ever, considering the actual trends of development towards integrally working decentralised teams with more independence and own responsibility. Numerous investigations in companies on the part of the Chamber of Commerce and Industry Dresden show that to the companies training professions with broad qualifications are of utmost importance, since these eliminate the classical differentiation between technical and commercial qualification profiles. Motives for this are on the one hand the increasing combination of production and service

Im Bereich des computerunterstützten Lernens hat die Berufsbildung eine Pionierrolle übernommen.

In the field of computer-aided learning, vocational education has taken on a pioneering role.

Berufsbildung

Dieser Trend interaktiver Begegnung wird durch moderne Lernmedien gestützt. Was gibt es da nicht alles auf CD-ROM! Und damit nicht genug. Viele dieser CD-ROM können auch im Internet online genutzt oder heruntergeladen werden. Lernen erfolgt schon lange nicht mehr nur in Schule und Universität. Lernen geschieht zu Hause in der Freizeit und zunehmend direkt am Arbeitsplatz. Gerade dieses, auf das Arbeitsgebiet bezogene Lernen ist ein Schlüssel für anhaltenden Unternehmenserfolg. Stabilität zu halten, sich dem Fortschritt zu stellen, neue Marktpositionen zu erobern – diese Firmenphilosophie wird nur aufgehen, wenn die human resources in das Konzept eingebunden sind.

Die zunehmende Komplexität von Arbeitsprozessen erfordert einen ständig steigenden Bildungsstand der Mitarbeiter. Aktive Personalentwicklung für das Unternehmen ist unverzichtbar. ∎

Hilfreich sind die gegenwärtigen Bemühungen, berufliche Ausbildung durch ein ergänzendes Modulsystem praxisgerechter und flexibler zu gestalten, sofern die geradezu strategischen Vorteile des ganzheitlichen Bildungskonzeptes grundsätzlich nicht preisgegeben werden. In der Diskussion um die Modernisierung stehen gegenwärtig Modellvorschläge im Wettbewerb, die alle zum Ziel haben, mit mehr Flexibilität auf veränderte Anforderungen zu reagieren, ohne das Berufskonzept zu verlassen. Es geht grundsätzlich darum, dem Ausbildungsbetrieb, aber auch dem Auszubildenden mehr Gestaltungsfreiräume für Bedarf und Neigung zu lassen.

Die Initiative „Verbundausbildung in den Berufen der Hochtechnologie" wird die Erkenntnisse zur Vorgehensweise zeitigen für die benötigte Flexibilisierung und Differenzierung von Ausbildung, die heutigen und künftigen Arbeitsplätzen entspricht.

Das enorme Tempo der wissenschaftlich-technischen Entwicklung macht es möglich, dass die Welt virtuell zusammenrückt. Geografische Entfernungen, politische Grenzen und vor allem aber die oft in Jahrzehnten gewachsenen Strukturen von Wirtschaftsbeziehungen scheinen im World Wide Web aufgelöst, sie werden mühelos überwunden. Die modernen Informations- und Kommunikationstechnologien ermöglichen es, sowohl Geschäftsanbahnungen, als auch Geschäftsbeziehungen und -abschlüsse vom PC aus abzuwickeln. Auch das virtuelle Unternehmen mit entwickeltem Intranet ist gar nicht mehr so weit entfernt.

Vor allem das auf das Arbeitsgebiet bezogene Lernen ist ein Schlüssel für anhaltenden Unternehmenserfolg.
Especially the learning related directly to one's area of work is a key element for the lasting success of a company.

Vocational Education

Im wachsenden Dienstleistungs-Sektor fehlen weitere moderne Berufsbilder, die zu einem Plus an Ausbildungsstellen und Beschäftigung beitragen können.
In the growing service sector images of modern professional careers are still missing, which could contribute to an increase in training places and employment.

provisions as well as on the other the generally growing significance of service activities in highly technical production processes.

Of great significance for the economic future of our country are the new "professions of the future" in the field of information and communications technologies. Nevertheless, greater efforts must be made: Especially in the growing tertiary sector, images of modern professional careers are still missing, which could contribute to an increase in training places and employment. The complete area of service provisions is growing tremendously. Both in the field of staff-related services there will be a rapid development as well as in the field of services in material goods or in kind through various methods of outsourcing. Above all, the establishment of e-Commerce with create new developments. Of marked significance for the greater area of Dresden is the securing of a specialist workforce in future growth branches like biotechnology and nanotechnology. Dresden is on its way to becoming the location for future technologies. The developing companies and institutions will require in the forecasted period expert staff, which can not be described at present neither in quality nor in quantity. Also, for this purpose there must be concerted action in order to counteract a possible shortage of specialists with preventive measures. However, each individual company, each single institute is still responsible for the specialist staff needed there, whereby there also exists an individual responsibility of each person for his or her own qualification and above all for his or her life-long learning as well.

In the field of computer-aided learning, the vocational education has taken on a pioneering role. Multimedia have found a firm place in educational work, providing the possibility of linking various technologies and instruments, databases and teaching programmes, forms of communication and information together. The future of vocational education lies in its ability to renew itself, in the ability to adjust constantly to new requirements.

Of great help are the present endeavours to structure professional training through a complimentary system of modules in a way more suitable to practical work and more flexible, as long as the almost strategic advantages of the concept of integral education is not given up in principle. At present, competing proposals of models are in the centre of discussions about modernisation, which all have the aim to react with more flexibility to changed requirements without leaving the concept of vocational education. In principle, the issue is about leaving room that is more creative to the company training apprentices as well as to the apprentice himself for the existing demand and for talents. The initiative "Unified Education in the Professions of High Technology" will bring about findings of methodology for the necessary flexibility and differentiation of vocational training, which corresponds to present and future workplaces. The enormous speed of the scientific and technical development enables that the world is moving closer together virtually. Geographic distances, political borders and, above all, the structures of economic relationships, often grown in the space of decades, seem to be vanished in the World Wide Web; they are overcome without any effort. Modern information and communications technologies enable to deal both with commencing businesses as well as with ensuing business relations and closing of contracts from the PC. Also, a virtual company with a developed intranet is not very far away any longer. This trend of interactive encounter is supported through modern teaching media. What a wealth of products are available on CD-ROM! And it does not stop here. Many of these CD-ROM can also be used in the Internet online or downloaded. Learning does not happen only at school or university any more. Learning happens at home in the spare time and increasingly directly at one's workplace. Especially this learning, related directly to one's area of work, is a key element for the lasting success of a company. The philosophy to maintain stability, to confront progress, to conquer new market positions will only bear fruit if the human resources are imbedded in the concept.

The increasing complexity of work processes requires a constantly growing level of education of employees. Active personnel development is thus indispensable for a company. ∎

Company Profile

KAMA weiter auf Wachstumskurs

KAMA still Heading for Growth

Polygraph KAMA GmbH

Geschäftsführer/Manager:
Marcus Tralau
Telefon +49 (351) 270 36 20
Mobil +49 (172) 400 90 11
E-Mail tralau@polygraph-kama.de

Jörg Schulze
Telefon +49 (351) 270 36 10
E-Mail schulze@polygraph-kama.de

Geschäftstätigkeit/Business Activity:
Entwicklung, Herstellung und Vertrieb von:
- Stanzautomaten
- Faltschachtelklebemaschinen
- Maschinenbaugruppen, Maschinenbauteilen und Schweißbaugruppen

Development, production and sale of:
- Automatic punching machines
- Folder-gluers
- Structural components, components for mechanical engineering and components for welding.

Gründungsjahr/Year of Foundation:
1994 Neugründung

Mitarbeiter/Employees: 76

Umsatz/Turnover:
6 Mio. Euro

Anschrift/Address:
Kurt-Beyer-Straße 4
D-01237 Dresden
Telefon +49 (351) 270 36 0
Telefax +49 (351) 270 36 90
E-Mail info@polygraph-kama.de
Internet www.polygraph-kama.de

Moderner Stanzautomat von KAMA.
Modern punching machine by KAMA.

Polygraph KAMA in Dresden.

Polygraph KAMA in Dresden.

Die KAMA ist ein Unternehmen für die Entwicklung und Fertigung moderner Stanzautomaten und Faltschachtelklebemaschinen für die Weiterverarbeitung von bedrucktem und unbedrucktem Papier, von Pappe und Micro-Wellpappe. Die weltweite Kundschaft schätzt die Maschinen, weil sie einfach zu bedienen, schnell umzurüsten und sehr robust sind. 1894 erstmals gegründet, fertigte sie schon damals Spezialmaschinen für die Papier- und Kartonagenverarbeitung. 1994 wurde die KAMA von drei im Unternehmen tätigen Managern neu gegründet. Gestartet wurde mit 21 Mitarbeitern, Ende 2000 sind bereits 76 Mitarbeiter beschäftigt, die einen Umsatz von rund 6 Mio. Euro erreichen. Für die nächsten drei Jahre ist eine Umsatzsteigerung auf 10 Mio. Euro geplant. Grund für das hohe Wachstum sind neue Absatzmärkte in Europa, USA, Südamerika und Afrika. Außerdem stimmen die guten Aussichten in Osteuropa und Deutschland, dem traditionellen Markt der KAMA, die Unternehmensleitung sehr optimistisch. Aufgrund einer Vertriebskooperation mit einem führenden Druckmaschinenhersteller stehen den Kunden in jedem Land der Welt Vertriebs- und Servicepartner zur Verfügung. Das zweite Geschäftsfeld der KAMA ist die Entwicklung und Fertigung von Baugruppen und Komponenten für den Maschinenbau. Auch dieser Bereich entwickelte sich in den letzten Jahren sehr stabil und trägt erheblich zur guten Kapazitätsauslastung bei. ■

KAMA is an enterprise for the development and production of modern automatic punching machines and folder-gluers for the further processing of printed and unprinted paper, of carton and micro-corrugated cardboard. Its worldwide clientele values the machines, because they are easy to operate, can be converted rapidly and are very robust. Founded in 1894 for the first time, it manufactured even back in those early days special machines for paper and carton processing. In 1994, three managers working in the company newly established KAMA. They started with 21 employees and at the end of 2000, already 76 employees were achieving a turnover of around 6 million Euro. For the next three years, an increase in turnover to 10 million Euros is planned. The reasons for this enormous growth are new sales markets gained in Europe, USA, South America and Africa. Furthermore, the good prospects in Eastern Europe and Germany, the traditional market of KAMA, are making the management feel very optimistic. Because of a sales co-operation with a leading printing machine manufacturer, the clients have in each country of the world a sales and service partner to their disposal. The second business field of KAMA is the development and production of structural components and components for mechanical engineering. Also this field has developed in the last years in a very stable way and contributes considerably to the good and full use of its capacities. ■

Company Profile

Elektronische Geräte und Baugruppen aus Dresden

Electronic Equipment and Components from Dresden

DELTEC electronic

DELTEC electronic GmbH

Geschäftsführer/Managing Director:
Reinhold Seligmann

Gründungsjahr/Year of Foundation: 1992

Mitarbeiter/Employees: 32

Geschäftstätigkeit/Business Activity:
1. Entwicklung und Fertigung elektronischer Geräte
2. Fertigung von elektronischen Baugruppen, Kabeln und Wickelerzeugnissen im Kundenauftrag
3. Fertigung und Vertrieb von Komponenten für Datennetze

1. Development and production of electronic equipment
2. Production of electronic components, cables and winding products customer-specific on client contract
3. Production and sale of components for data networks

Anschrift/Address:
Heidelberger Straße 18
D-01189 Dresden
Telefon   +49 (351) 430 39-30
Telefax   +49 (351) 430 39-33
E-Mail   DELTEC@deltec.de
Internet www.deltec.de

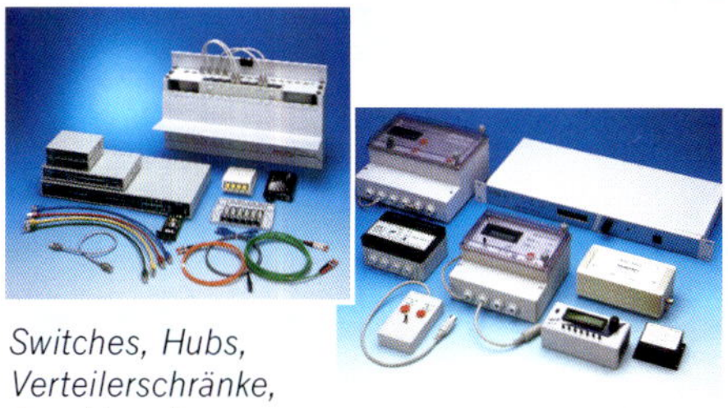

Dresden ist traditionell ein Zentrum der Elektrotechnik/ Elektronik. Im Gewerbegebiet Coschütz/Gittersee hat die DELTEC electronic GmbH eine moderne Fertigungsstätte für elektronische Baugruppen und Geräte errichtet. Sie beschäftigt sich mit Entwicklung, Herstellung und Vertrieb innovativer Produkte für die Elektronikindustrie und Datenkommunikation wie z. B. Temperaturdifferenzregler für Solaranlagen, elektronische Vorschaltgeräte für Halogenlampen, Überwachungselektronik für Netzwerkschränke u. a. Neben den eigenen Produkten werden auch verschiedenste Baugruppen im Kundenauftrag gefertigt. Dazu gehören Elektronikboards in SMD- und konventioneller Montagetechnik, komplette elektronische Geräte sowie auch konfektionierte Kabel (NF, HF, HV u. a.) und Wickelerzeugnisse (Spulen, Drosseln, Übertrager, Hochspannungstrafos u. a.). Modernste technische Anlagen ermöglichen es in allen Technologiebereichen rationell zu fertigen und höchste Qualitätsansprüche zu erfüllen. Ein motiviertes und qualifiziertes Team von Mitarbeitern steht zur Verfügung. Viele Kunden nutzen das umfangreiche Erfahrungspotenzial für eine intensive Zusammenarbeit, beginnend mit der Entwicklung neuer Erzeugnisse bis zur Serienfertigung. Dieses Vertrauen beruht auf vielfach nachgewiesene Zuverlässigkeit und fachliche Kompetenz.

Für den Aufbau von Datennetzen bietet die DELTEC electronic GmbH ein umfangreiches Sortiment von Hardwarekomponenten (Anschlussdosen, Kabel, Hubs, Switches, USV, Messtechnik) an. Diese werden zum Teil selbst gefertigt (Verbindungskabel, Verteilerschränke, Rack-Security) sowie mittels Import- u. Distributionsverträgen von verschiedenen Herstellen bezogen. Die Komponenten sind zueinander passfähig, sowohl für kleine Netze als auch für komplexere Netzwerklösungen. Den Kunden wird bei Projektierung und Auswahl der Komponenten umfangreicher Support geboten. ∎

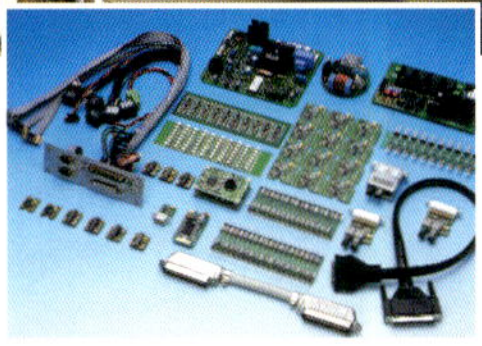

Firmensitz in Dresden; rechts: Elektronikbaugruppen, Kabelkonfektion, Planartrafos.

The company's seat in Dresden; right: electronic components, ready-made cables, and planar transformers.

Dresden is traditionally a centre of electro technology and electronics. In the industrial area of Coschütz/Gittersee, the DELTECT electronic GmbH has established a modern production place for electronic components and equipment. It deals with the development, manufacture and sales of innovative products for the electronic industry and data communication like for example, temperature difference adjuster for solarplants, electronic lamp ballast for halogen bulbs, surveillance electronic for computer network cases, etc. Apart from our own products, also the most varied components are produced on assignment for our clients. This includes electronic boards in SMD and conventional assembly technique, complete electronic equipments as well as ready-made cables (NF, HF, HV etc.) and winding products (coils, chokes, transformers, high-voltage transformers etc.). The most modern technical plants enable us to manufacture produce in all technological fields economically and to meet the highest quality standards. A motivated and qualified team of staff is permanently available. Many customers use the extensive potential of experience for an intensive co-operation, starting from the development of new products up to serial production. This trust is a result of our repeatedly proven reliability and expert competence.

For building up data networks, DELTEC electronic GmbH has an extensive assortment of hardware components on offer (connector boxes, cables, wobbler dispersions, switches, USV, measuring technology). These are partly self-produced (distributor cases, rack security) as well as procured by means of import and distribution agreements from various manufacturers. Forms of components are suitable to each other, both for small networks and for more complex network solutions. The clients receive extensive support on projection and selection of the components. ∎

Switches, Hubs, Verteilerschränke, Anschlussdosen, Patchkabel, LWL-Technik, Temperaturdifferenzregler für Solarheizungen, Überwachungselektronik für Netzwerkschränke, MP3-Player, elektronische Vorschaltgeräte für Halogenlampen.

Switches, wobbler dispersions, distributor cases, connector boxes, patch cables, LWL technology, temperature difference adjuster for solar heaters, surveillance electronic for network cases, MP3-players, electronic top equipment for halogen bulbs.

THEEGARTEN PACTEC

PACTEC Verpackungsmaschinen-
Fabrik Theegarten GmbH & Co. KG

Geschäftsführer/Manager:
Name der Geschäftsführer
Christa Rustler-Theegarten
Erhard Rustler
Gerd Schwarze

Gründungsjahr/Year of Foundation:
Die heutige THEEGARTEN-PACTEC gründet
auf den Zusammenschluss der Firmen
Rose-Theegarten Köln und
Pactec Dresden im Jahre 1994.
The present Theegarten-Pactec company
originates from the merger of the companies
Rose-Theegarten Cologne and Pactec Dresden
in the year 1994.

Rose-Theergrarten wurde 1934 von
Justus und Franz Theergarten gegründet.
Rose-Theegarten was established in 1934 by
Justus and Franz Theegarten.

Die Firma Pactec geht 1990 aus dem
Kombinat Nagema hervor.
The Pactec company emerges in 1990 from the
combinate Nagema.

Der Verpackungsmaschinenbau in Dresden reicht
historisch bis ins 19. Jahrhundert zurück.
Historically, the production of packaging
machines dates back to the 19th Century in
Dresden.

Mitarbeiter/Employees:
260

Umsatz/Turnover:
65 Mio. DM

Geschäftstätigkeit/Business Activity:
Herstellung von Verpackungsmaschinen und
Anlagen für die Nahrungsmittelindustrie
(mit Schwerpunkt Süßwarenindustrie) sowie
für den Non-Food-Bereich
Manufacture of packaging machines and
plants for the food industry (with main focus
on confectionery industry) as well as for the
non-food sector

Anschrift/Address:
Breitscheidstraße 46
D-01237 Dresden
Telefon   +49 (351) 25 73-0
Telefax   +49 (351) 25 73-329
E-Mail   pactec@theegarten-pactec.de
Internet www.theegarten-pactec.de

Company Profile

Maschinenbau-Spezialist in der dritten Generation

Machine Construction Specialist in its third Generation

Der Unternehmenssitz in Dresden.

The company's headquarter in Dresden.

Verpackungsmaschinenbau in Dresden reicht historisch bis ins 19. Jahrhundert zurück. Die heutige Theegarten-Pactec gründet auf den Zusammenschluss der Firmen Rose-Theegarten Köln und Pactec Dresden im Jahre 1994. Die Gründungsphasen: Die Firma Rose-Theegarten wurde 1934 von Justus Theegarten und seinem Sohn Franz in Köln gegründet. Die Firma Pactec geht 1990 aus dem Kombinat Nagema hervor.

Stärke und Erfolg der beiden Unternehmen liegen in der Beschränkung auf ein relativ kleines, hochspezialisiertes Marktsegment. 1994 übernahm die Firma Rose-Theegarten die Firma Pactec von der Treuhand und rundete somit ihr Produktionsprogramm Verpackungsmaschinen- und Anlagenbau für die Nahrungsmittel-, mit Schwerpunkt auf die Süßwarenindustrie, ab. 1997 wurden die bis dahin getrennten Standorte auf den heutigen Firmensitz in Dresden konzentriert.

Die Theegarten-Pactec Erzeugnisse sind in der Leistungsfähigkeit, Funktionssicherheit und Lebensdauer als Spitzenleistungen weltweit bekannt. Rund 260 hochmotivierte Mitarbeiter tragen dazu bei, dass die Maschinen stets auf dem neuesten technischen Stand sind.

Der hohe Exportanteil von mehr als 85 % wird durch ein weltweites Vertreternetz betreut.

Trotz allem hat Theegarten seinen Charakter als mittelständischer Maschinenbauer – in der dritten Generation im Familienbesitz – bewahrt. ∎

Historically, the production of packaging machines dates back to the 19th century in Dresden. The present company Theegarten-Pactec originates from the merger of the companies Rose-Theegarten Cologne and Pactec Dresden in the year 1994. The stages of foundation are: Rose-Theegarten was established in 1934 by Justus Theegarten and his son Franz, in Cologne. The Pactec company emerges in 1990 from the combinate Nagema.

The strength and success of both companies lies in their focussing on a relatively small yet high-specialised market segment. In 1994, the company Rose-Theegarten took over the company Pactec from the Treuhand (Federal Trust Company) and thus rounded off its production programme of packaging machines and plants for the food stuff industry, while concentrating on the confectionery industry in particular. In 1997, the separated locations were joint on the present company location in Dresden.

Products made by Theegarten-Pactec are renowned worldwide for their efficiency, functional safety and their durability at top performance. Around 260 highly motivated employees contribute to the machines constantly being on the latest technical level.

The high share of exports of more than 85 % is serviced by a worldwide network of agents. On the other hand, Theegarten has maintained its character as a middle-sized machine manufacturer and as family business owned by its third generation. ∎

Company Profile

Traditionsunternehmen auf Erfolgskurs

Traditional Company on Heading for Success

Die APOGEPHA Arzneimittel GmbH ist ein mittelständisches Unternehmen in Dresden, das nach der Enteignung 1972 dank der deutschen Einheit heute wieder wirtschaftlich selbstständig ist. Verantwortung gegenüber Arzt, Apotheker und Patient sowie das Ziel, moderne Arzneimittel zu entwickeln, in bester pharmazeutischer Qualität herzustellen und mit einem guten Service zu vertreiben, sind das gemeinsame Anliegen von Unternehmensleitung und Mitarbeitern.

Die Geburtsstunde des Unternehmens fällt bereits in das Jahr 1882, als der Laboratoriumsbetrieb der damaligen Dresdner Kronenapotheke den Schritt zum selbstständigen Industrieunternehmen wagte. Nach mehrfachem Wechsel der Besitzverhältnisse führten Umbildungen 1933 zur „APOGEPHA-Fabrik chemisch-pharmazeutischer Präparate". Der nahezu vollständigen Zerstörung in der Nacht vom 13. zum 14. Februar 1945 folgte der mühsame Wiederaufbau, doch erst nach dem Zusammenbruch der DDR konnte das Unternehmen seine Erfolgsstory fortsetzen. Schon kurz nach der Wende war APOGEPHA wieder auf dem Markt vertreten, viele Ärzte und Apotheker freuten sich, die Medikamente wieder einsetzen zu können. Das mittelständische Unternehmen ist bekannt für seine hohe Kompetenz auf dem Spezialgebiet Urologie, die es den Ärzten schnell und unbürokratisch, ihren Bedürfnissen entsprechend, anbietet. Die Urologie bildet gleichzeitig den Forschungsschwerpunkt des Unternehmens. Hier ist es das Ziel, neue Arzneistoffe zu entwickeln und durch Verbesserung der Darreichungsformen deren Wirksamkeit und Verträglichkeit zu optimieren.

Als alt eingesessenes Unternehmen investiert APOGEPHA in der sächsischen Landeshauptstadt und hat für 27 Millionen DM in Dresden-Lockwitz eine neue Produktionsstätte errichtet. ∎

Eine neue Produktionsanlage in Dresden-Lockwitz.
A new prodution plant in Dresden-Lockwitz.

The APOGEPHA Arzneimittel GmbH is a medium-sized company in Dresden, which after expropriation in 1972 is today again economically independent thanks to the German Unification. Common tasks of the company management the employees are the responsibility to the medical profession, pharmacists and patients as well as the aim to develop modern medication of best pharmaceutical quality and to sell these products while providing a good service.

The company was founded in 1882, when the laboratory of the former Dresden Kronen pharmacy risked the step to establish an independent industrial enterprise. After various changes of proprietors, restructurisations led to the birth of "APOGEPHA-Fabrik chemisch-pharmazeutischer Präparate" (factory for chemical pharmaceutical preparations) in 1933. After its almost complete destruction in the night of 13th to 14th February 1945, followed its arduous reconstruction; but only after the collapse of the GDR, the company was able to continue its story of success. Shortly after the political change, APOGEPHA was present on the market again, many doctors and pharmacists were glad to use the medicines again.

The medium-sized company is known for its high level of competence in the special field of urology, which is offered to the doctors according to their needs, fast and unbureaucratic. At the same time, urology is the focal point of research of the company. In this respect, it aims to develop new pharmaceutical agents and to optimise their efficiency and tolerance by improving forms of dispensing.

Being a traditional local company, APOGEPHA invests in the Saxon regional capital and has established for 27 million DM a new production plant in Dresden-Lockwitz. ∎

APOGEPHA ARZNEIMITTEL GMBH

APOGEPHA Arzneimittel GmbH

Geschäftsführerin/Managing Director:
Henriette Starke

Geschäftsführender Gesellschafter/Managing Partner:
Dr. Christian Starke

Gründungsjahr/Year of Foundation:
1882

Mitarbeiter/Employees:
183

Umsatz/Turnover:
52,3 Mio. DM

Geschäftstätigkeiten/Business Activities:
Entwicklung, Herstellung und Vertrieb von Arzneimitteln
Development, production and sale of medicines

Anschrift/Address:
Kyffhäuserstraße 27
D-01309 Dresden
Telefon   +49 (0351) 33 63-3
Telefax   +49 (0351) 33 63-440
E-Mail   apo@apogepha.de
Internet www.apogepha.de

Der Sitz des Unternehmens (oben) und der Produktionsneubau in Dresden Lockwitz.
The company's headquarters (above) and the newly built production hall in Dresden Lockwitz.

Chip-Produktion

Speicherchips und Logikbausteine, gefertigt mit modernster Technologie

Memory chips and logic components produced with the most modern technology

Wer mit dem Flugzeug nach Dresden kommt, entdeckt vom Fenster aus beim Anflug einen modernen, beeindruckenden Industriekomplex – gelegen zwischen dem Stadtzentrum und dem Flughafen Klotzsche. Auf dem großen Campus hat Infineon Technologies Dresden eine der weltweit modernsten Chip-Produktionsstätten für Speicherchips und Logikbausteine errichtet, in der mehr als 3.300 Mitarbeiter nicht nur hoch integrierte Schaltungen der neuesten Generation fertigen, sondern auch die weltweit ersten Chips auf Siliziumwafern mit 300-mm-Durchmesser produzieren. Infineon Technologies setzt damit von Dresden aus weltweit die neusten Standards in der Fertigungstechnologie.

Die Siemens AG hat Dresden als Standort für seine Halbleiteraktivitäten im Frühjahr 1990 erstmals vorgeschlagen. Sowohl die Stadt Dresden als auch das Land Sachsen haben in Gesprächen ihren Willen gezeigt, die Stadt zu einer weltweit angesehenen Hightech-Metropole zu machen. Bei dieser Absichtserklärung ist es nicht geblieben: Dresdens Image in der Welt hat sich gewandelt. Neben der Barockstadt prägt sich auch langsam der Hightech-Standort Dresden ein.

Eines der bedeutenden Standortkriterien für die Siemens AG waren damals die technisch hoch qualifizierten Arbeitskräfte – immerhin war Dresden schon früher ein Zentrum der Hochtechnologie mit dem Zentrum für Mikroelektronik (ZMD) und dem Potenzial der Hochschulen und Forschungsinstitute. Die Akzeptanz durch den Freistaat Sachsen, industrielle Hightech-Unternehmen anzusiedeln, und die gezielten Fördermaßnahmen für Investitionen in den neuen Bundesländern trugen ebenfalls mit zur Entscheidung bei. Da solche wirtschaftlichen Entwicklungsaktivitäten wesentlich den Standort Deutschland in der Hochtechnologie stärken, förderte auch das Bundesministeriums für Bildung und Forschung (BMBF) den Aufbau von Infineon Technologies Dresden. Vor dem Hintergrund dieser günstigen Rahmenbedingungen hat Siemens in Dresden – vier Jahre nach der Errichtung der ersten Bauabschnitte – 1998 ein Gemeinschaftsunternehmen (Joint Venture) mit Motorola gegründet, das unter dem Namen SEMICONDUCTOR300 die Entwicklung der Fertigungstechnologie auf 300-mm-Wafern zum Ziel hatte.

Dr. Peter Kücher

Der Autor wurde in Mühldorf am Inn geboren. Nach dem Physikstudium an der Universität in Regensburg und der Dissertation auf dem Gebiet der Angewandten Physik begann er 1988 seine berufliche Laufbahn bei der Siemens AG in München, Bereich Halbleiter. Dr. Kücher initiierte und koordinierte verschiedene europäische Projekte für Prozess-, Equipment- und Materialentwicklung innerhalb JESSI und ESPRIT. Von 1993 bis 1996 leitete er in East Fishkill, New York, USA, das IBM-, Siemens-, Toshiba-256M-DRAM-Projekt, in dem Strukturen mit 0.25 Mikrometer entwickelt wurden. Seit 1997 verantwortete er das 300-mm-Programm.

The author was born in Mühldorf on the Inn. After studying physics at the University of Regensburg with a thesis in the field of applied physics, he started his professional career at Siemens AG in Munich in 1988 in the area of semiconductor. Dr. Kücher initiated a co-ordinated various European projects for process, equipment and materials development within JESSI and ESPRIT. From 1993 until 1996, he headed the IBM, Siemens and Toshiba 256M-DRAM-project in East Fishkill, New York, USA, in which structure with 0.25 micrometers were developed. Since 1997, he has been responsible for the 300-mm-programme.

Infineon Technologies Dresden eine der modernsten Chip-Fabriken Europas, hat sich seit der Gründung im Jahr 1994 weltweit zu einem Referenzstandort der Technologie-Entwicklung für die Infineon-Standorte entwickelt. Das Werk beschäftigt derzeit mehr als 3.300 Mitarbeiter.

Infineon Technologies Dresden, one of the most modern chip factories of Europe, has evolved since its foundation in 1994 worldwide into a reference location for technology developments for the Infineon locations. The works presently employ more than 3,300 staff members.

Bislang wurden die Chips weltweit auf Siliziumscheiben (Wafern) im Durchmesser von 200 Millimetern produziert. Schafft es dieses Joint-Venture, die Fertigungsprozesse auf 300-mm-Wafer zu beherrschen? So lautet die große technische

Chip-Production

chips per wafer
64 Mb DRAM

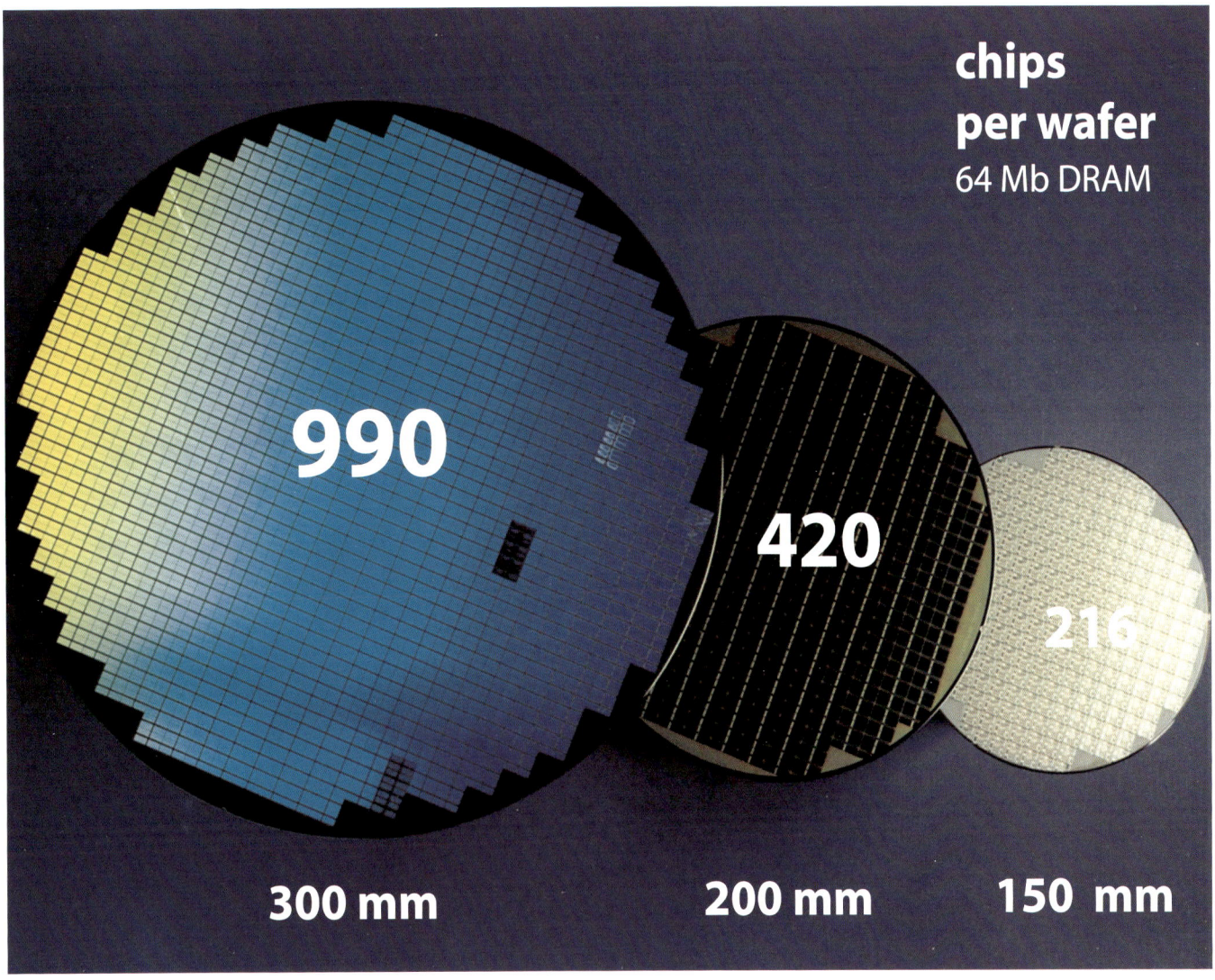

990 — 300 mm
420 — 200 mm
216 — 150 mm

300mm-Wafer – ein Beitrag zur Produktivitätssteigerung.

300mm-Wafer – a contribution to the increase of productivity.

Whoever travels to Dresden by plane, discovers through the window while approaching a modern, impressive industrial complex situated between the city centre and the Klotzsche airport. Infineon Technologies Dresden has established one of the world's most modern chip production halls for memory chips and logic components on the large campus, in which more than 3,300 employees not only produce highly integrated circuits of the latest generation, but also the worldwide first chips on silicon wafers of 300-mm-diameter. Infineon Technologies is thus setting worldwide the latest standards of production technology from Dresden.

In spring 1990, Siemens AG had proposed Dresden as location of its semiconductor activities for the first time. Both the City of Dresden and the regional government of Saxony have shown their willingness in talks to make the city one of the worldwide renowned high-tech metropolitan places. But, it did not stop at this declaration of intention: Dresden's image in the world has changed completely. Apart from "Baroque City" slowly also the "high-tech location Dresden" is becoming significant.

One of the important location criteria for Siemens AG was in those days the technically highly qualified workforce – indeed, Dresden had been in former times a centre of high technology with the Zentrum für Mikroelektronik (ZMD) and the potential of universities and research institutes. Also crucial in determining the decision were the acceptance of Free State of Saxony to settle industrial high-tech companies and the targeted promotional measures for investments in the new East German provinces. Furthermore, the Federal Ministry of Education and Research (BMBF) supported the establishment of Infineon Technologies Dresden, since such economic development activities strengthen the location Germany in the field of high technology essentially. Against the background of these favourable frame conditions, Siemens in Dresden founded in 1998 – four years after the completion of the first construction phases – a joint venture with Motorola named SEMICONDUCTOR300, which had the aim to develop a production technology on 300-mm-wafers.

Until now, chips were produced worldwide on silicon wafers of 200 mm-diameter. Will this joint venture manage to control production processes on 300-mm-wafers? This was the great technical challenge. After all, on a wafer of 300 mm-diameter it is possible to produce more than double the amount of chips per wafer. The semiconductor market requires an increase of productivity of around 30 percent each year. One contribution to achieve this aim is the

Chip-Produktion

Blick in den SC300 Reinraum mit Transportsystem für FOUPs.
View into the SC300 clean-room with transport system for FOUPs.

Herausforderung. Schließlich können auf einem Wafer im Durchmesser 300 Millimeter mehr als doppelt soviele Chips pro Wafer hergestellt werden. Der Halbleitermarkt verlangt eine Produktivitätssteigerung von circa 30 Prozent pro Jahr. Ein Beitrag, um dieses zu erreichen, ist der Wechsel hin zu einem größeren Waferdurchmesser, der damit einen entscheidenden Wettbewerbsvorteil darstellt. Die Steigerung der Wafergrößen hat die Halbleiterindustrie in der Vergangenheit etwa alle sechs bis acht Jahre vollzogen – wesentlich getrieben durch amerikanische Halbleiterhersteller und verbunden mit immensen Kosten.

Um die Chip-Herstellungsprozesse auf der neue Wafergröße von 300 Millimetern zu entwickeln, waren weltweit Kooperationen mit Material- und Anlagenherstellern notwendig, die mehrere Milliarden Euro kosteten. Zwei Vereinigungen von Halbleiterherstellern in den USA, in dem auch die Infineon Technologies AG Mitglied ist, sowie in Japan haben zunächst Standards für Wafer, Anlagen und den Materialtransport in einer Fertigung definiert sowie erste Prototypen getestet.
In der Pilotlinie von SEMICONDUCTOR300, einem Joint Venure von Infineon und Motorola, die in der Dresdner Infineon-Chipfabrik untergebracht war, wurde 1998 die weltweit erste Entwicklungslinie mit allen notwendigen Geräten installiert. Zielsetzung war die Basis für eine Beurteilung der Reife von Anlagen, Materialien und Prozessen zu erstellen. Eine Mannschaft von 450 hochqualifizierten internationalen Wissenschaftlern und Technikern, die das Know-how für diese Technologie entwickelt, musste erst einmal zusammengestellt werden. Mit einem Aufwand von rund 1,5 Milliarden Mark, gefördert durch das BMBF und das Land Sachsen, konnte ein Netzwerk von Firmen, die Anlagen, Materialien und Dienstleistungen aus der ganzen Welt bereitstellen, aufgebaut werden. Doch nicht nur aus aller Welt wurden Firmen in dieses Projekt mit eingebunden, sondern auch Unternehmen aus der Region arbeiteten an dem Schlüsselprojekt für die Halbleiterindustrie mit.
Der bahnbrechende Erfolg des Joint Ventures SEMICONDUCTOR300 in Dresden kann sich sehen lassen: Die Dresdener Entwicklungs- und Pilotlinie hat als erste Halbleiterlinie in der Welt einen kompletten Fertigungsprozess auf 300-mm-Wafern entwickelt. Ende 1999 wurden die ersten voll funktionsfähigen Produkte, Speicherchips der Generation 64M DRAM mit 0,25 µm Strukturbreite hergestellt. Damit war eine Referenz zur Beurteilung des Entwicklungsfortschritts geschaffen.

In der zweiten Stufe wurden die prozesstechnischen Anforderungen erhöht und Strukturbreiten um 0,2 µm realisiert. Das entsprechende Test-Produkt sind Chips mit 256 Megabite Speicherkapazität. Hiermit ist Dresden weltweit führend! Parallel zur Anlagen- und Prozessentwicklung wurde im Projekt „Fab of the Future" die planerischen Grundlagen für eine Volumenfertigung gelegt, um den Kostenvorteil von 30 % gegenüber 200 mm realisieren zu können. Um den Wettbewerbsvorsprung weiter auszubauen und vor allem um die gewaltigen Entwicklungsvorleistungen zu nutzen, hat Infineon Technologies beschlossen, in Dresden die erste 300-mm-Volumenproduktion zu errichten. Im Frühjahr 2000 wurde der Grundstein für die Fabrik, das Modul 3, gelegt – gemeinsam mit dem Bundeskanzlers Gerhard Schröder, der Bundesforschungsministerin Edelgard Bulmahn und Ministerpräsident Professor Kurt Biedenkopf.

Mit ungeheurem Aufwand und in Rekordzeit begann dann die Errichtung der Reinraumhalle für die Fertigung. Mehr als 800 Spezialisten arbeiten täglich am Rohbau, mehr als 1.200 Spezialisten werden notwendig sein, um die Halle mit Geräten zu bestücken. In der Endausbaustufe soll das weltweit erste 300-mm-Fertigungsmodul 1500 Mitarbeiter beschäftigen und circa 6.000 Wafer pro Woche verarbeiten. Das heißt, pro Woche werden mehr als fünf Millionen DRAM-Chips die neue Fertigungslinie verlassen.

Einer der Initiatoren der 300-mm-Aktivitäten ist Dr. Peter Kücher, bis Ende September 2000 Geschäftsführer des Joint Ventures SEMICONDUCTOR300 und jetziger Geschäftsführer von Infineon Technologies SC300, zusammen mit Dr. Klaus Müller und Wolfgang Schmid.

Nach dem Ausscheiden von Motorola – alle Entwicklungsziele wurden erreicht – sind in dem Unternehmen neben Infineon auch der Freistaat Sachsen und die Firma M&W Zander als Gesellschafter vertreten. ∎

Chip-Production

change to a larger wafer diameter, which signifies a decisive competition advantage. The semiconductor industry has executed in the past increases of wafer sizes about every six to eight years, usually driven by American semiconductor producers and linked to tremendous costs.

Several billions of Euros were necessary to cover the costs of worldwide co-operations with material and equipment producers in order to develop the chip production processes on the new wafer size of 300 mm. Two affiliations of semiconductor producers in the USA, of which also Infineon Technologies AG is a member, as well as in Japan have at first defined the standards for wafers, plants and the transport of material within a production as well as tested the first prototype.

In 1998, the worldwide first development line with all necessary equipments was installed in the pilot line of SEMICONDUCTOR300, a joint venture of Infineon and Motorola, which is housed in the Dresden Infineon chip factory. The aim was to create a basis for the evaluation of the maturity of plants, materials and processes. A team of 450 highly qualified international scientists and technicians that developed the expertise for this technology had to be first put together. It was achieved to build up a network of companies, which provided plants, materials and services from all over the world, at an expense of around 1.5 billion DM with the support of the BMF and funds of the Regional State of Saxony. However, not only companies from all over the world were involved in this project, but also local companies of the region worked on this key project for the semiconductor industry.

The pioneering success of the joint venture SEMICONDUCTOR300 in Dresden is certainly something to be proud of: The Dresden development and pilot line has developed as first semiconductor line in the world a complete production process on 300-mm-wafers. The first fully functional products, memory chips of the 64M-DRAM generation with 0.25 mm structural width were manufactured at the end of 1999. Thus, a reference criterion for monitoring development progress was created.

In the second phase, the technical process requirements were increased and structural width realised around 0.2 mm. The corresponding test products are chips of 256 Megabite memory capacity. Thus, Dresden is leading worldwide! Basic plans for production of large volumes were made parallel to plant and process developments within the project "Fab of the Future", in order to realise the cost advantage of 30 % against 200 mm. Infineon Technologies decided to establish in Dresden the first 300 mm-volume-production, in order to extend the competition advantage further and, above all, to use the enormous advance development performances. In spring 2000, the foundation for the construction of the factory, Module 3, was laid – together with Chancellor Gerhard Schröder, Federal Research Minister Mrs. Edelgard Bulmahn and Minister President Professor Kurt Biedenkopf.

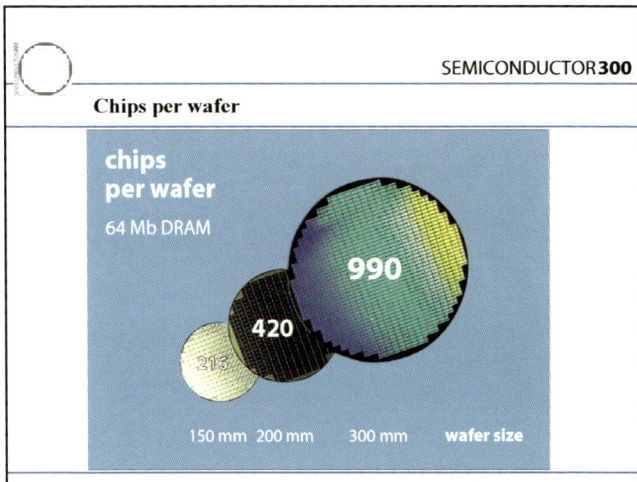

With a tremendous effort and in record time the erection of the clean-room hall for production was started. More than 800 specialists worked daily on the construction site, more than 1,200 specialists will be needed to provide the hall with equipments. The worldwide first 300-mm production module is designed to employ 1,500 staff members in the final construction phase and to process approx. 6,000 wafers per week. This means that more than five million DRAM chips per week will leave the new production line.

One of the initiators of the 300-mm-activities is Dr. Peter Kücher, until the end of September 2000 Managing Director of the joint venture SEMICONDUCTO300 and now Managing Director of Infineon Technologies SC300 together with Dr. Klaus Müller and Wolfgang Schmid.

After the withdrawal of Motorola – all development aims have been achieved – the Free State of Saxony and the company M&W Zander are partners in the company apart from Infineon.

Grundsteinlegung im Mai 2000.

Laying of the foundation stone in May 2000.

Company Profile

Im Focus: Zusammenschluss von Anorganischer Chemie und Festkörperphysik

In the Spotlight:
Merger of Inorganic Chemistry with Solid-State Physics

MAX-PLANCK-GESELLSCHAFT

Max-Planck-Gesellschaft zur Förderung der Wissenschaften e. V.
Max-Planck-Institut für Chemische Physik fester Stoffe

Geschäftsführender Direktor/
Managing Director:
Professor Dr. Rüdiger Kniep

Direktoren am Institut/Directors at the Institute:
Professor Dr. Rüdiger Kniep
Professor Dr. Frank Steglich
Dr. Yuri Grin

Gründungsjahr/Year of Foundation: 1995
Arbeitsaufnahme/Beginning of Operation: 1996

Mitarbeiter/Employees:
140 (geplant ist das Institut mit vier Direktoren und ca. 230 Mitarbeitern/the institute is planned with four directors and approx. 230 employees)

Themenspektrum/Spectrum of Topics:
- Intermetallische Phasen und Übergänge zu kovalenten Verbindungen
- Neue intermetallische Verbindungen mit stark korrelierten Elektronen
- Unkonventionelle Ordnungsphänomene
- Struktur/Eigenschafts-Beziehungen
- Entwicklung neuer Syntheseverfahren
- Intermetallic phases and transitions to covalent compounds
- New intermetalic compounds with strongly correlated electrons
- Unconventional ordering phenomena
- Structure/property relationship
- Development of new synthesis methods

Anschrift/Address:
Öffentlichkeitsarbeit
Dr. Liane Schröder
Nöthnitzer Straße 40
D-01187 Dresden
Telefon   +49 (351) 46 46-36 02
Telefax   +49 (351) 46 46-10
E-Mail   schroede@cpfs.mpg.de
Internet www.cpfs.mpg.de

„Begegnungsturm" des Instituts.
"Tower of Encounters" in the institute.

Vorderansicht des Instituts entlang der Nöthnitzer Straße.
Front view of the institute along the Nöthnitzer Straße.

Das Max-Planck-Institut für Chemische Physik fester Stoffe (CPfS) widmet sich der experimentellen Erforschung intermetallischer Verbindungen mit neuartigen chemischen und physikalischen Eigenschaften. Die Hauptforschungsgebiete der drei zurzeit arbeitenden Forschungsbereiche Festkörperphysik und Anorganische Chemie sind orientiert auf:
- Intermetallische Phasen und Übergänge zu kovalenten Verbindungen
- Neue intermetallische Verbindungen mit stark korrelierten Elektronen
- Unkonventionelle metallische Eigenschaften, quantenkritische Phänomene
- Unkonventionelle Ordnungsphänomene (Ladungsordnung, magnetische Ordnung, Supraleitung) und Charakterisierung von Schwere-Fermionen-Verbindungen, Spin-Peierls-Systemen und metallorganischen Supraleitern
- Suche nach neuen stark korrelierten Halbleitern („Kondo-Isolatoren")
- Struktur/Eigenschafts-Beziehungen
- Entwicklung neuer Syntheseverfahren
- Phasengleichgewichte, Phasenumwandlungen, Nichtstöchiometrie
- Valenzzustände und chemische Bindung.

Zur Lösung dieser Fragestellungen tragen die Kompetenzgruppen Materialentwicklung, Hohe Drücke, Tiefe Temperaturen, Theorie, Struktur, Analytik und Metallographie bei, deren wissenschaftliche Leiter eigene Forschungsprojekte verfolgen. ∎

The Max-Planck-Institute for Chemical Physics of Solids (CPfS) is dedicated to the experimental investigation of intermetallic phases with new chemical and physical properties. The main research areas of the three presently active research fields solid-state physics and inorganic chemistry are oriented towards:
- Intermetallic phases and transitions to covalent compounds
- New intermetalic compounds with strongly correlated electrons
- Unconventional metallic properties, quantum-critical phenomena
- Unconventional ordering phenomena (charge order, magnetic order, superconductivity) and characterization of heavy-fermion compounds, spin-Peierls system and metal-organic superconductors
- Search for new strongly correlated semiconductors (Kondo-insulators)
- Structure/property-relations
- Development of new synthesis methods
- Phase equilibrium, phase changes, non-stoichiometry
- Valence conditions and chemical bonding.

The competence groups materials development, high pressures, low temperatures, theory, structure, analysis and metallography provide contributions to these issues and their scientific heads of department follow their own research projects. ∎

Im Eingangsbereich.
In the entrance hall.

Company Profile

Physikalische Forschung, experimentelle Workshops

Physical Research, Experimental Workshops

Im November 1992 beschloss der Senat der Max-Planck-Gesellschaft die Gründung des Instituts in Dresden. Bereits im Juli 1993 wurden die wissenschaftlichen Aktivitäten aufgenommen.

Im Mai 1994 erfolgte die offizielle Einweihung des Instituts durch den Präsidenten der Max-Planck-Gesellschaft, zwei Jahre später konnten der Institutsneubau sowie die Gästehäuser bezogen werden.

Das Konzept

Das Institut betreibt theoretische Physik, vorgesehen ist dabei auch eine enge, zeitlich begrenzte Zusammenarbeit mit experimentellen Gruppen. Das Konzept des Instituts sieht die Organisation und Durchführung von ein- bis dreimonatigen Seminaren und Workshops vor. So hat es sich inzwischen zum Treffpunkt für den Nachwuchs der Hochschulen mit auf dem Fachgebiet international führenden Wissenschaftlern entwickelt.

Systematisch arbeitet das Dresdner Max-Planck-Institut mit nationalen und internationalen Forschungseinrichtungen zusammen. Besonders enge Beziehungen bestehen zu dem israelischen Minerva Center for Nonlinear Physics of Complex Systems und der University of Tokyo. Ein umfangreiches Gästeprogramm (ca. 80 Gäste können gleichzeitig betreut werden) ist die Grundlage der wissenschaftlichen Zusammenarbeit. ■

Das Max-Planck-Institut für Physik komplexer Systeme.
The Max-Planck Institute for Physics of Complex Systems.

In November of 1992, the Senate of the Max-Planck-Institute decided to found a new institute in Dresden. As early as in July 1993, scientific activities began. In May 1994, the official inauguration of the institute by the president of the Max-Planck-Society took place, two years later the new buildings of the institute as well as the guesthouses were ready to be occupied.

The Concept

The institute is concerned with theoretic physics, whereby also a close, time limited co-operation with experimental groups is planned. The concept of the institute intends the organisation and realization of one- to three-months seminars and workshops. Thus, it has meanwhile become the meeting point for up and coming young academics of universities with scientists that are international leading experts in this field.

The Max-Planck-Institute Dresden systematically works together with national and international research institutions. Particularly close relations exist to the Israeli Minerva Center for Nonlinear Physics of Complex Systems and to the University of Tokyo. An extensive programme for guests (approx. 80 guest can be accommodated simultaneously) is the basis of this scientific co-operation. ■

Der Neubau wurde 1997 eingeweiht.
The new building was inaugurated in 1997.

Max-Planck-Institut für
Physik komplexer Systeme

Geschäftsführender Direktor/
Managing Director:
Prof. Dr. Peter Fulde

Direktor 2. Abteilung/
Director of 2nd Department:
Prof. Dr. Jan-Michael Rost

Gründungsjahr/Year of Foundation: 1992

Mitarbeiter/Employees:
Planstellen: 37
Gastwissenschaftler und Doktoranden: 52
Stipendiaten: 81

Forschungsschwerpunkte/
Main Research Topics:
- Korrelierte Elektronen
- Endliche Systeme
- Nichtlineare Zeitreihenanalyse
- Quantenchaos und mesoskopische Systeme
- Strukturbildung
- Quantenchemie
- Wellen in komplexen Medien und mesoskopische Phänomene
- Electronic Correlations
- Finite Systems
- Non-linear Time Series Analysis
- Quantum Chaos and Mesoscopic Systems
- Patternformation
- Quantum Chemistry
- Waves in Complex Media and Mesoscopic Phenomena

Anschrift/Address:
Nöthnitzer Straße 38
D-01187 Dresden
Telefon +49 (351) 871-0
Telefax +49 (351) 871-19 99
E-Mail   gneisse@mpipks-dresden.mpg.de
Internet www.mpipks-dresden.mpg.de

Öffentlichkeitsarbeit/Public Relations:
Priv.-Doz. Dr. Sergej Flach
Telefon +49 (351) 871-21 03
Uta Gneiße
Telefon +49 (351) 871-11 05

Das Gebäude bietet Platz für 80 Gäste.
The building provides space for 80 guests.

TechnologieZentrum

TechnologieZentrumDresden – Brutstätte für Unternehmen und Ideen

TechnologyCentreDresden – Place of Procreation for Enterprises and Ideas

Dresden 1990: Viele gute Projektideen, aber kein Mittelstand

Schon zum Ende Jahres 1989 war man sich in der Technischen Universität Dresden darüber klar geworden, dass neue Formen der wirtschaftlichen Verwertung der Forschungsergebnisse gefunden werden müssen. Mit Unterstützung des TechnologieZentrumDortmund, eines der ersten deutschen Technologiezentren überhaupt und bereits sehr erfolgreich, wurde der Aufbau des TechnologieZentrumDresden als Gründerzentrum und Keimzelle für Innovationen vereinbart und realisiert. Die Idee fand ein breites Echo. Noch in der ersten Hälfte des Jahres 1990 lagen mehr als 50 Anfragen für Unternehmensgründungen und Ansiedelung im TechnologieZentrumDresden vor. Daher war das erste Domizil schon am ersten Tage voll ausgelastet. Die Gründerunternehmen kamen vornehmlich aus der TU Dresden. Dort waren in den letzten Jahren viele anwendungsreife Forschungsergebnisse entstanden, deren Schöpfer nun unter den neuen wirtschaftlichen Rahmenbedingungen auf ihre Nutzung drängten. So lief der Aufbau des Zentrums selbst und die ersten Existenzgründungen parallel ab. Mit dem ersten betreuten Existenzgründern qualifizierte sich auch das Dresdner Zentrumsmanagement. Das Deutsch-Deutsche Gemeinschaftsunternehmen mit Dortmunder Unterstützung konnte noch im Sommer 1990 seine erste Existenzgründung verbuchen.

Das Profil der Technischen Universität Dresden mit seinen High-Tech-Disziplinen prägte von Anfang an die inhaltlichen Akzente der Unternehmen im TechnologieZentrumDresden. So dominierten bereits in dieser Zeit Ideen rund um die Mikroelektronik, Sensortechnik und Informationstechnologie.

TechnologieZentrumDresden Dienstleister für Existenzgründungen

Nach dem erfolgreichen Start und Umzug an einen neuen Standort mit entsprechendem Potenzial an Erweiterungsflächen konnte sich das Zentrum

Das Hauptgebäude des TechnologieZentrumDresden.
The main building of the TechnologyCentreDresden.

Dr. Bertram Dressel

Der Autor, 1955 in Meerane geboren, studierte von 1975 bis 1980 Verfahrenstechnik an der Technischen Universität in Dresden mit dem Abschluss als Dipl.-Ing. Anschließend war er als Wissenschaftlicher Assistent, später als Oberassistent und als Referent im Prorektorat für Wissenschaften der TU tätig. 1982 erfolgte die Promotion zum Dr.-Ing., 1988 die Habilitation. Seit 1990 ist Dr. Bertram Dressel Geschäftsführer der TechnologieZentrumDresden GmbH.

The author, born in 1955 in Meerane, studied processing technology at the Technical University in Dresden from 1975 until 1980, graduating as a Certified Engineer. Afterwards he worked as scientific assistant, later as chief assistant and as head of department in the protectorate for sciences at the TU. In 1982, he attained his PhD in engineering, in 1988 his postdoctoral lecturing qualification. Since 1990, Bertram Dressel is Managing Director of the TechnologyCentreDresden GmbH.

auch inhaltlich weiter profilieren. Beim Auf- und Ausbau des TechnologieZentrumDresden und seiner fachlichen Profilierung leistete die Stadt Dresden als ein Gesellschafter besonders durch das Amt für Wirtschaftsförderung von Anfang an bis heute wertvolle Unterstützung. Bis 1993 wurden insgesamt 35 Existenzgründungen erfolgreich betreut. Die Arbeit des Zentrums war von Anfang an sehr stark von Kundenorientierung geprägt. Es verstand sich schon zu dieser Zeit als Infrastrukturdienstleister und Partner der Existenzgründer, kurz gesagt selbst als Unternehmen. Besonderer Wert wurde auf die Entwicklung eines attraktiven, synergieträchtigen

Technology Centre

Ein attraktives Arbeitsumfeld schafft ein gutes Klima für Innovationen.

An attractive working environment creates a good climate for innovations.

Dresden 1990: Many excellent project ideas, but no middle-size business sector.

Already by the end of 1989, one had it clear at the Technical University of Dresden that new forms of economic exploitation of research findings had to be found. With the support of the Technology Centre Dortmund, one of the first German technology centres at all and already being very successful, the creation of the Technology Centre Dresden was agreed and realized as a centre for start-ups and a breeding cell for innovations. The idea found a broad acceptance. Even in the first half of the year 1990, more than 50 enquiries for company start-ups and settlements were presented to the Technology Centre Dresden. For this reason, the first building was complete occupied on the first day. The company start-ups came mainly from the TU Dresden. In the past years, many research findings had been developed that were ready to be applied and their creators were eagerly pushing for their utilization under the new economic frame conditions of the free market. Thus, the establishment of the centre itself and the first company start-ups occurred in parallel. Indeed, the centre's management qualified itself through the service provided to first company founder. The joint company founded in East-West-German co-operation with the support from Dortmund was able to show its first company start-up as early as in the summer of 1990.

From the very beginning, the profile of Technical University of Dresden characterised the contents of the trends set in the companies of the Technology Centre Dresden with its high-tech disciplines. Even in the early hours, ideas around microelectronics, sensor technology and information technology dominated plans.

TechnologyCentreDresden Service Provider for Company Start-ups

After the successful start and relocation to a new site with corresponding potential of areas for expansion, the centre was also able to extend its profile in terms of contents. As partner, the City of Dresden, particularly through its Department of Economic Promotion, rendered valuable support through the establishment and extension of the Technology Centre Dresden and the definition of its specialized technical profile. Until 1993, a total of 35 company start-ups were accompanied successfully. The work of the centre was very customer-oriented right from the beginning. Even in the early days, it saw itself as provider of an infrastructure and partner of the young entrepreneurs, in short, as an enterprise itself. Special attention was given to the development of an attractive mix of companies generating fruitful synergies. Thus, from the beginning onwards, companies of differing development stages were placed next to each other.

As an important foundation of its work, a close co-operation was established with other institutions of technology transfer in Dresden and its region. This co-operation is documented in the publication Dresdner Transferbrief, among others. The Dresdner Transferbrief is published

TechnologieZentrum

Unternehmensmixes gelegt. So wurden von Anfang an Firmen unterschiedlicher Entwicklungsstadien nebeneinander untergebracht.

Die enge Kooperation mit anderen Einrichtungen des Technologietransfers Dresdens und der Region wurde als wichtige Arbeitsgrundlage etabliert. Dokumentiert wird diese Kooperation u.a. durch den Dresdner Transferbrief. Der Dresdner Transferbrief wird gemeinsam vom TechnologieZentrumDresden, der Technischen Universität Dresden und der BTI-Beratungsgesellschaft für Technologietransfer und Innovationsförderung GmbH herausgegeben und bietet eine solide Plattform für Transferangebote wissenschaftlicher Einrichtungen und Unternehmen einerseits und dient gleichzeitig aktiv dem Marketing sächsischer KMU. Nunmehr bereits im 9. Jahrgang erfolgreich und gefragt ist der Transferbrief in dieser Form einzigartig in den neuen Bundesländern.

Bis 1995 konnte die Anzahl der betreuten Firmen auf 50 erhöht werden. Mit der PRO-DV GmbH Dresden zog das erste Unternehmen nach erfolgreicher Entwicklung wieder aus dem Inkubator aus. Es besitzt heute ein eigenes Firmengebäude im TechnologieParkDresden-Nord und gehört zur bundesweit tätigen PRO-DV AG. Zahlreiche heute noch im TechnologieZentrumDresden ansässige Firmen haben sich sehr erfolgreich entwickelt und sind weltweit auf dem Markt aktiv.

So verkauft z. B. die SITA Messtechnik GmbH ihr selbst entwickeltes Oberflächenspannungsmessgerät über Vertriebsfirmen in Australien, Japan, Korea, den USA und zahlreichen EU-Staaten. Die DAS Dünnschicht Anlagen Systeme GmbH agiert weltweit als gefragter Lieferant von Abgasentsorgungstechnik für die Halbleiterindustrie, u. a. in Taiwan, Südostasien, den USA und Europa.

Branchenorientierung ermöglicht bessere Firmenbetreuung

Mit der Entwicklung der Mikroelektronik als Kernbranche Dresdens erfolgte auch im TechnologieZentrumDresden eine stärkere Fokussierung auf diese Unternehmen. Dem Bedarf folgend wurde ein zweiter Standort in unmittelbarer Nähe der Halbleiterproduzenten im Dresdner Norden aufgebaut. Die Ausrichtung auf einige besonders wichtige und zukunftsträchtige Technologiefelder ermöglicht eine zielstrebige Betreuung der Firmen sowohl mit zugeschnittener technischer und organisatorischer Infrastruktur als auch durch vertiefte Kenntnisse von Branchenspezifika. Neben der Mikroelektronik wurde für das TechnologieZentrumDresden die Kommunikationstechnik als Schwerpunkt definiert.

Integration in regionale und überregionale Netzwerke schafft Zusatzkompetenz bei der Unternehmensbetreuung.

In die Betreuung der Existenzgründer bezieht das Zentrumsmanagement kompetente Partner ein. Dazu wurde ein regionales Netzwerk aufgebaut, das alle Bereiche der Betreuung von der Aufstellung der Unternehmenskonzepte über die Marktbeurteilung bis hin zur Finanzierung beinhaltet. Aber auch überregional engagiert sich das TechnologieZentrumDresden frühzeitig innerhalb verschiedener Kompetenznetzwerke. Hierbei spielt die Arbeitsgemeinschaft Deutscher Technologie- und Gründerzentren (ADT e. V.) als der Bundes-

Der Start erfolgte im Altbaubereich der ehemaligen Ziegelei in Dresden-Gostritz.
The start took place in the part of the old building of the former brickworks in Dresden-Gostritz.

Technology Centre

Technologiepark Dresden.

Technology Park Dresden.

together by the Technology Centre Dresden, the Technical University Dresden and the BTI-Beratungsgesellschaft für Technologytransfer (Consulting Company for Technology Transfer) and Innovationsförderung GmbH (Innovation Promotion) and provides a solid platform for transfer proposals of scientific institutions and companies on the one hand and at the same time its serves actively to promote the marketing of KMU in Saxony. Meanwhile successful and sought after in its 9th volume, the Transferbrief is unique in this form in the East German Federal States.

Until 1995, the number of attended companies had increased to 50. After it's successful development, the PRO-DV GmbH Dresden was the first company to move out of the incubator again. Today, it possesses its own company building in the Technology Park Dresden-North and belongs to the nationally active PRO-DV AG. Numerous companies that are still located in the Technology Centre Dresden have had a successful development and are active worldwide on the market.

As for example, the SITA Messtechnik GmbH sells her self-developed surface tension measuring equipment via distributing agents in Australia, Japan, Korea, the USA and numerous EU states. The DAS Dünnschicht Anlagen Systeme GmbH (Thin Coating Plant Systems) is active worldwide as a supplier in great demand of waste gases disposal technology for the semi-conductor industry, including in Taiwan, South East Asia, the USA and Europe, among others.

Branch-orientation enables a better support of companies

With the development of microelectronics as a core branch of Dresden also a more intensive focus on these companies ensued in the Technology Centre Dresden. Following the demand, a second location was established in direct vicinity to the producers of semi-conductors in the North of Dresden. The orientation towards particularly important and promising fields of technology enables a targeted support of the companies both with a custom-made technical and organisational infrastructure as well as through the deep knowledge of branch specific issues. Apart from microelectronics, communications technologies have been defined as a main focus for the Technology Centre Dresden.

Integration in regional and supraregional networks creates additional competence for the support of companies.

The management of the centre involves competent partners in the support of start-ups. For this, a regional network has been built up that comprises all fields of support parting from elaboration of the company concept across market evaluation up to financing. But the Technology Centre Dresden is also engaged timely in various supraregional networks of competence. In this respect, the Arbeitsgemeinschaft Deutscher Technologie- und Gründerzentren (ADT e. V.) being the Federal Association of technology

TechnologieZentrum

verband der Technologiezentren eine besondere Rolle. Durch die Kontakte und den Erfahrungsaustausch innerhalb dieses Verbandes konnte die Qualität der Firmenbetreuung entscheidend verbessert werden.

So wurden bisher insgesamt mehr als 120 Existenzgründungen betreut. 90 Firmen sind heute im TechnologieZentrumDresden ansässig.

Im Jahr 2000 wurde auf Initiative des TechnologieZentrumDresden das Kompetenznetzwerk „Silicon Saxony" als Verein gegründet. Dieses Netzwerk bildet für Hochschulen, branchenspezifische Forschungseinrichtungen, Großunternehmen der Halbleiterindustrie, KMU als Zulieferer oder Serviceunternehmen und Bildungseinrichtungen eine gemeinsame Plattform. Zielsetzung ist die Vertiefung der Zusammenarbeit, Schaffung effektiver Instrumente des Technologietransfers, Unterstützung von Firmengründungen, Ansiedelungen, Marketing, Vermittlung von Kooperationspartnern und Service sowie die Bildung einer Brücke zu anderen Netzwerken in der Region und im Ausland.

Ausbau des Technologie ZentrumDresden zum TechnologiePark

Nach zehnjähriger erfolgreicher Entwicklung des TechnologieZentrumDresden wurde 2001 der Aufbau des TechnologieParkDresden begonnen. Nunmehr können im TechnologieZentrumDresden gewachsene Technologiefirmen sich auf Dauer unmittelbar benachbart zu den Existenzgründern anzusiedeln. Im ersten Gebäude des TechnologieParks sind bereits fünf Unternehmen mit insgesamt mehr als 120 Mitarbeitern eingezogen. An den derzeitig zwei Standorten des TechnologieZentrumDresden (Gostritzer Straße und Dresden Nord) sind damit mehr als 1.500 Mitarbeiter in den Unternehmen tätig.

Die Mikrobiologie – Nanotechnologie – ist ein zukünftiges Technologiefeld des TechnologieZentrumDresden.

Mit dem Bioinnovationszentrum Dresden wird in Zusammenarbeit mit der TU Dresden ein Forschungs- und Existenzgründerzentrum für den Bereich der Molekularbiologie geschaffen. Es wird Bestandteil sein eines ganzen Komplexes an Vorhaben zu diesem Fachgebiet, die fachlich geprägt werden vom Max Planck Institut für Molekulare Zellbiologie und Genetik und der Technischen Universität Dresden.

Die ingenieurwissenschaftliche Umsetzung der biologischen Grundlagenforschung in neue Verfahren und Produkte unter einem Dach gewährleisten Innovation und Effektivität. Das Zentrumsmanagement wird mit professioneller Hilfe die wirtschaftliche Verwertung fördern. Das Bioinnovationszentrum soll sich somit zu einem tragenden Pfeiler des Dresdner Biotechnologiegebäudes entwickeln. ∎

TechnologieZentrumDresden.

TechnologyCentreDresden.

Technology Centre

TechnologieZentrumDresden.

TechnologyCentreDresden.

centres plays an important role. Through contacts and exchange of experiences within this association the quality of company support has been decisively improved.

Thus, a total of more than 120 company start-ups have been supported. 90 companies are located today in the Technology Centre Dresden.

In the year 2000, the competence network "Silicon Saxony" was established as an association on the initiative of the Technology Centre Dresden. This network establishes a common platform for universities, branch-specific research institutes, large companies of the semi-conductor industry, KMU as a supplier or service provider and educational institutes.

The targeted aim is the intensification of co-operation, creation of effective instruments of technology transfer, support of company start-ups, settlements, marketing, mediation of co-operation partners and service as well as establishing a bridge to other networks in the region and abroad.

Extension of the Technology Centre Dresden into a Technology Park

In 2001, the construction of the Technology Park Dresden was started after ten years of successful developments at the Technology Centre Dresden. Now it is possible for technology companies that have grown within the Technology Centre Dresden to settle directly in the neighbourhood of the company start-ups. Already five enterprises with a total of more than 120 employees have moved into the first building of the Technology Park. In the present two locations of the Technology Centre Dresden (Gostritzer Strasse and Dresden North), there are thus working more than 1,500 staff members.

Microbiology – nano technology is a future field of technology in the Technology Centre Dresden

In co-operation with TU Dresden a research and company start-up centre for the field of molecular biology is being created with the Bioinnovationszentrum Dresden (Bio Innovation Centre Dresden). It will be one component of a whole complex of projects in this special field, which is being influenced by experts from the Max Planck Institute for Molecular Cell Biology and Genetics and the Technical University of Dresden.

The realization in terms of engineering science of the biological basic research into applications of new procedures and products under one roof guarantees innovation and effectiveness. The management of the centre will promote the economic exploitation with professional help. The Bio Innovation Centre is designed to develop into a supporting pillar of the Dresden building of biotechnology.

Company Profile

HTW Dresden:
Lehre und Forschung für die Wirtschaft

HTW Dresden: Research and Teaching for the Economy

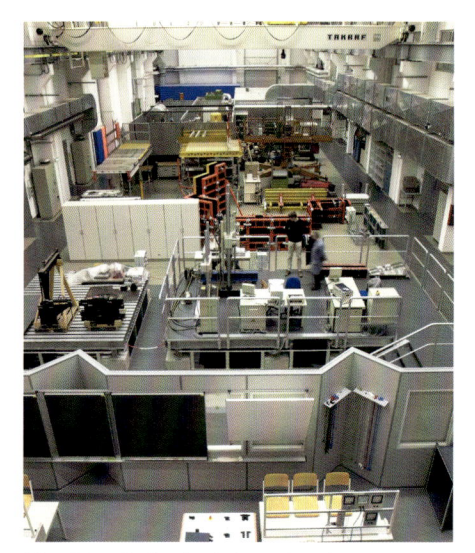

Maschinenhalle des Laborgebäudes.
Machine hall of the laboratory building.

Nahe dem Dresdner Hauptbahnhof befinden sich die aus den frühen sechziger Jahren stammenden Gebäude der ehemaligen Hochschule für Verkehrswesen „Friedrich List". In ihnen hat seit 1992 die Dresdner Hochschule für Technik und Wirtschaft (FH) ihren Platz. Heute ist sie mit 180 Professoren und über 4.800 Studenten die zweitgrößte Hochschule der Landeshauptstadt.

Die acht Fachbereiche Bauingenieurwesen/Architektur, Elektrotechnik, Gestaltung, Informatik/Mathematik, Landbau/Landespflege, Maschinenbau/Verfahrenstechnik, Vermessungswesen/Kartografie und Wirtschaftswissenschaften bilden in 21 Studiengängen aus. Dabei reicht die Palette des Studienangebotes von der Agrarwirtschaft bis zum Wirtschaftsingenieurwesen. Dazwischen liegen Allgemeiner Maschinenbau, Architektur, Bauingenieurwesen, Betriebswirtschaft, Chemieingenieurwesen/Umwelttechnik, Computertechnik/Automatisierungstechnik, Elektrotechnik/Elektronik, Fahrzeugtechnik, Gartenbau, Informatik, International Business Studies, Kartografie, Kommunikationstechnik, Landespflege, Medieninformatik, Produktgestaltung, Produktionstechnik, Vermessungswesen und Wirtschaftsinformatik. Einige von ihnen, so den „grünen" Studienbereich und die Verbindung zwischen Vermessungswesen und Kartografie, gibt es in Sachsen nur an der HTW Dresden.

Moderne Laborkomplexe, ein leistungsfähiges Rechenzentrum, eine neuzeitlich eingerichtete Bibliothek und ein Sprachenzentrum tragen in Verbindung mit dem individuellen Studium, dem obligatorischen praktischen Studiensemester und weit reichenden Auslandskontakten dazu bei, dass die Markenzeichen der deutschen Fachhochschulen: „ausgeprägte Berufsnähe zur Wirtschaft und Gesellschaft" und „Befähigung zur interkulturellen Kommunikation durch international anerkannte Studienabschlüsse" auch in Dresden mit Leben erfüllt werden.

Eine Hochschule mit aktuellem Anspruch ist jedoch nicht nur Platz zur Vermittlung von Fachwissen, sondern sie muss zugleich Heimstatt der Forschung und Entwicklung sein. Hier stützt sich die HTW auf die Ergebnisse ihres Forschungsinstituts Fahrzeugtechnik sowie die Arbeiten zur technischen Elektrostatik, Prozessmesstechnik und Umformtechnik.

Erfassung von Klimadaten im Gewächshaus.
Compiling climatic data in the greenery.

Seit 1998 arbeiten Spezialisten aus dem Bauingenieurwesen, der Elektrotechnik, dem Maschinenbau und der Verfahrenstechnik in einem Zentrum für angewandte Forschung und Technologie e. V. an der Hochschule gemeinsam an innovativen Systemlösungen.

Lehre und Forschung sind niemals, schon gar nicht im Hinblick auf wachsende Globalisierung, national begrenzt. Im Rahmen umfassender Kooperation unterhält die HTW Dresden deshalb enge Verbindungen zu zahlreichen wissenschaftlichen Einrichtungen in Europa, Afrika, Amerika, Asien und Australien. ∎

Im Labor für elektrische Maschinen und Antriebe.
In the laboratory for electrical machines and engines.

Company Profile

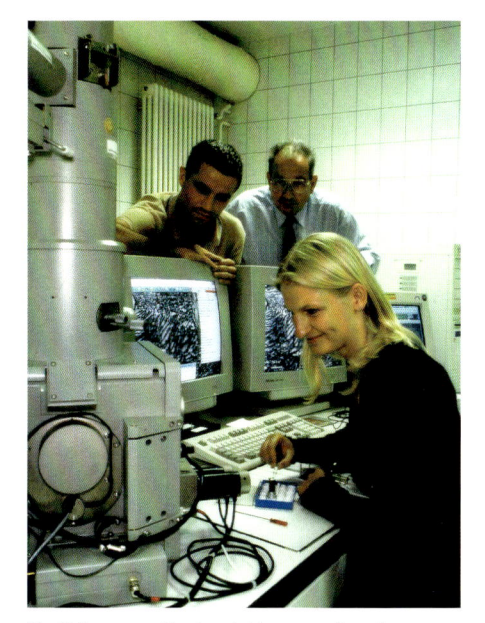

Praktikum am Rasterelektronenmikroskop.
Practical training at the scanning electron microscope.

The buildings of the former University for Transport Systems "Friedrich List" originating from the sixties is situated in the vicinity of the main train station of Dresden. Since 1992, the "Dresden Hochschule für Technik und Wirtschaft (FH)" Dresden University of Applied Sciences is located there now. Today, it is with 180 professors and over 4,800 students the second largest university of the regional capital. The eight faculties civil engineering/architecture, electro technology, design, computer science, mathematics, agricultural engineering/land conservation, mechanical engineering/process technology, surveying technology/cartography and economics educate students in 21 courses.

The range of the study provision extends from agricultural economy to industrial engineering. In between are general mechanical engineering, architecture, civil engineering, business economics, chemical engineering/environmental technology, computer science/automation technology, electro technology/electronics, automobile technology, horticulture, information technology, international business studies, cartography, communications technology, land conservation, computer science in media, product design, production technology, surveying technology and business computing. Some of these like for example the "green study fields and the link between surveying and cartography, are only available in Saxony at the HTW Dresden.

Rechnergestützte Kartenherstellung.
Computer aided map construction.

Modern laboratory facilities, an efficient computer centre, a library equipped to the latest standards and a language centre contribute in connection with an individual study, the obligatory practical training semester and far-reaching contacts abroad to the established image of the German universities that is also upheld in Dresden: "a marked nearness to the sectors of economy and society" and "capacitating intercultural communication through internationally recognised degrees".

A university of modern demands, however, is not only a place for the transmission of expert knowledge, but must also be the homestead of research and development. The HTW is backed up in this by the findings of its research institute for automobile technology as well as the work for technical electrostatics, process measuring technology and conversion technology. Since 1998, specialists from civil engineering, electro technology, mechanical engineering and process technology work together in the Centre for Applied Research and Technology e.V. at the university searching for innovative system solutions.

Education and research are never limited with regard to national boundaries, especially not in view of the growing globalisation. Within the framework of extensive co-operations, the HTW Dresden maintains close connections to numerous scientific institutions in Europe, Africa, America, Asia and Australia. ∎

HTW

Hochschule für
Technik und Wirtschaft Dresden (FH)
University of applied sciences

Rektor/Rector:
Prof. Dr.-Ing. Dr. h.c. Günther Otto

Gründungsjahr/Year of Foundation:
1992

Professoren/professors.:
180

Studenten/students:
4.800

Anschrift/Address:
Friedrich-List-Platz 1
D-01069 Dresden
Telefon   +49 (351) 462 31 02
Telefax   +49 (351) 462 21 85
E-Mail   rektor@htw-dresden.de
Internet www.htw-dresden.de

In einem der Rechnerlabore.
In one of the computer laboratories.

Biotechnologie

Biotechnologie

Die Biotechnologie entwickelt sich zu einem strukturbedeutsamen Teil der Dresdner Wirtschaft. In einem Netzwerk unter dem Namen BioMeT arbeiten Forschungseinrichtungen, Unternehmen und Unterstützer aus dem Finanzbereich und der Verwaltung zusammen. Geplant ist ein Bio-Innovationszentrum, ein ausschließlich der Biotechnologie vorbehaltenes Technologiezentrum.

BioParc Bioinformationszentrum

Bioinnovationszentrum Tatzberg BIOZ

TU Dresden Medizinische Fakultät

Entwicklungsareal Tatzberg

Max-Planck-Institut für Molekulare Zellbiologie u. Genetik

Zentrum für Biomaterialien

TU Dresden

Was verstehen wir unter Biotechnologie?

Biotechnologie ist der Einsatz biologischer Prozesse im Rahmen technischer Verfahren und industrieller Produktionen. Ihren großen Schub bekam die Biotechnologie bereits 1940 mit der Entdeckung und Produktion der Antibiotika, besonders des Penicillins. Jedoch erst die Gentechnik ermöglicht es, das Erbprogramm DNA aus Organismen zu isolieren und mit der so gewonnenen DNA Mikroorganismen und Zellen neu zu programmieren.

Biotechnology

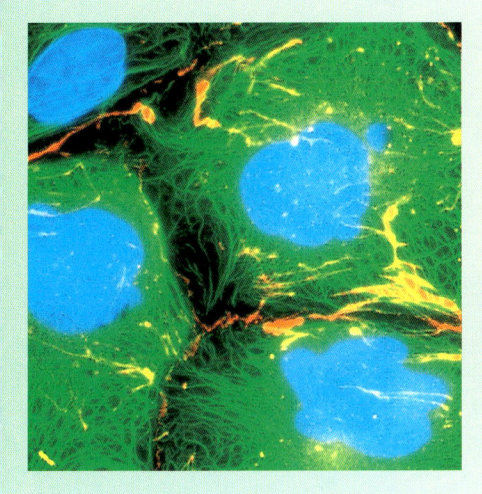

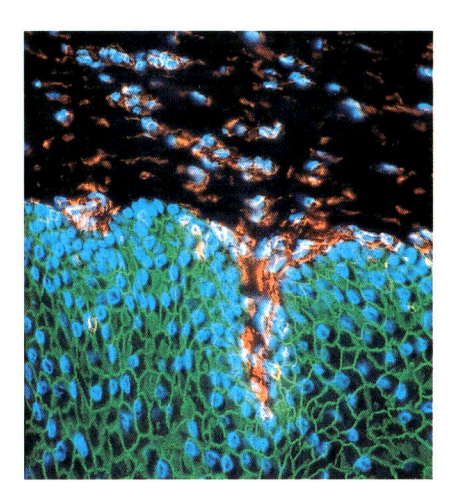

Biotechnology

Biotechnology is evolving to become an important structural part of Dresden's economy. Research institutions, enterprises and supports from the fields of finance and administration work together within a network by the name of BioMeT. It is planned to create a bio innovation centre, a technology centre exclusively reserved for biotechnology.

What do we mean by biotechnology?

Biotechnology is the application of biological processes in the framework of technical procedures and industrial production. Biotechnology received its great thrust as early as 1940 with the discovery and production of antibiotics, particularly of penicillin. However, only since the advent of gene technology, it is possible to isolate the genetic programme DNA from organisms and to reprogramme with newly gained DNA microorganisms and cells.

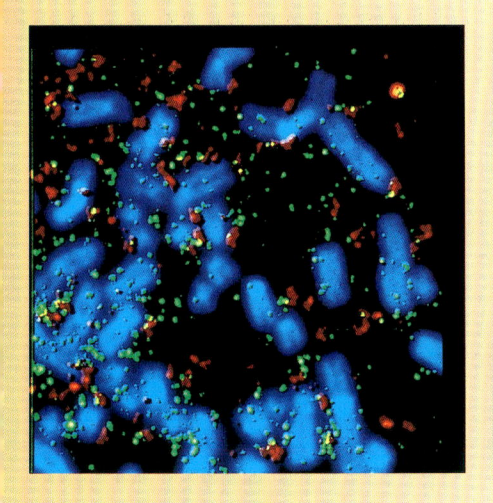

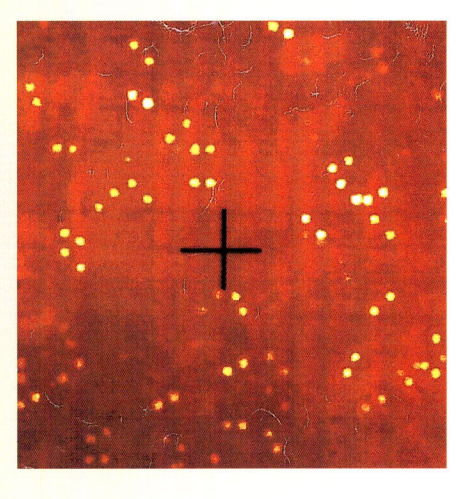

Company Profile

AMI-Service für Europa aus Dresdener Headquarter

AMI – Service for europe in their Dresden headquarter

American Microsystems GmbH

Geschäftsführer/Manager:
Harold A. Blomquist
Heiner Lohse

Gründungsjahr/Year of Foundation: 1993

Mitarbeiter/Employees: 66

Umsatz/Turnover: 1999: 17.400.000,00 Euro

Geschäftstätigkeit/Business Activity:
Entwicklung und Produktion von kundenspezifischen, integrierten Schaltkreisen.
Development and Production of customer-specific, integrated switch circuits (AMI)

Anschrift/Address:
Bertolt-Brecht Allee 22
D-01309 Dresden
Telefon   +49 (351) 315 30 0
Telefax   +49 (351) 315 30 11
E-Mail   europe_inquiry@amis.com
Internet   www.amis.com

American Microsystems Inc. (AMI), mit seinem Hauptsitz in San Diego/Kalifornien und seinem europäischen Hauptsitz in Dresden/Deutschland, leistete 1966 Pionierarbeit in der Entwicklung von kundenspezifischen integrierten Schaltkreisen (ASICs). Während dieser 34 Jahre zählt AMI zu den führenden Halbleiterherstellern, dazu verpflichtet, die besten Gesamtlösungen unter Nutzung der neuesten digitalen und analogen Technologien anzubieten.

American Microsystems, Inc. (AMI), with worldwide headquarters in San Diego, California, and European headquarters in Dresden, Germany, pioneered the development of application specific integrated circuits (ASICs) in 1966. Over the last 34 years, AMI has remained a leading semiconductor supplier committed to providing the best total solutions that employ the latest digital and analogue capabilities.

Qualität – AMI ist nach ISO 9001 und QS 9000 zertifiziert.
Quality – AMI is ISO 9001 and QS 9000 certified.

Die AMI GmbH in Dresden als Headquarter und Entwurfszentrum der American Microsystems, Inc. in Europa …
- bietet europäischen Kunden mit einem hochmotivierten, in Deutschland und USA hervorragend ausgebildeten Team den vollen Service der weltweiten AMI- Organisation,
- leistet insbesondere mit dem größten AMI Entwurfszentrum außerhalb AMI in USA jegliche wissenschaftlich-technische Unterstützung für kundenspezifische Schaltkreisentwürfe,
- kooperiert mit europäischen Forschungsinstituten, Universitäten und anderen Entwurfszentren bei der Entwicklung innovativer Produkte und Verfahren,
- koordiniert alle Entwicklungs- und Verkaufsaktivitäten der AMI in Europa.

AMI verfügt über umfangreiche Kooperationserfahrungen sowohl mit internationalen Marktführern als auch mit Erstanwendern aus der klein- und mittelständischen Industrie. Höchstmögliche Flexibilität bestimmt die kundenorientierte Arbeitsweise der AMI- Entwurfszentren. Sie können auf jeder denkbaren Arbeitsstufe in die Zusammenarbeit mit uns eintreten – gleich, ob Sie nur die Spezifikation vorgeben wollen, einen fertigen Schaltplan haben, Netzlisten in irgendeiner Beschreibungssprache besitzen oder ein bereits fertiges Layout realisiert haben möchten – immer finden Sie einen potenten Partner. Und wir beraten Sie in allen Fragen – von der Machbarkeit einer Systemidee bis zur optimalen Teststrategie. ∎

Founded in 1993, AMI GmbH, Dresden, is the location of AMI's European Headquarter and design center …

AMI GmbH offers:
- Complete customer service with a highly motivated, USA-trained, German team,
- The largest design center outside of AMI Headquarters with complete technical support,
- Cooperation with European research institutes, universities, and other design centers for the development of innovative products and processes,
- Coordination of development and sales activities for AMI in Europe.

AMI provides critical resources and an attitude of partnership and responsiveness to our customers' needs. You can trust AMI's experience with market leaders worldwide to bring success to your specific application.

Flexibility is the key to design methodology at the AMI design center. Now you can turn your analog or mixed-signal development over to AMI with complete confidence, AMI's unique „virtual interface" option allows you to be as involved in the design process as you like. You can provide source data at any entry point from chip specification to GDSII tape, and in nearly any format from captured schematic to netlists. With AMI as your partner you can be confident that your projects will become reality. ∎

Company Profile

Weltweit führender Smart Label-Hersteller

Worldwide leading Smart Label Manufacturer

KSW Microtec gehört weltweit zu den führenden Unternehmen auf dem Gebiet der Herstellung von aktiven und passiven „Smart Labels", basierend auf einer speziellen Flip-Chip Technologie und einer neuartigen papierdünnen Batterie. Diese superdünnen intelligenten Etiketten werden in Applikationslösungen für die Bereiche industrielle Automation, Logistik, Materialförderung und Zugangskontrollen eingesetzt. Eine umweltfreundliche und papierdünne Batterie ermöglicht selbst die Dokumentation des Produktlebenszyklus. Das Unternehmen ist international bekannt für die Technologieentwicklung und die Produktion von komplexen elektronischen Baugruppen auf kleinstem Raum. KSW ist weiterhin bekannt sowohl als Zulieferer von Smart Label Inlays für die Industrie als auch als Anbieter von kompletten Lösungen mit kompatiblen Lese- und Schreibgeräte (Reader bzw. Scanner). Durch eine spezielle Chip-Montage, auch Adhesive Flip Chip Technik genannt, erfolgen Montage des Chips und die Kontaktierung des Chips gleichzeitig, was eine Kostensenkung zur Folge hat. Der Chip wird dabei direkt auf den Anschlusspads der Antenne montiert. KSW bietet ihren Kunden standard- und kundenspezifische Chips, um eine breite Palette von Funktionalitäten und Speichergrößen zu gewährleisten. Größe und Form der Etiketten sind in einem weiten Bereich variabel. KSW bietet neben Standard Smart Label Inlays in den Größen 50 x 50 mm und 80 x 50 mm auch eine breite Palette von kundenspezifischen Lösungen an.

Die Smart Label Inlays von KSW Microtec wurden für sehr hohe Anforderungen entwickelt und sind geeignet für den Einsatz in vielen unterschiedlichen Applikationen und weisen damit gegenüber herkömmlichen Transpondersystemen deutliche Vorteile auf. Die selbstklebenden Etiketten sind so gestaltet, dass sie auch unter Extrembedingungen wie zum Beispiel Kälte, Hitze, Schmutz, Staub, Stöße sowie Vibrationen zuverlässig arbeiten. Für spezielle Einsatzbedingungen bietet KSW auch spezielle Smart Label an.

Die neueste Entwicklung von KSW Microtec ist ein Temperatursensor-Etikett, basierend auf eine speziell auf den Einsatzzweck abgestimmte Chipentwicklung von KSW. Dieses mit einer papierdünnen Batterie ausgestattete Etikett ermöglicht dem Anwender, neben einer eindeutigen Produktidentifikation auch die Temperatur innerhalb eines Bereiches zu überwachen und Über- bzw. Unterschreitungen mit Datum und Uhrzeit zu dokumentieren. ∎

KSW Microtec belongs to the worldwide leading companies in the field of manufacture of active and passive "smart labels" based on a special flip-chip technology and a newly developed paper-thin battery. These super thin intelligent labels are employed in application solutions for the fields of industrial automation, logistics, material conveyance and access controls. An ecologically benign and paper-thin battery enables even the documentation of the lifecycle of the product. The company is internationally known for the technological development and production of complex microelectronic packaging solutions. KSW is furthermore known as supplier of smart label inlays for the industrial sector as well as provider of comprehensive solutions with compatible reading and scanning equipment. Through a special chip assembly, also called the adhesive flip chip technnology, the assembly and contacting of the chips occur simultaneously, thus resulting in a cost reduction. The chip is hereby mounted directly on the connecting pad of the antenna. KSW offers its clients standard and customer-specific chips, in order to ensure a broad range of functionalities and sizes of memory. Size and forms of the labels are variable to a great extend. KSW provides apart from standard smart labels in the sizes 50 x 50 mm and 80 x 50 mm also a broad range of customer-specific solutions.

The smart label inlays of KSW Microtec have been developed for very high requirements and are suitable for use in many varied applications and thus show distinct advantages against common transponder systems. The self-adhesive labels are designed in such way that they work reliably also under extreme conditions like for example cold, heat, dirt, dust, impact shocks as well as vibrations. For special conditions of use KSW also offers special smart label inlays.

The latest development of KSW Microtec is a temperature sensory label based on a special chip development of KSW matched with the purpose of use. This label, furnished with a paper thin battery enables the user, besides clearly identifying the product, to control also the temperature and to record any temperature outside the allowed temperature range with date and time. ∎

KSW Microtec GmbH

Gesellschafter/*Corporate member*:
Dr.-Ing. habil. Thomas Seidowski
Dr.-Ing. Frank Kriebel
Trierenberg Holding AG

Gründungsjahr/*Year of Foundation*:
1.11.1994

Mitarbeiter/*Employees*:
35

Geschäftstätigkeit/*Business Activity*:
Mikrosystemtechnik, Smart Label Systeme
Micro Packaging, Smart Label Systems

Fertigungsfläche/*Production areas*:
über 1.000 m², inklusive klimatisierter Reinraum
more than 1,000 m², including acclimatised clean room

Office Bereich/*Office space*:
600 m²

Anschrift/*Address*:
Gostritzer Straße 63
D-01217 Dresden
Telefon   +49 (351) 871 80-40
Telefax   +49 (351) 871 84-11
E-Mail   office@ksw-microtec.de
Internet www.ksw-microtec.de

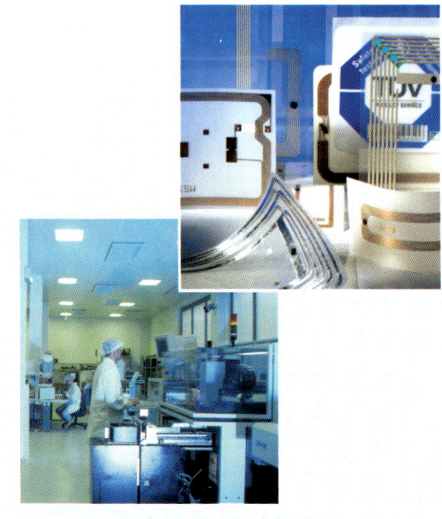

Oben: Smart Label Produkte.
Unten: Reinraum.
Above: Smart Label Products.
Below: Clean room.

Technische Universität

TU Dresden: Brückenschlag zwischen Wissenschaft und Wirtschaft

TU Dresden: Building Bridges between Science and the Economic Sector

Dort liegt Europa, sagte der Schriftsteller Erich Kästner mit Fingerzeig auf seine Heimatstadt Dresden. Nach zahlreichen Zerstörungen und Wiederaufbauten in den vergangenen Jahrhunderten, nach der friedlichen Revolution 1989 behauptet Dresden noch immer seinen Platz in Europa, was sich im gesamten urbanen, wirtschaftlichen, kulturellen und geistigen Leben der sächsischen Landeshauptstadt widerspiegelt. Das gilt auch für die Technische Universität Dresden, mit deren Unterstützung die Brückenstadt Dresden überhaupt erst viele Brücken, damit auch dauerhafte Verbindungen aufbauen konnte. Der zu jederzeit innovative Wirtschaftsstandort Dresden

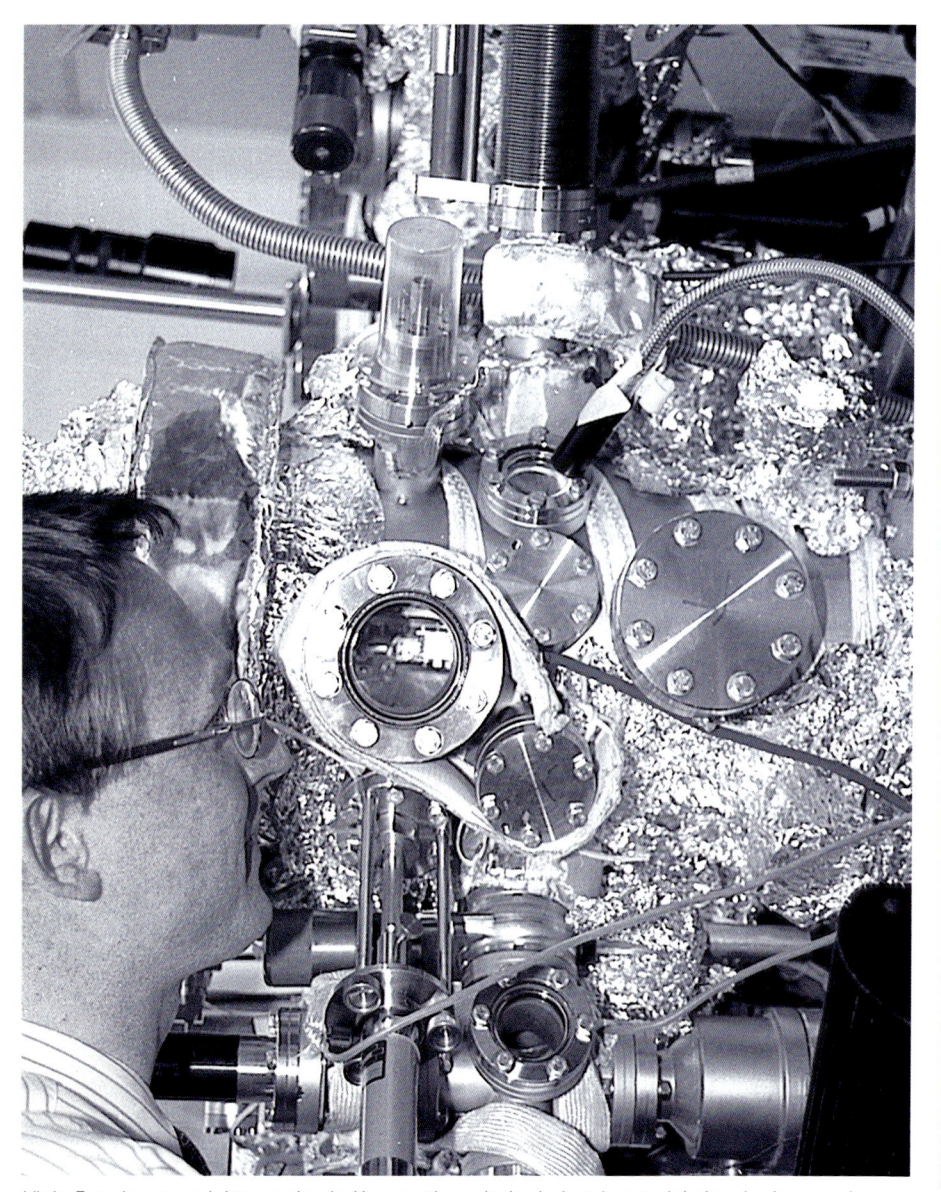

Alfred Post

Der Autor wurde 1942 in Wesel geboren und absolvierte nach dem Abitur eine Bankausbildung. Von 1963 bis 1964 leistete er den Wehrdienst. Als Geschäftsführer war er von 1965 bis 1969 für ein Großhandelsunternehmen tätig. Danach studierte er Rechtswissenschaften in Berlin, München und Münster. Das Studium schloss der Autor nach dem Referendariat 1974 mit dem 2. Staatsexamen ab. In den Jahren 1974 und 1975 war er als Rechtsanwalt tätig. Von 1976 bis 1990 arbeitete er als Dezernent für Personal und Organisation sowie als stellvertretender Kanzler an der Universität Essen. Seit Anfang 1991 ist Alfred Post Kanzler der Technischen Universität Dresden.

The author was born in 1942 in Wesel and after his A-levels; he completed training as a bank officer. From 1963 until 1964, he completed his military service. He worked as Managing Director for a wholesale company from 1965 until 1969. Afterwards he studied law in Berlin, Munich and Münster. After working as a Referendar (judicial service trainee), the author completed his studies graduating with the Second State Examination in law and admission to the bar in 1974. He worked as a lawyer in the years 1974 and 1975. From 1976 until 1990, he worked as head of department for personnel and organisation as well as deputy chancellor at the University of Essen. Since the beginning of 1991, Alfred Post is chancellor of the Technical University of Dresden.

Viele Forschungsprojekte werden in Kooperation mit der Industrie entwickelt, wie das von der VW-Stiftung geförderte Projekt am Institut für Angewandte Photophysik, zu dem diese Abscheideranlage gehört.

Many research projects are developed in co-operation with the industrial sector, like the project supported by the VW Educational Trust at the Institute for Applied Photo Physics, which is working on this separator plant.

Technical University

Tausende sächsische Schüler stürmen jedes Jahr zum „Tag der offenen Tür" den Campus und informieren sich über Studiengänge.
Each year, thousands of schoolchildren rush across the campus on "Open Day" and obtain information about study courses.

There lies Europe; the writer Erich Kästner said pointing to his hometown of Dresden. After numerous destructions and reconstructions in the past centuries, after the peaceful revolution of 1989, Dresden still manages to holds its ground in Europe, which is mirrored in the whole urban, economic, cultural and intellectual life of the Saxon regional capital. This is also valid for the Technical University of Dresden, which has given great support to the outgoing City of Dresden for it to build such bridges at all in order to establish lasting connections. The always-innovative economic location of Dresden was and is unthinkable without the Technical University.

This important reciprocal stimulation between the sectors of economy and science was recognised already at the beginning of the 19th Century both by King Anton of Saxony and the State Economy Manufacture and Commerce Deputation as well as the Economic Society, which in 1928 signed the statute for one of the eldest technical education institutes of Germany, the present Technical University of Dresden. In the following years, Saxony developed into one of the leading economic regions of Europe with an industrial sector oriented towards export. The regional capital of Dresden was involved to a great extent in the process of industrialisation: Thus, Ludwig Gehe relocated his factory for chemical and pharmaceutical products to Dresden. Johann Andreas Schubert, who was professor at the Technical Education Institute, had opened in 1836 his machine construction factory in the fishing village Übigau on the outskirts of the residential city, where he built the first operational German steam locomotive "Saxonia". The entrepreneur Friedrich Siemens achieved in 1856 with the regenerative process and the tank furnace developed by him a worldwide recognised technological innovation: the industrial glass production. For this, he received in 1900 the first doctor honoris causa of the Technical University Dresden. Further examples for innovations Made in Dresden are the foundations for the synthesis of salicylic acid, the chemical basis of the painkiller Aspirin, the first photographic camera or the research of the Dresden scientist Heinrich Barkhausen, without which modern communications technology would be unthinkable. Thus, it is not surprising that before 1945 most patents and inventions of Germany came from Saxony. Also after the Second World War, the urge for research at the Technical University did not stop: The history of the Personal Computer does not start neither in Japan or the USA, but in Dresden. Professor N. Joachim Lehmann built the first desk computer of the world called "DA4" in 1962/63.

The reason that after the reunification the global companies like AMD and Infineon Technologies settled in Dresden is due to the availability of excellently trained young people especially in computer technology as well as to the continuous investigations in the field of microelectronics at the Technical University. Both chip producers point the way towards a high-tech region Dresden in the environment of the university. Finally, the co-operation between sciences and the economy enhances also the intellectual assets of the regional capital Dresden.

Since 1994, the university unites under one roof now a broad range of scientific disciplines from the fields of engineering science, humanities and social sciences, natural science and medicine. After the peaceful revolution, this was preceded by extensive staffing and structural subject innovations: the new establishment of faculties primarily in humanities and social sciences, the integration of the pedagogic university, the institute

Technische Universität

Praxisnahes Studium für Studenten der Kommunikationswissenschaft: ihr Ausbildungskanal „035eins" bei „Dresden Fernsehen".

Study near to practical work for students of communication science: their education channel "035eins" at "Dresden Television".

war und ist ohne die Technische Universität nicht denkbar.

Das wichtige Wechselspiel zwischen der Wirtschaft und der Wissenschaft erkannten bereits zu Beginn des 19. Jahrhunderts neben König Anton zu Sachsen auch die Landes-Ökonomie-Manufaktur- und Kommerziendeputation sowie die Ökonomische Gesellschaft, die das Statut für eine der ältesten Technischen Bildungseinrichtungen Deutschlands – die heutige Technische Universität Dresden – 1828 unterzeichneten. Sachsen entwickelte sich in den Folgejahren zu einem der führenden Wirtschaftsgebiete Europas mit einer auf Export orientierten Industrie. Die Landeshauptstadt Dresden wurde in die Industrialisierung in großem Umfang einbezogen: So verlegte Ludwig Gehe seine chemisch-pharmazeutische Fabrik nach Dresden. Johann Andreas Schubert, Professor an der Technischen Bildungsanstalt, hatte 1836 seine Maschinenfabrik in dem Fischerdorf Übigau am Rande der Residenzstadt eröffnet, wo er die erste betriebsfähige deutsche Dampflok „Saxonia" baute. Dem Unternehmer Friedrich Siemens gelang 1856 mit dem von ihm entwickelten Regenerativverfahren und dem Wannenofen eine weltweit beachtete technologische Neuerung: die industrielle Glaserzeugung. Hierfür erhielt er 1900 den ersten Ehrendoktor der Technischen Hochschule Dresden. Die Grundlagen für die Synthese der Salicylsäure, der chemischen Basis des Schmerzmittels Aspirin, die erste Fotokamera oder auch die Forschungen des Dresdner Wissenschaftlers Heinrich Barkhausen, ohne die die moderne Kommunikationstechnologie nicht denkbar wäre, sind weitere Beispiele für Innovationen Made in Dresden. So ist es nicht verwunderlich, dass vor 1945 die meisten Patente und Erfindungen Deutschlands aus Sachsen kamen. Auch nach dem Zweiten Weltkrieg ließ der Forscherdrang an der Technischen Hochschule nicht nach: Die Geschichte des Personal Computers beginnt weder in Japan oder den USA, sondern in Dresden. Professor N. Joachim Lehmann baute 1962/63 mit dem „DA4" den ersten Tischcomputer der Welt.

Gerade in der Informationstechnologie gut ausgebildete junge Menschen sowie kontinuierliche Forschungen im Bereich Mikroelektronik an der Technischen Universität waren mit der Ausschlag dafür, dass nach der Wende die Weltunternehmen AMD und Infineon Technologies sich in Dresden angesiedelt haben. Beide Chipfabriken weisen den Weg zu einer Hightech-Region Dresden – im Umfeld der Universität. Letztlich fördert die Kooperation zwischen den Wissenschaften und der Wirtschaft damit auch den ökonomischen wie geistigen Reichtum der Landeshauptstadt Dresden.

Seit 1994 vereint die Universität nun ein breites Spektrum wissenschaftlicher Disziplinen aus den Gebieten Ingenieurwissenschaften, Geistes- und Sozialwissenschaften, Naturwissenschaften und Medizin unter einem Dach. Vorausgegangen waren nach der friedlichen Revolution umfassende personelle und fachlich-strukturelle Erneuerungen: die Neugründung von Fakultäten vor allem in den Geistes- und Sozialwissenschaften, die Integration der Pädagogischen Hochschule, der Hochschule für Verkehrswesen und der Medizinischen Akademie Dresden sowie von Wissenschaftlern aus den alten Bundesländern. Die Dresdner Hochschule mit ihren 14 Fakultäten verfügt heute über ein Spektrum an Wissensdisziplinen, das ihresgleichen unter den Technischen Universitäten Deutschlands suchen kann. Neben den traditionell stark vertretenen Ingenieurwissenschaften studieren von den mehr als 25.000 eingeschriebenen Studenten etwa die Hälfte Geistes- und Sozialwissenschaften, Medizin sowie Naturwissenschaften. So bietet die TU Dresden beispielsweise bundesweit als einen der wenigen internationalen geisteswissenschaftlichen Studiengänge „German Studies" an, den der Deutsche Akademische Austauschdienst fördert. Ebenso ist der interdisziplinäre Studiengang „Internationale Beziehungen" einmalig in Deutschland. Für die 30 Studienplätze pro Jahr bewerben sich weltweit mittlerweile mehr als 500 junge Menschen. Hier werden Kenntnisse aus den Bereichen Internationale Wirtschaft, Internationales Recht, Internationale Beziehungen und Geschichte – verbunden mit einem Auslandssemester – vermittelt.

Internationalität wird an der TU Dresden groß geschrieben. Der Anteil ausländischer Studienanfänger – auch aus dem westlichen Ausland – steigt weiter stark an (10,8 Prozent Studienanfänger zum Wintersemester 1998/99 gegenüber 8,6 Prozent im Jahr zuvor). Neben vielfältigen internationalen Forschungskontakten und Studentenaustauschprogrammen gibt es mittlerweile 16 internationale Studiengänge, teilweise Vorlesungen in englischer Sprache sowie gemeinsame Studiengänge mit anderen europäischen Universitäten. In sieben Fakultäten und zwölf Studiengängen können Studenten den Bachelor-Abschluss erwerben, in elf Studiengängen den Master-Abschluss. Mit dem Wintersemester 1999/2000 wurde an der TU Dresden deutschlandweit erstmalig der Bakkalaureus im universitären technischen Fernstudium eingeführt. Derzeit studieren mehr als 1.600 ausländische Studenten aus über 100 Ländern an der Universität.

Mit Interdisziplinarität ist ein weiterer Grundzug der jüngsten Universitätsentwicklung zu benennen. Dieser ständig wachsende Anspruch an Forschung und Lehre der Dresdner Volluniversität wird unter anderem in dem auf fünf Jahre angelegten Bundesleitprojekt „Intermobil" verwirklicht, an dem neben mehr als 20 Wissenschaftlern aus zwei Fakultäten der TU ebenso andere Forschungseinrichtungen, das Land Sachsen, Industriepartner, die Deutsche Bahn AG und Träger

Technical University

for transport systems and the Medical Academy Dresden as well as of scientists from West-Germany. The Dresden University today disposes with its 14 faculties of a range of expert disciplines that is difficult to find among the technical universities of Germany. Apart from the traditionally strong presence of engineering sciences around half of the more than 25,000 enrolled students study humanities and social sciences, medicine and natural sciences. Furthermore, the TU Dresden offers nationally one of the few international humanities courses of "German Studies" that is promoted by the German Academic Exchange Service. Also, the interdisciplinary course of "International Relations" is unique in Germany. Meanwhile, more than 500 young people apply worldwide for only 30 available places each year. Here, expert knowledge from the fields international economy, international law, international relations and history are taught, in connection with a semester spent abroad.

An international outlook is of utmost importance at the TU Dresden. The share of foreign students beginning their studies – also from foreign Western countries – is continuously increasing (10.8 percent study beginners in the winter semester 1998/99 compared to 8.6 percent in the previous year). Apart from numerous international research contacts and student exchange programmes there are now 16 international study courses, lectures partly given in English language and mutual study courses together with other European universities. Students are able to acquire a bachelor degree in seven faculties and twelve study courses and the master's degree in eleven study courses. In the winter semester of 1999/2000, the Bakkalaureus was introduced for the first time in Germany within the technical university remote study sector. At present, more than 1,600 foreign students from over 100 countries study at the university.

Another basic characteristic of the latest developments at the university worth mentioning is its interdisciplinary approach. This constantly growing demand of the comprehensive Dresden university towards research and teaching is accomplished, among other things, in the Federal Guidance Project "Intermobil", which is planned for five years and at which are participating apart from more than 20 scientists from two faculties of the TU also other research institutions, the regional government of Saxony, industrial partners, the Deutsche Bahn AG (German Railways) and bodies of the local public passenger transport. It is intended to elaborate in Dresden until the year 2004 with a budget amounting to 61 million DM, an exemplary integral strategy for an ecological, flexible mobility and transport routing and to implement it in the Southeast corridor "Dresden-Sächsische Schweiz (Switzerland of Saxony)". Also, the newly founded Bio Innovation Centre (BIOZ), which also houses six disciplines of the university among others, will not be able to cope without interrelated subject research. In the field of molecular bioengineering, scientist will search together in projects of modern biology and biochemistry for medicine, technology and foodstuff development. One of the lecturers involved in this, Wolfgang Pompe from the Institute for Material Science, contributes with his working group for example his knowledge and developments of tailor-made ceramic bones up to the installation of live bacteria into ceramic filters. Competence centres and interdisciplinary research centres like the BIOZ gather their resources effectively. For this reason, the TU has presently established 14 such research unions, including the Research Union Public Health Saxony, the Media Design Center, the Center for High-speed Computing and the Center for Microtechnical Production.

Of great significance is also the mutual research with extra-university research institutions in the region, for example, with the Research Center Rossendorf, three Max-Planck-Institutes, six Fraunhofer-Institutes, the BioParc Dresden – Klaus Tschira Stiftung gGmbH, the Verband der Elektrotechnik Elektronik Informationstechnik e. V. (Association of Electro Technology, Electronics and Information Technology Dresden) as well as with the institutes of the Intellectual Society Gottfried Wilhelm Leibniz (former Blaue Liste/Blue List).

The university is active in and also promotes both pure research and applied research equally in order to provide the students with practically oriented studies on the one hand that renders an ideal qualification for the labour market, and on the other, to secure third party funds for the TU Dresden. Because, it is not possible nowadays for a German university to provide high-quality teaching and research with government funding

Der Rektor der TU Dresden, Professor Achim Mehlhorn (rechts), verliest die Urkunde zur Ehrenpromotion von UN-Generalsekretär Kofi Annan. Links im Bild der Dekan der Fakultät Wissenschaften, Professor Werner Esswein.
The rector of TU Dresden, Professor Achim Mehlhorn (right), reads the document on the award of doctor honoris causa to UN General Secretary Kofi Annan. Left in the picture, the dean of the faculty of science, Werner Esswein.

Technische Universität

Regelmäßig besuchen Industrievertreter die TU Dresden – im Foto der Ressortkreis Forschung der DaimlerChrysler AG – um neue Forschungsprojekte kennenzulernen.

Representatives of the industrial sector regularly visit the TU Dresden – pictured is the department of research of DaimlerChrysler AG – in order to become familiar with new research projects.

des Öffentlichen Personennahverkehrs beteiligt sind. Mit einem Budget von insgesamt 61 Millionen Mark soll bis zum Jahr 2004 in Dresden eine vorbildliche, ganzheitliche Strategie für eine umweltgerechte, flexible Mobilität und Verkehrsführung erarbeitet und im Südost-Korridor „Dresden - Sächsische Schweiz" umgesetzt werden. Ebenso kommt das neu gegründete Bioinnovationszentrum (BIOZ), in dem unter anderem sechs Disziplinen der Universität vertreten sind, ohne fächerübergreifende Forschungen nicht aus. Auf dem Gebiet des Molecular Bioengineering werden Wissenschaftler gemeinsam an Projekten der modernen Biologie und Biochemie für die Medizin, Technik und Nahrungsmittelentwicklung forschen. Einer der daran beteiligten Professoren, Wolfgang Pompe vom Institut für Werkstoffwissenschaft, bringt mit seiner Arbeitsgruppe beispielsweise seine Kenntnisse und Entwicklungen vom maßgeschneiderten Knochen aus Keramik bis hin zum Einbau von lebenden Bakterien in Keramikfiltern ein. Kompetenzzentren und Interdisziplinäre Forschungszentren wie das BIOZ bündeln effektiv Ressourcen. Deshalb hat die TU zurzeit 14 derartige Forschungsverbünde eingerichtet, darunter den Forschungsverbund Public Health Sachsen, das Media Design Center, das Zentrum für Hochleistungsrechnen und das Zentrum für mikrotechnische Produktion.

Einen hohen Stellenwert hat die gemeinsame Forschung mit außeruniversitären Forschungseinrichtungen in der Region, unter anderem mit dem Forschungszentrum Rossendorf, drei Max-Planck-Instituten, sechs Fraunhofer-Instituten, BioParc Dresden - Klaus Tschira Stiftung gGmbH, dem Verband der Elektrotechnik Elektronik Informationstechnik Dresden e. V. sowie Instituten der Wissenschaftsgemeinschaft Gottfried Wilhelm Leibniz (ehemals Blaue Liste).

Grundlagenforschung und angewandte Forschung betreibt und fördert die Universität gleichermaßen, um zum einen den Studenten ein praxisorientiertes Studium anzubieten, das sie für den Arbeitsmarkt optimal qualifiziert, und zum anderen Drittmittelgelder an die TU Dresden zu binden. Denn alleine von staatlichen Geldern kann heute keine bundesdeutsche Universität mehr eine qualitativ hochwertige Lehre und Forschung betreiben. So hat die TU Dresden 1999 insgesamt mehr als 142 Millionen Mark über Forschungsprojekte eingeworben. Eine besondere Anerkennung der Dresdner Universität durch die Wirtschaft ist die Finanzierung von Stiftungsprofessuren. Zehn Professuren werden zurzeit von Unternehmen wie SAP, Mannesmann Mobilfunk oder Siemens finanziert.

Die Technische Universität ist nicht nur ein interessanter Kooperationspartner für große Firmen und Institutionen sowie mittlere und kleinere Firmen in der Region, sondern sie sorgt auch aktiv für Erfindungen und Ausgründungen. Das an der Universität angesiedelte Patentinformationszentrum steht als Dienstleister für Forschung und Wirtschaft gleichermaßen zur Verfügung. 1999 meldete die TU 74 Schutzrechte an, davon 54 nationale und 20 internationale. In dem von der Universität 1990 mitgegründeten TechnologieZentrum Dresden haben sich bis heute 45 Ausgründungen von Wissenschaftlern angesiedelt. Die Tochtergesellschaft der TU, die Gesellschaft für Wissens- und Technologietranfer der TU Dresden mbH (GWT) verwertet zunehmend erfolgreich Schutzrechte der Forscher und führt anwendungsorientierte Forschungs- und Entwicklungsprojekte im Auftrag der Wirtschaft durch. Im Geschäftsjahr 1999 waren mehr als 80 Mitarbeiter in der Tochtergesellschaft beschäftigt und erwirtschafteten ein ansehnliches Ergebnis für die TU Dresden. Das vom Bund geförderte universitäre Projekt „Dresden exists", an dem unter anderem der SAP-Stiftungslehrstuhl für Technologieorientierte Existenzgründung und Innovationsmanagement beteiligt ist, hat ein Beratungs- und Unterstützungsnetzwerk entwickelt und damit letztlich auch die Grundlage für viele weitere Firmengründungen in und um Dresden.

Ohne eine moderne, innovative Universitätsverwaltung könnte die vom Stifterverband für die Deutsche Wissenschaft als Reformuniversität ausgezeichnete TU Dresden diese Leistungen nicht erbringen. Als eine der ersten bundesdeutschen Hochschulen haben die Dresdner das Universitätsmarketing als eigenständiges Sachgebiet eingeführt. Um transparent und wirtschaftlich die Universität zu leiten, hat die TU das Prinzip der Kosten- und Leistungsrechnung als eine der ersten deutschen Universitäten zum festen Bestandteil ihrer Leistungs- und Führungsinstrumente gemacht.

Damit wird deutlich, dass die Universität erhebliche Anstrengungen unternimmt, Brücken zur Stadt, Gesellschaft sowie Wirtschaft aufzubauen. Ein beständiger Dialog zwischen Wissenschaft und Gesellschaft wird geführt, um Anregung und Orientierung zu geben. Die Technische Universität Dresden ist nicht nur ein Kompetenzzentrum für Wissen, sondern eine umfassende Bildungs- und Kulturinstitution. Öffentliche Vorlesungen wie das Studium Generale, Einrichtungen wie die Seniorenakademie, die Bibliotheken, das Universitätsorchester, Kulturveranstaltungen im modernsten Hörsaalzentrum Ostdeutschlands, die wissenschaftlichen Sammlungen und die Botanischen Gärten sind längst unverzichtbarer Bestandteil im Leben der Landeshauptstadt Dresden. Bereits zehn Jahre nach der politischen Wende gehört die Technische Universität Dresden in die erste Reihe der deutschen und europäischen Hochschulen.

Die Stadt Dresden schätzt ihre Technische Universität, und die TU fühlt sich wohl im prosperierenden Dresden. ∎

Technical University

Eine von unzähligen Erfindungen der Dresdner Wissenschaftler: Minigreifer mit Formgedächtnis-Aktor vom Institut für Feinwerktechnik können sehr kleine, empfindliche oder nachgiebige Bauteile greifen.

One of the numerous inventions of Dresden scientists: Mini-graspers with form memory-actor from the Institute for Precision Engineering are able to hold very small, sensitive or yielding components.

alone. Thus, the TU Dresden has acquired funds totalling more than 142 million DM by means of research projects in 1999. A very special recognition of the Dresden University by the economic sector is the financing of sponsored lectureships. Companies like SAP, Mannesmann Mobilfunk or Siemens are financing ten lectureships presently.

The Technical University is not only an interesting co-operation partner for large companies and institutions as well as middle-size and small companies in the region, but it also seeks actively to create inventions and new establishments. The Patent Information Centre situated at the university is also available as service provider for the sectors of research and economy. In 1999, TU Dresden registered 74 licences, thereof 54 national and 20 international ones. Until to today, 45 new establishments of scientist have settled in the Technology Centre Dresden, which was co-founded in 1990 by the university.

The subsidiary of the TU, the Gesellschaft für Wissens- und Technologietransfer der TU Dresden mbH/GWT (Society for knowledge and technology transfer of the TU Dresden), increasingly exploits licences of the researchers successfully and carries out application-oriented research and development projects on contract of the economic sector. In the business year 1999, more than 80 employees worked in the subsidiary and achieved an impressive result for the TU Dresden. The university project "Dresden exists" – supported by the Federal State and in which the SAP sponsored lectureships for Technology-oriented Company Start-ups and Innovation Management is participated, among others – has developed a consulting and support network and thus finally also produced the foundation for many more company foundations in and around Dresden.

Without a modern, innovative university administration the TU Dresden, which has been awarded the title of "Reformuniversität" by the Stifterverband für die Deutsche Wissenschaft (Assocation of Educational Trusts of German Science), would not be able to provide these services. Dresden was one of the first German universities to introduce university marketing as an independent subject matter. In order to manage the university in a transparent and economic way, the TU has established the principle of cost and performance account as a firm component of its performance and management instruments as one of the first German universities. This clarifies that the university is taking considerable efforts to build bridges to the city, society and the economy. A constant dialogue between science and society is being held in order to offer stimulation and orientation. The Technical University Dresden is not only a competence centre for expert knowledge, but also an extensive educational and cultural institution. Public lectures, like the general studies, facilities like the seniors' academy, libraries, the university orchestra, cultural events in the most modern auditory centre of East Germany, the scientific collections and the Botanic Gardens are long an undeniable part of life in the regional capital Dresden. Only ten years after the political change, the Technical University of Dresden belongs to first ranking German and European universities.

The City of Dresden values its Technical University and the TU feels good in prospering Dresden. ■

Durchblick im neuen Hörsaalzentrum der TU Dresden, dem technisch modernsten Ostdeutschlands, der nicht nur für Seminare und Vorlesungen genutzt wird, sondern auch für Ausstellungen und Konzerte.

Vista in the new auditory centre of the TU Dresden, the most modern of East Germany, which is not only used for seminars and lectures, but also for exhibitions and concerts.

Company Profile

Industrienahe Forschung mit Plasma und Elektronstrahl

Research with Plasma and Electron Beam Related to Industry

Fraunhofer Institut Elektronenstrahl- und Plasmatechnik

Fraunhofer-Institut für
Elektronenstrahl- und Plasmatechnik (FEP)

Institutsleitung/Head of the Institute:
Prof. Dr. Günter Bräuer
Dr. Volker Kirchhoff

Gründungsjahr/Year of Foundation:
1992

Mitarbeiter/Employees:
98

Geschäftsfelder/Business Fields:
- Beschichtung von Flachsubstraten mit optischen Schichten und Schichtssystemen
- Beschichtung von Kunststofffolien
- Beschichtung metallischer Platten und Bänder
- Oberflächenbearbeitung und -behandlung mit dem Elektronenstrahl
- Beschichtung von Bauteilen und Werkzeugen
- Beschichtung von Komponenten mit elektrischen, optischen und magnetischen Schichten und Schichtsystemen
- Coating with flat substrates with optical thin films
- Coating of plastic foils
- Coating of metal plates and strips
- Surface treatment with electron beams
- Coating of tools and machine parts
- Coating of electrical, optical and magnetic components

Anschrift/Address:
Winterbergstraße 28
D-01277 Dresden
Telefon +49 (351) 25 86-0
Telefax +49 (351) 25 86-105
E-Mail info@fep.fhg.de
Internet www.fep.fhg.de

Im FEP steht neueste Technologie zur Verfügung.

In the FEP, the latest technology is available.

Die Hauptaufgabe des FEP besteht darin, neue Elektronenstrahl- und Plasmatechnologien zu entwickeln und damit neue Anwendungsfelder zu erschließen. Ein besonderer Schwerpunkt ist dabei die Erprobung der neuen Technologien unter industrienahen Bedingungen und die Überführung in die Produktion. Zu diesem Zweck wurden in den letzten Jahren im Institut eine Vielzahl von großtechnischen Anlagen auf einer Fläche von ca. 4.000 m² installiert. Die z. Z. im FEP betriebenen Forschungsanlagen verkörpern eine Gesamtvolumen von ca. 20 Mio. Euro. Diese Technik kann sowohl für die Entwicklung von Hardwarekomponenten mit zugehöriger Technologie als auch für die Produktentwicklung und die Pilotproduktion unserer Kunden genutzt werden.

The main task of the Fraunhofer-Institut für Elektronenstrahl und Plasmatechnik (FEP) consists in developing and thus opening up new fields for its practical application. One particular focal point is the testing of new technologies in conditions that comparable to industrial situations and to transfer these into production systems. For this purpose, in an area of approx. 4,000 m² a number of large technical plants were installed in the past years. Presently, the research plants operated in the FEP comprise a total volume of approx. 20 million Euro. This technology may both be used for the development of hardware components with their pertinent technology as well as for product development and pilot production of our clients.

Leistungen des FEP:
- Angewandte Forschung
- Machbarkeitsstudien
- Abschätzungen zu wirtschaftlichen Aspekten
- Entwicklung, Bau und Lieferung von Spezialkomponenten und Technologie
- Produktentwicklung
- Pilotproduktion
- Integration von Spezialkomponenten in bestehende Beschichtungsanlagen
- After-Sales-Service sowie laufende Prozessberatung

Services of the FEP:
- Applied research
- Feasibility studies
- Estimates regarding economic aspects
- Development, construction and supply of Special components and technology
- Product development
- Pilot production
- Integration of special components into Existing coating systems
- After-Sales-Service as well as constant process consulting

Company Profile

Automatisierung des Systementwurfs

Automation of System Design

Analog-Digital-Wandler.
Analog-to-Digital converter.

Zum Fraunhofer-Institut für Integrierte Schaltungen gehört die Dresdner Außenstelle Entwurfsautomatisierung EAS. Die Mitarbeiter, überwiegend Ingenieure und Wissenschaftler, entwickeln Methoden und Werkzeuge für den rechnergestützten Entwurf elektronischer und heterogener Systeme sowie Prototypen von Hardware-Software-Systemen. Die Anwendungen liegen hauptsächlich im Bereich der Telekommunikation, des digitalen Rundfunks und der Mikrosystemtechnik. Die Werkzeuge dienen in erster Linie dem Schließen von Lücken in Entwurfsabläufen bzw. sie verbessern den Leistungsumfang vorhandener kommerzieller Werkzeuge. In der EAS werden auch umfassende Kundenberatungen sowie Seminare und Schulungen durchgeführt.

Die Außenstelle ist seit ihrer Gründung dynamisch gewachsen. Im Rahmen von gemeinsamen F&E-Projekten bzw. Auftragsarbeiten konnte eine fruchtbare Kooperation mit führenden Unternehmen (z. B. Bosch, Infineon, Siemens, TechniSat) aufgebaut werden. Die Zusammenarbeit mit Universitäten und Hochschulen sichert den notwendigen methodischen Vorlauf und den Aufbau neuen Wissens.

Studenten der Fakultäten Elektrotechnik und Informatik finden hier als wissenschaftliche Hilfskräfte, Praktikanten und Diplomanden ein praxisnahes Betätigungsfeld bei der Lösung anspruchsvoller Aufgaben.

Das Institut ist eines von derzeit 47 Einrichtungen der Fraunhofer-Gesellschaft, die als führende Trägerorganisation für angewandte Forschung in Deutschland agiert. ∎

The Dresden branch lab Design Automation belongs to the Fraunhofer Institute for Integrated Circuits. Its employees, mainly engineers and scientists, develop methods and tools for computer-aided design of electronic and heterogeneous systems as well as prototypes of hardware-software systems. The applications are primarily for the field of telecommunications, digital radio and micro system technology. The tools are principally intended to close gaps in design flows or they improve the performance of existing commercial tools. The EAS also provides extensive consulting as well as seminars and training.

The branch lab has grown dynamically since its foundation. Within common R&D projects or contract work a fruitful co-operation with leading enterprises (e. g. Bosch, Infineon, Siemens, TechniSat) has been established. The co-operation with universities and research institutes ensures the necessary methodical approach and building up of new knowledge. Students of the faculties electrical engineering and computer sciences will find here fields of activities that are close to practical work in occupations as scientific assistants, practical trainees and students preparing for their diplomas while solving demanding tasks.

The institute is one of presently 47 institutions of the Fraunhofer-Society that acts as leading organisation for applied research in Germany. ∎

Fraunhofer Institut
Integrierte Schaltungen

Fraunhofer-Institut für
Integrierte Schaltungen
Angewandte Elektronik
Außenstelle Entwurfsautomatisierung

Leiter der Außenstelle/Head of the Branch:
Prof. Dr. Günter Elst

Gründungsjahr/Year of Foundation:
1992

Mitarbeiter/Employees:
60

Anschrift/Address:
Zeunerstraße 38
D-01069 Dresden
Telefon   +49 (351) 46 40-701
Telefax   +49 (351) 46 40-703
E-Mail   info@eas.iis.fhg.de
Internet www.eas.iis.fhg.de

Das Institut bietet optimale Forschungsmöglichkeiten.
The institute offers optimal research possibilities.

Company Profile

IPF – wissenschaftlicher Partner der Unternehmen

IPF – a scientific partner of companies

Institut für Polymerforschung Dresden e. V.

Vorstand/Executive Board:
Wissenschaftlicher Direktor/*Scientific Director:*
Prof. Dr. Klaus Lunkwitz
Kaufmännischer Direktor/*Administrative Director:*
Günter Mateika

Kuratorium/Committee:
Min.-Rätin Dr. Petra Karl (Vors./Chairman)
Reg.-Dir. Dr. Klaus Heller (stellv. Vors./Cochairman)
Prof. Dr. Achim Mehlhorn

Gründungsjahr/Year of Foundation: 1992

Mitarbeiter/Employees: 279 (12/2000)

Geschäftstätigkeit/Business Activity:
Anwendungsorientierte Grundlagenforschung zu Polymeren
Application-oriented fundamental research on polymers

Anschrift/Address:
Hohe Straße 6
D-01069 Dresden
Telefon +49 (351) 46 58-0
Telefax +49 (351) 46 58-284
E-Mail   ipf@ipfdd.de
Internet www.ipfdd.de

Untersuchungen zur Polymerverarbeitung und -modifizierung: Versuchsstand zur reaktiven Extrusion.
Investigations on polymer processing and modification: Test stand for reactive extrusion.

Untersuchung des Verhaltens von Zellen an Polymeroberflächen (Entwicklung von Polymermaterialien für die Medizin).
Investigation of the behaviour of cells on polymer surfaces (Development of polymer materials for medicine).

Gebäudekomplex des IPF; hier entsteht noch ein neues Laborgebäude für Biomaterialien.
Building complex of IPF; a new laboratory is being built here for biomaterials.

Das Institut für Polymerforschung Dresden e. V. ist ein durch das Bundesministerium für Bildung und Forschung und das Staatsministerium für Wissenschaft und Kunst des Landes Sachsen gefördertes Forschungsinstitut und gehört der Wissenschaftsgemeinschaft G. W. Leibniz an.

Die Forschung am Institut beinhaltet chemische Synthese, Modifizierung, Charakterisierung sowie Verarbeitung und Prüfung von polymeren Werkstoffen. Schwerpunkte sind die Untersuchung des Einflusses von Grenzflächen in Mehrphasensystemen und bei der Polymerverarbeitung sowie die gezielte Gestaltung von Oberflächen. Für das IPF typisch und Basis vieler anwendungsrelevanter Ergebnisse ist die enge interdisziplinäre Kooperation von Naturwissenschaftlern und Ingenieuren.

Die drei Teilinstitute des IPF verfolgen die Hauptarbeitsrichtungen:
- Definierte Polymerstrukturen durch Polymersynthese und Reaktionen in Schmelzen
- Wechselwirkungsmechanismen an Grenzflächen und deren Steuerung
- Polymere Werkstoffe/Funktionalisierung und Veränderung von Oberflächen und Grenzschichten

Die Direktoren der Teilinstitute sind gleichzeitig Professoren an der Technischen Universität Dresden, wodurch eine enge Kooperation mit der Universität garantiert ist. Außerdem arbeitet das IPF mit einer Reihe von Dresdner Instituten und Forschungsgruppen im Materialforschungsverbund Dresden und Netzwerken u. a. zur Nanotechnologie und Biomaterialforschung zusammen. Durch zahlreiche Projekte ist das IPF in die internationale Forschung integriert und anerkannter Partner von Industrieunternehmen. ∎

The Institut für Polymerforschung Dresden e. V. (Institute of Polymer Research) is a research institute supported by the Federal Ministry of Education and Research and the Saxon State Ministry of Science and Art and belongs to the Wissenschaftsgemeinschaft G. W. Leibniz.

Research at the institute includes chemical synthesis, modifications, characterization and testing of materials and technological investigations on polymer processing. Main focus is the investigation of the influence of interfaces in multiphase systems, in polymer processing, and on deliberate modification of surfaces. The close co-operation of scientists and engineers is both typical for IPF and the basis of many application-oriented findings.

The three sub-institutes of the IPF are engaged in the following main research areas:
- Defined polymer structures by polymer synthesis and modification of melts
- Elucidation of interactions at interfaces and their control
- Polymeric materials/Functionalization and modification of surfaces and interphases

The heads of the sub-institutes are at the same time professors at the Dresden University of Technology, which ensures close cooperation between the independent institute and the university. In addition, the IPF works together with a number of Dresden institutes and research groups in the Dresden Materials Research Association and networks, for example on the field of nano technology and biomaterials research. Through numerous projects, IPF is integrated into the international scientific community and a recognised partner of industrial enterprises. ∎

Herstellung von Tailored Fibre Placement-Preforms für beanspruchungsgerecht verstärkte Faserverbund-Werkstoffe mit Achtkopf-Stickmaschine.
Production of Tailored Fibre Placement-Preforms for high-performance fibre reinforced composites with eight-head stitching machine.

Company Profile

Forschung für die Wirtschaft

Research for the Economic Sector

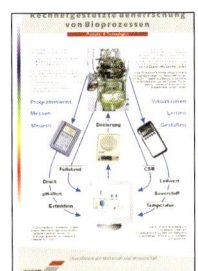

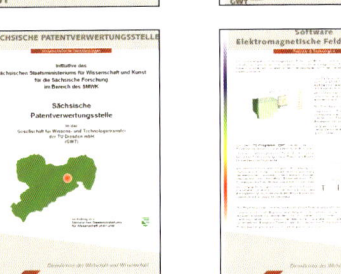

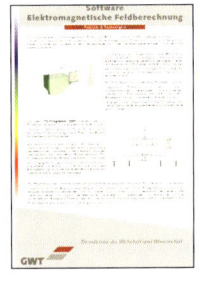

GWT

Gesellschaft für Wissen- und
Technologietransfer der TU Dresden GmbH

Geschäftsführer/Manager:
Herr Reinhard Sturm
Herr Dr. Claus Martin

Gesellschafter/Corporate member:
TU Dresden Aktiengesellschaft (TUDAG)

Gründungsjahr/Year of Foundation:
1996

Handelsregister/Commercial Register:
HRB 13840

Anschrift/Address:
Chemnitzer Straße 48b
D-01187 Dresden
Telefon   +49 (351) 463 17 20
Telefax   +49 (351) 463 77 71

Die GWT agiert an der von Innovation und Wettbewerb dominierten Schnittstelle von Wissenschaft und Wirtschaft. Als kompetenter Ansprech- und Vertragspartner für Ihren Bedarf an wissenschaftlichen Leistungen und F/E-Ergebnissen bündelt die GWT die an der Technischen Universität Dresden vorhandenen Kompetenzen zur effizienten Nutzung durch den freien Markt. Die GWT ist ein von der Universität rechtlich unabhängiges marktwirtschaftliches Unternehmen.

Über die TU Dresden hinaus nutzt die GWT aber auch die Kompetenzen anderer Universitäten, Hochschulen und außeruniversitären Forschungseinrichtungen.

Unser Leistungsangebot:

- **Auftragsforschung/Technologietransfer**
- Anwendungsorientierte Autragsforschung und -entwicklung
- Bedarfs- und anwendungsorientierter Technologietransfer
- Patentverwertung für universitäre und außeruniversitäre Forschungseinrichtungen Sachsens
- **Wissenschaftliche Dienstleistungen für Wirtschaft und Wissenschaft**
- Wissenschaftlich-organisatorische Dienstleistungen u. a. Projektmanagement
- Wissenschaftlich-technische u. -medizinische Dienstleistungen
- EU-Forschungsfachberatung
- **Forschungsnahe Produkte und Technologien** ■

GWT is active at the point of interface of the sectors of science and economy that dominated by innovation and competition. GWT bundles existing competences available at the Technical University of Dresden for efficient use by the free market, being a competent contact and contract partner for Your requirement of scientific services and R&D findings. The company is a free enterprise legally independent from the university.

However, beyond the limits of TU Dresden, competences of other universities, extra-university polytechnics and research institutes are also employed.

Our service provision:

- **Contracted research/Technology transfer**
- Application-oriented contracted research and development
- Requirement- and application oriented technology transfer
- Exploitation of patents for university and extra-university research institutes in Saxony
- **Scientific services for the sectors of economy and science**
- Organisational scientific services including project management
- Technical and medical scientific services
- Expert research consulting for the EU
- **Products and technologies near to research** ■

Gläserne Manufaktur

Ein Juwel für Dresden und eine Krone für den Automobilbau in Deutschland

A Jewel for Dresden and a crown for the automobile industry in Germany

Als am 27. Juli 1999 am Straßburger Platz in Dresden der Grundstein für die „Gläserne Manufaktur" der Volkswagen AG gelegt wurde, begann ein Projekt, das so ungewöhnlich ist wie noch keines zuvor in der Geschichte des Wolfsburger Automobilkonzerns.

In unmittelbarer Nähe des barocken Kernes von Dresden baut der Volkswagen-Konzern ein Automobilwerk, das weltweit seinesgleichen sucht. Es ist ein exklusives Werk, etwas, was jenseits von dem liegt, was man sich unter einem Automobilwerk vorstellt: Ein neues Juwel für Dresden und eine Krone für den Automobilbau in Deutschland. Und die „Gläserne Manufaktur" steht in gewissem Sinne symbolisch auch für die Unternehmenspolitik des Volkswagen-Konzerns, der sich als eine Gemeinschaft weltoffener und transparenter Unternehmen auszeichnet.

Bereits jetzt glitzert dieses Juwel in vielen Facetten, wenn sich das Sonnenlicht in den rund 4.300 Glasscheiben der Fassaden spiegelt. In wenigen Monaten wird zu diesem Licht der Glanz der hochwertigen Fahrzeuge, die hier gefertigt werden, hinzu kommen.

Dresden, so der erklärte Wille von Volkswagen, wird das Kompetenzzentrum für die automobile Oberklasse von Volkswagen. In Form einer hochwertigen, handwerklich geprägten Endmontage weitgehend vormontierter Teile werden hier Fahrzeuge entstehen, die das Herz eines jeden Automobil-Liebhabers höher schlagen lassen werden.

Und hier wird Autobau und Autokauf künftig regelrecht zelebriert werden. Die Fahrzeuge werden hier in der Manufaktur vor den Augen des Kunden ihren letzten Schliff bekommen. Der Kunde weiß dann, es ist wirklich sein Auto, was er aus der Manufaktur nach Hause fahren kann. Das ist eine völlig neue Dimension des Autokaufes. Es wird ein einzigartiger Bogen gespannt werden, zwischen Hightech, Kunst und Kultur.

Für außergewöhnliche Darstellungen ist VW bekannt.

VW is known for unusual design.

Werner Ulrich

Der Autor, 1937 in Egestorf geboren, absolvierte von 1954 bis 1957 im Volkswagenwerk Wolfsburg eine Lehre als Modellbauer, von 1958 bis 1962 besuchte er die Fachschule für Maschinentechnik. Danach arbeitete er bis 1967 als Konstrukteur der Abteilung Mechanisierungskonstruktion und Werkzeuge im Volkswagenwerk Wolfsburg. Als Fertigungsingenieur war er bis 1977 in der Fertigungsplanung tätig. Dann wechselte er in die Produktionsplanung, wo ihm 1980 die Leitung übertragen wurde. 1986 wurde er zum Leiter der Technologieplanung ernannt. Von 1989 bis 1999 war Werner Ulrich Hauptabteilungsleiter der Fertigungsplanung Lackiererei, Montagen und Kunststoffteile. Werner Ulrich wurde 2000 zum Geschäftsführer der Automobilmanufaktur Dresden GmbH berufen. Außerdem wurde ihm zum gleichen Zeitpunkt die Leitung der Markenplanung Volkswagen übertragen.

The author, born in 1937 in Egestorf, completed an apprenticeship as model maker in the Volkswagenwerk from 1954 until 1957 and from 1958 until 1962, he visited the Technical College of Machine Technology. Until 1967 he worked as design engineer in the department of mechanization construction and tools at the Volkswagenwerk Wolfsburg. He worked until 1977 as production engineer in process planning. Later he changed to production planning, where he headed the department from 1980. In 1986, he was appointed head of technology planning. From 1989 until 1999, Werner Ulrich held the position of main head of department for production planning of the paint shop, assembly and plastic parts. Werner Ulrich was appointed Managing Director of the Automobilmanufaktur Dresden GmbH in the year 2000. Furthermore, he assumed the management position of head of brand planning for Volkswagen at the same time.

Glass Manufacturing Hall

In der Gläsernen Manufaktur.

Inside the Glass Manufacturing Hall

Gläserne Manufaktur

Ein Modell der Anlage.

A model of the plant.

Autokauf im Spannungsfeld zwischen Tradition und Moderne

So wird der Kauf eines hochwertigen Fahrzeuges zugleich zum kulturellen Erlebnis im Spannungsfeld zwischen Technik und Kultur, zwischen Tradition und Moderne – eine reizvolle Konstellation. Für die Umsetzung einer solch weltweit bislang beispiellosen Philosophie bedarf es eines ganz besonderen Flairs rund um die Manufaktur. Und dieses Flair hat die Dresdner Innenstadt ohne Zweifel zu bieten. Hier verbinden sich in einer einzigartigen Weise große kulturelle Traditionen mit dem Ambiente einer modernen Landeshauptstadt. Hier wurden seit jeher architektonische Glanzpunkte gesetzt, etwa mit dem Zwinger, der Semperoper, der wieder im Aufbau befindlichen Frauenkirche und dem neuen Landtag.

Dresden war von Beginn an für dieses Projekt von Volkswagen „allererste Wahl". Der Bau der Manufaktur auf der „Grünen Wiese" gleich neben der Autobahn wäre ebenso undenkbar gewesen wie die Ansiedlung in einer rein industriell geprägten Umgebung.

Skepsis ist der Vorfreude gewichen

Freilich gab es zu Beginn des Projektes nicht nur Zustimmung. Vor allem in der Bevölkerung gab es skeptische Stimmen. Man fürchtete um die Attraktivität des Straßburger Platzes, um die Parkeisenbahn und um den Großen Garten. Heute, kurz vor der Vollendung des Baus, sind die Skeptiker verstummt. Die Vorfreude auf dieses neue Highlight in der sächsischen Landeshauptstadt überwiegt.
Der Bau, wird dem Straßburger Platz zu neuer Attraktivität verhelfen. Die aus einem rechtwinkligen Fertigungsgebäude, einem 40 Meter hohen Fahrzeugturm und einem attraktiven Erlebnisbereich für Kunden und Besucher bestehende lichtdurchflutete Anlage greift traditionelle Elemente der früheren Bebauung des Platzes auf und setzt zugleich Zeichen für die Zukunft. 20.000 Quadratmeter Glas, 16.000 Tonnen Stahl und 60.000 Tonnen Beton dominieren die Gebäude. Harmonisch mit Wasser und Begrünung gestaltete Freiflächen schaffen einen nicht nur optischen Übergang zum angrenzenden Großen Garten.

Nach Entwürfen Dresdner Schulklassen entstand im Architektenbüro Henn ein neuer Bahnhof für die Dresdner Parkeisenbahn, die vorbei an der „Gläsernen Manufaktur" auch künftig ihre Runden durch den Großen Garten drehen wird.

„Grüne Lunge" von Dresden wird weiter atmen

Der Große Garten, jene einzigartige „Grüne Lunge" von Dresden, Heimat zahlreicher wertvoller und seltener Pflanzen und Tiere, wird durch das Volkswagen-Projekt nicht gefährdet. In Zusammenarbeit mit zahlreichen Experten wurde die „Gläserne Manufaktur" auf die besonderen Bedingungen am Straßburger Platz

Glass Manufacturing Hall

A project began that is unusual as no other before in the history of the automobile corporation from Wolfsburg, when the foundation stone for the "Glass Manufacturing Hall" of Volkswagen AG was laid at the Strassburger Platz in Dresden on 27 July 1999.

In direct vicinity to the baroque city centre of Dresden, the Volkswagen Group is building an automobile work that will hardly find comparison worldwide. It is a very exclusive work, something that lies beyond one's imagination of an automobile work: A new jewel for Dresden and a crown for the automobile industry in Germany. In a certain sense, the "glass manufacturing hall" also stands symbolically for the company policy of the Volkswagen Group, which distinguishes itself as a community of transparent and cosmopolitan companies.

Already this jewel is glittering in many facets, when the sunlight is reflected in the façade's around 4,300 glass panes. In a few months, the glamour of high-quality vehicles that are produced here will be added to this light.

the tense field between technology and culture, between tradition and modernism – a delightful constellation. A very special flair around the manufacturing hall is needed for the realization of such a hitherto worldwide unprecedented philosophy. And this flair without doubt is certainly provided by the Dresden inner city. In a unique way, great cultural traditions are combined with the

capital is stronger. The construction will help the Strassburger Platz to attain new attractiveness. The translucent plant consisting of a right-angled production building, a vehicle tower 40 meters high and an attractive event area for customers and visitors pick up traditional elements of the former development of the square and sets trends for the future at the same time. 20,000 square meters

Der Zwinger.

The Zwinger.

Volkswagen has declared its intention to make Dresden the competence centre for the upper class of automobiles made by Volkswagen. Vehicles will be created here that will make any automobile lover's heart beat faster by means of high-calibre mainly pre-assembled parts put together in a final assembly characterised by skilled handicraft.

Indeed, in this place, car construction and car buying will be blatantly celebrated in future. The vehicles will receive here in the manufacturing hall in front of the customers their last finish. The customer will then know that it is really his car that he is driving home from the manufacturing hall. This is a completely new dimension of car buying. A unique arch will be drawn between high-tech, art and culture.

Car buying in the tense field between tradition and modernism.

Thus, the purchase of high-quality vehicles will result at the same time into a cultural event within

ambience of a modern regional capital here. Always, architectural highlights have been set here, like with the Zwinger, the Semperopera, the Frauenkirche presently in reconstruction and the new regional parliament. Dresden has been "first choice" for this Volkswagen project from the beginning. It would have been just as unthinkable to build the manufacturing hall on the "green meadow" next to the motorway, as would be a settlement in a purely industrial environment.

Scepticism has given way to anticipation.

Of course, at the beginning of the project there was not only agreement. Above all, among the population there were sceptical voices. It was feared that the attractiveness of the Strassburger Platz, the Parkeisenbahn and the Great Garden was in danger.

Today, shortly before the completion of the construction the sceptics are silenced. Anticipation about this new highlight in the Saxon regional

of glass, 16,000 tons of steel and 60,000 tons of cement dominate the building. Open areas harmonically designed with water and grass plants not only create an optical crossover to the adjoining Great Garden.

A new train station was created after the designs of Dresden school classes in the architect's office Henn for the Dresden Parkeisenbahn, which will also make in future it's rounds through the Great Garden, passing the "Glass Manufacturing Hall".

Dresden's "green lung" will continue to breath

The Great Garden, Dresden's unique "green lung", home of numerous valuable and rare plants and animals will not be endangered by the Volkswagen project. The "Glass Manufacturing Hall" has been adjusted to the particular conditions at Strassburger Platz in co-operation with numerous experts. 98 meters is the distance between the assembly hall and the Botanical Garden Dresden

Gläserne Manufaktur

abgestimmt. Der Abstand zwischen dem Montagegebäude und dem Botanischen Garten Dresden, der östlich an das Grundstück grenzt, beträgt 98 Meter. Natriumdampf-Lampen im Außenbereich arbeiten mit Licht im gelben Spektralbereich, das Insekten nicht stört. Die Tiefe des Gesamtgebäudes wurde so gewählt, dass kein Eingriff in das Grundwasser erfolgt. Die versiegelte Fläche am Straßburger Platz verringert sich durch den Manufaktur-Bau von 6,7 Hektar auf 4,8 Hektar. Eine spezielle, indirekte Innenbeleuchtung der Manufaktur gewährleistet, dass nur so viel Licht nach außen abgegeben wird, wie die Pflanzen, insbesondere Nachtblüher, im Botanischen Garten vertragen. Während des Manufaktur-Betriebes werden durch eine Spezialdämmung nahezu keine Geräusche nach außen dringen.

Logistik-Konzept steht „Glasbau" in keinster Weise nach

All jenen, die mit der Volkswagen-Ansiedlung am Straßburger Platz eine erhöhte Verkehrsbelästigung durch Teileanlieferungen befürchtet hatten, setzt Volkswagen ein Logistik-Konzept entgegen, das so einzigartig ist wie das Gesamtprojekt: Für den umweltfreundlichen Transport der Autoteile zwischen dem ebenfalls neu entstandenen VW-Logistikzentrum in Dresden-Friedrichstadt und der „Gläsernen Manufaktur" werden speziell konstruierte Güterstraßenbahnen eingesetzt. Dazu wird das vorhandene Straßenbahnnetz der Dresdner Verkehrsbetriebe genutzt. 60 Meter lang und in volkswagenblau lackiert, werden die Transportstraßenbahnen das Straßenbild von Dresden für jeden sichtbar beleben. Somit setzt Volkswagen auch hiermit Zeichen für Dresden. Einer der wichtigsten Effekte dieses Logistikkonzeptes aber ist neben der enormen Entlastung der Umwelt, dass die Dresdner und ihre Gäste keine Angst davor haben müssen, ständig zwischen irgendwelchen Autotransportern und sonstigen VW-Zuliefer-Lkws im innerstädtischen Stau zu stehen.

Wirtschaftliche „Folgeerscheinungen" stärken positiven Eindruck

Der positive Eindruck des Gesamtkonzeptes wird durch seine voraussichtlichen wirtschaftlichen Folgeerscheinungen für den Standort Dresden noch verstärkt.

In der „Gläsernen Manufaktur" und im VW-Logistikzentrum in Dresden-Friedrichstadt werden insgesamt etwa 800 Mitarbeiter tätig sein.

Der Große Garten, die „Grüne Lunge" von Dresden, wird durch das Volkswagen-Projekt nicht gefährdet.

Weitere 1.700 bis 2.600 neue Stellen werden im Zuliefer-, Service- und Logistikbereich externer Partner für das Volkswagen-Projekt entstehen. Volkswagen investiert in die gläserne Manufaktur rund 365 Millionen DM, weitere 30 Millionen DM in das VW-Logistikzentrum. Durch das Volkswagen-Engagement wird Dresden nach heutigen Prognosen jährlich zusätzliche Steuereinnahmen in beachtlicher Höhe erzielen.
Die zusätzliche Wertschöpfung für Dresden wird durch die VW-Ansiedlung voraussichtlich insgesamt rund eine Milliarde DM pro Jahr betragen.
Und die Zulieferbranche wird von der Ansiedlung in der Sachsenmetropole profitieren.

Fazit: Ansiedlung ist Bekenntnis zum Standort

Die „Gläserne Manufaktur" ist ein weiteres Bekenntnis von Volkswagen zu den neuen Bundesländern und zum Standort Deutschland. Sachsen, die Heimat solch bedeutender Namen des Automobilbaus wie Autounion und Horch, ist aus Volkswagen-Sicht ein hervorragender Standort für den Bau hochwertiger Fahrzeuge.

Wir sind froh und stolz, ein solch einzigartiges Konzept wie das der „Gläsernen Manufaktur" hier in Dresden umsetzen zu dürfen. ∎

Glass Manufacturing Hall

The Great Garden, the "green lung" of Dresden, is not endangered by the Volkswagen project.

that borders on the Eastern side of the premises. In the outer areas, natrium vapour lamps work with yellow lighting in a spectral region that does not disturb insects. The depth of the total building was chosen is such way that the groundwater is not affected. The sealed area at Strassburger Platz is reduced by the manufacturing hall construction from 6,7 ha. to 4,8 ha. A special indirect interior lighting system of the manufacturing hall ensures that only that much light comes through as the plants, particularly the night blossoming ones, can endure in the Botanical Gardens. Through a special dead sounding system, almost no noises will get out during operations in the manufacturing hall.

The logistics concept does not take second place of the "Glass Construction" in any way

All those people that had feared an increased traffic disturbance by parts suppliers for the Volkswagen settlement at the Strassburger Platz, Volkswagen is meeting with a logistics concept that is just as unique as the total project: Specially constructed freight tramlines are used for the ecological transport of car parts between the also newly built VW logistics centre in Dresden-Friedrichstadt and the "Glass Manufacturing Hall". For this purpose, the existing tramway network of the Dresdener Verkehrsbetriebe (Dresden transport company). These transportation trams, 60 metres long and lacquered in volkswagen-blue, will revitalize the street scene of Dresden visibly to everyone. Thus, Volkswagen is also creating symbols for Dresden. One of the most important effects of this logistic concept, however, is, apart from the enormous relief of the environment, that Dresden citizens and their guest do not have to fear to be constantly standing in an inner-citytraffic jam between some car transporters and other VW supplier lorries.

Economic "Consequences" strengthen a positive Image

Through its expected economic consequences for the location of Dresden, the positive image of the total concept in intensified. In the "Glass Manufacturing Hall" and in the VW logistics centre in Dresden–Friedrichstadt a total of around 800 employees will be working. In the supply, service and logistics fields of external partners further 1,700 to 2,600 new workplaces will be created for the Volkswagen project. Volkswagen is investing in the glass manufacturing hall around 365 million DM and further 30 million DM in the VW logistics centre. Through Volkswagen's engagement, the City of Dresden will achieve yearly additional tax income of considerable amounts according to present forecasts.

Through the VW settlement additional expected net profits for Dresden will amount to a total of around one billion DM per year. And the supply branch will also profit from the settlement in the Saxon cosmopolitan city.

Conclusion: The settlement is a declaration of faith in the location

Volkswagen has also declared its faith in the new East German region and in the economic location of Germany as a whole through the "Glass Manufacturing Hall". From a Volkswagen point of view, Saxony – the home of such important names of automobile construction like Autounion and Horch – is an excellent location for the construction of high-quality vehicles.

We are happy and proud to be able to realize such a unique concept as the "Glass Manufacturing Hall" here in Dresden. ∎

Company Profile

Technisch-wissenschaftliche Forschung & Dienstleistung

Technical and scientific research and service provision

IMA Matrialforschung und Anwendungstechnik GmbH

Geschäftsführer/Manager:
Dr.-Ing. Wilhelm Hanel

Gründungsjahr/Year of Foundation:
1993

Mitarbeiter/Employees:
95

Geschäftstätigkeit/Business Activity:
Dienst- und Forschungsleistungen auf den Gebieten der Werkstoff-, Bauteil- und Produktprüfung bzw. -begutachtung
Research work and service provision on the fields of materials, component parts and product testing and analysis

Anschrift/Address:
Hermann-Reichelt-Straße (am Flughafen)
D-01109 Dresden
Telefon +49 (351) 88 37-303
Telefax +49 (351) 880 43 13
E-Mail ima@ima-dresden.de
Internet www.ima-dresden.de

Stoßfolge- und Schwingungsprüfung.

Testing of impact cycles and vibration.

Betriebslastensimulation an einem LKW-Führerhaus.

Operational load simulation on the driver's cabin of a lorry.

Die IMA GmbH Dresden ist eine technisch-wissenschaftliche Dienstleistungs- und Forschungseinrichtung. Sie entstammt der Dresdner Flugzeugindustrie und dem daraus hervorgegangenen Institut für Leichtbau (IfL) und fühlt sich dieser Tradition verpflichtet.

In der IMA GmbH Dresden werden praxisorientierte Aufgaben zur Werkstoffforschung, zur Prüfung, Berechnung und Qualitätssicherung von Werkstoffen, Bauteilen und Produkten, zum Werkstoffeinsatz, zur Werkstoffinformation und zum Verschleißschutz für den Maschinen-, Anlagen- und Apparatebau, den Straßen- und Schienenfahrzeugbau, die Kunststoffindustrie, die Eisen- und Stahlindustrie und den Stahl- und Leichtmetallbau bearbeitet.

Geschäftsfelder
- Bauteil- und Produktprüfung
- Metalle
- Kunststoffe
- Informationszentrum Werkstoffanwendung

Ein besonderer Schwerpunkt der Unternehmenstätigkeit ist die Bearbeitung von Aufgaben für die Luft- und Raumfahrtindustrie. Gegenwärtig befinden sich die Vorbereitungsarbeiten für den gemeinsam mit der IABG Ottobrunn durchzuführenden Betriebsfestigkeitsversuch an der Gesamtstruktur des größten europäischen Flugzeuges Airbus A340-600 in der Endphase. ∎

The IMA Materialforschung und Anwendungstechnik GmbH (IMA Material Research and Application Technology Ltd.) is a technical and scientific service and research institution. It originates from the Dresden aviation industry and the Institut für Leichtbau/IfL (Institute for Lightweight Construction) that emerged from it and feels committed to continue in this tradition.

IMA GmbH Dresden carries out practice-oriented tasks in materials research work, testing, calculating and quality assurance of materials, component parts and products for material application, material information and for the protection of wear and tear in machine, equipment and apparatus construction, road and railway vehicle construction, the plastics industry, the iron and steel industry and the steel and light alloy construction.

Business fields:
- Component and product testing
- Metals
- Plastics
- Information Centre for materials application

One particular main focus of the company's activities is the management of tasks for aeronautical and aerospace industry. At present, the preparatory work for the operational strength test to be carried out together with IABG Ottobrunn on the total structure of the largest European airplane, the Airbus A340-600, has reached its final stage. ∎

Maßgeschneiderte Lösungen für den Kunden

Tailor-made Solutions for the Customer

Der Unternehmenssitz in Dresden.
The company's headquarters in Dresden.

Vollautomatische Verpackungsanlage.
Fully automatic packaging plant.

Der Firmenverbund IBN, ALS und BIOCONSENS vereint erfolgreich mehrere Geschäftsfelder unter einem Dach. Das Aufgabengebiet der IBN Gesellschaft für industrielle Forschung und Technologie mbH umfaßt die Bearbeitung von Forschungs- und Entwicklungsleistungen in der Biotechnologie, im Lebensmittel- und Industriebereich sowie die Tätigkeit als technisch-technologischer Consultant für verarbeitende Industrie und Maschinenbau.

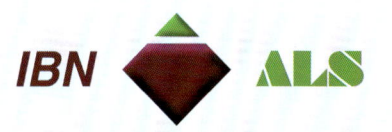

Mit der ALS Anlagentechnik und Sondermaschinen GmbH und der neugegründeten BIOCONSENS GmbH, welche sich mit der Entwicklung biotechnologischer Verfahren sowie der Herstellung und dem Vertrieb dieser Produkte und Wirkstoffe beschäftigt, entstand ein sehr effizient arbeitender Firmenverbund.

Durch die interdisziplinäre Besetzung ergeben sich Synergieeffekte, die Reibungsverluste minimieren, Projektabläufe vereinfachen und einen ständigen Informationsaustausch gewährleisten. Maßgeschneiderte Lösungen für die Kunden sind das Erfolgsrezept, beginnend mit der Konzeption, der Verfahrensentwicklung, der Konstruktion, der Automatisierungslösung bis hin zur Fertigung und Inbetriebnahme beim Kunden. ∎

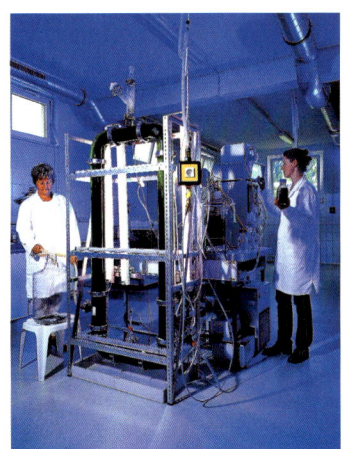

Phototrophe Fermentation zur Wirkstoffgewinnung.
Phototropic fermentation for the production of substances.

The association of companies IBN, ALS and BIOCONSENS successfully unites several business fields under one roof. The area of tasks of the company IBN Gesellschaft für industrielle Forschung und Technologie mbH comprises the handling of research and development services in biotechnology, food stuff and industrial areas as well as activities as a technical and technological consultant to the processing industry and machine construction.

Together with ALS Anlagentechnik und Sondermaschinen GmbH and the newly founded BIOCONSENS GmbH – that is concerned with the development of biotechnological processing methods as well as the manufacture and sale of such products and materials – a very efficiently working union of companies has been established.

Through the interrelated fields of work certain effects of synergy are resulting that minimize loss through competition, simplify project procedures and guarantee a constant exchange of information. Tailor-made solutions for customers are the secret of our success starting with conception, development of procedures, construction, solutions for automation up to the production and implementation at the client's premises. ∎

IBN Gesellschaft für industrielle Forschung und Technologie mbH

ALS Anlagentechnik und Sondermaschinen GmbH

BIOCONSENS GmbH
biologische Wirkstoffe und Verfahren

Geschäftsführer/Manager:
Dr. Ing. Hans-Jürgen Steiger
Dr. Ing. Gerd Arnold
Dipl.-Betriebswirt Frank Lippert

Gründungsjahr/Year of Foundation:
IBN 1990, ALS 1995, Bioconsens 2000

Mitarbeiter/Employees: 70

Geschäftstätigkeit/Business Activity:
- Verarbeitung von Nahrungsmitteln
- Abfüllung und Verpackung von Produkten einschließlich logistischer Einbindung
- Spezielle Bereiche der Umwelttechnik
- Biotechnologische Verfahrensentwicklung und Biodetektion
- Biotechnologische Produkte
- Spezialsensorik und Messtechnik
- Automatisierungs- und Steuerungstechnik
- Maschinentechnik für spezifische und sensible Einsatzbereiche
- Entwicklung und Fertigung von kundenspezifischen Sondermaschinen
- Verpackungs- und Abfülltechnik
- Planung und Realisierung von Anlagen
- Analytische Dienstleistungen
- Processing of food stuff
- Filling and packaging of products including logistics
- Speciality fields in environmental techniques
- Development of methodology in biotechnology and bio-detection
- Biotechnology products
- Special sensors and measuring technique
- Automation and control technology
- Machine engineering for specific and sensitive fields of use
- Development and production of customer-specific speciality machines
- Packaging and filling technology
- Planning and realization of plants
- Analytical services provision

Anschrift/Address:
Heidelberger Straße 12
D-01189 Dresden
IBN
Telefon +49 (351) 40 38-60
Telefax +49 (351) 40 38-699
E-mail info@ibn-dresden.de
Internet www.ibn-dresden.de

ALS
Telefon +49 (351) 40 38-60
Telafax +49 (351) 40 38-688
E-Mail info@als-dresden.de
Internet www.als-dresden.de

Bioconsens
Telefon +49 (351) 403 86-60
Telefax +49 (351) 403 86-66
E-Mail info@bioconsens.de
Internet www.bioconsens.de

Company Profile

Digitale Kommunikation auf höchstem Niveau

Digital Communication on the Highest Level

In Medias Res

IMR In Medias Res
Gesellschaft für vernetzte Kommunikation mbH

Geschäftsführer/Managing Director:
Kai Lewerenz

Gründungsjahr/Year of Foundation:
2000

Geschäftstätigkeit/Business Activity:
Die Beratung, Schulung, Konzeption, Realisierung und Produktion von Interaktiven Media- und Printprojekten, die Bereitstellung zur Einwahl ins Internet, die Herstellung von Festverbindungen, Web-homing und Web-housing, der Betrieb von Internetshop-lösungen, EDV-und Internetservice sowie Beratung, Verkauf, Reparatur und Installation von Standard-Computer- und Serversystemen inklusive Softwareapplikationen, Verkauf von Standardsoftwareprodukten, Netzwerkinstallationen und die Integration von Internetdiensten im Firmennetzwerk
Consulting, training, conception, realization and production of interactive media and print projects, provision of access to the Internet, establishing land lines, Web-homing and Web-housing, operation of Internet shop-solutions, computer and Internet service as well as consulting, sales, repair and installation of standard computer and server systems including software applications, sale of standard software products, network installations and integration of Internet services into company networks

Anschrift/Address:
Heidelberger Landstraße 68
D-64297 Darmstadt
Telefon +49 (6151) 702 88-0
Telefax +49 (6151) 702 88-10

Zweigstelle/Dependance:
Bismarckstraße 56
D-01257 Dresden
E-Mail info@in-medias-res.net
Internet www.in-medias-res.net

Eine Visionärin, die prozessoptimierte Lösungen integriert – so lässt sich in kurzen Worten die in Darmstadt-Eberstadt ansässige Firma IMR In Medias Res beschreiben. Technisches Knowhow in Kombination mit Marketingkompetenz schafft ein kreativ und zielorientiert agierendes Team. Die Eberstädter befassen sich mit der Realisierung von Internetauftritten und der Optimierung und Schaffung von kommunikativer Interaktion auf Basis der Internettechnologie. Neben beratenden, konzeptionellen, kreativen und programmiertechnischen Leistungen bietet die Gesellschaft für vernetzte Kommunikation Content-Pflege und -Research, Soft- und Hardwaresupport, Schnittstellenprogrammierung und die Integration existierender Medien in ihrem Spektrum an.

Auszüge des Leistungsspektrums

Beim Computer Based Training bekommen Kunden Lernsysteme auf CD-Rom, als lokale Insellösung oder gar als weltweites Lernnetz zur Verfügung gestellt. Weboptimierung befasst sich mit der Optimierung bereits bestehender Webauftritte. Hierbei wird größter Wert auf Unternehmensintegration gelegt. IMR In Medias Res erstellt vollständige Konzepte zur effektiven Umsetzung von Datenbanken, Shop-Lösungen und Logistikabläufen im nationalen und internationalen Verkehr. Um das angebotene Spektrum an Datenbanklösungen optimal bereitstellen zu können, betreibt IMR In Medias Res direkt am Hauptknoten in Frankfurt am Main eigene Datenbankserver, denn nichts ist wichtiger als ein verlässlicher Provider.

Referenzen und Standorte

Das umfangreiche Leistungsspektrum kommt an bei den Kunden. Namen aus unterschiedlichsten Bereichen wie Viva Medien AG, Jenapharm, Enviro Chemie, Wella, Planet Radio, Tetra Pak, ABC Verlag, Peugeot Deutschland, Michael Jackson oder Schloss Wachenheim zieren bereits die Referenzliste der von Kai Lewerenz geführten IT-Firma, die neben Darmstadt auch in Dresden eine Dependance hat. Planung: Sommer 2001: Wiesbaden, Winter 2001: Berlin.

Auf Messen wie der Systems 2000 in München war das Unternehmen präsent. Bei solchen Gelegenheiten darf eine beispielhafte interaktive Agentur eben auf keinen Fall fehlen. ■

A visionary that integrates process-optimised solutions – this may be the best way to describe in few words the company IMR In Medias Res located in Darmstadt-Eberstadt. Technical expertise combined with marketing competence empowers a creative and target-oriented active team. The Eberstadt Company deals with the realization of Internet appearances and optimising and creating communicative interaction on the basis of Internet technologies. Apart from consulting, conceptual, creative and technical programming services, the company offers Internet access for networked communication, all Provider services (Hosting, SMS, Wap, Payment, etc.) and complete solution as a one-stop shop. Computer-based training, Web-optimising, databases, shop-solutions, services (training, consulting, project-accompaniment, content-care and –research, soft and hardware support, interface programming) and video presentations are the pillars of the company.

Service range

In computer-based training, customers receive learning systems on CD-ROM as local isolated solutions or even as worldwide learning network to their disposal. In this relation, great importance is given to company integration and the discussion of useful effects. IMR In Medias Res creates complete concepts for the realization of databases, shop-solutions and logistic runs in national and international transport/ traffic. In order to provide an ideal range of database solutions IMR In Media Res operates directly at the main node in Frankfurt on the Main it's own database server, since nothing is more important than a reliable Provider.

References and Locations

Our clients like our extensive service range. The reference list of the IT company managed by Kai Lewerenz, which apart from Darmstadt also has a subsidiary in Dresden, is decorated with names of the most different branches like for example, Viva Medien AG, Jenapharm, Enviro Chemie, Wella, Planet Radio, Tetra Pak, ABC Verlag, Peugeot Deutschland, Michael Jackson or Schloss Wachenheim. Further strategic subsidiaries are being established in 2001 (Summer: Wiesbaden, Winter: Berlin). The company has been present on fairs like the Systems 2000 in Munich. An exemplary interactive agency cannot miss such occasions, by no means. ■

Company Profile

Industrienahe Forschung in Sachsen

Industry-near Research in Saxony

Neubau des Instituts in der Winterbergstraße.
New building of the institute in Winterbergstraße.

Das Fraunhofer Institut für Werkstoff- und Strahltechnik (IWS) betreibt angewandte Forschung und Entwicklung auf den Gebieten der Laser- und Oberflächentechnik. Über spezielle Kompetenzen verfügt es beim Laserstrahlfügen, -trennen und -abtragen sowie bei der Oberflächenbehandlung und der Spritztechnik.

Eine Besonderheit des Instituts sind die Erfahrungen in der Strahl- und Schichttechnik in Kombination mit fundiertem Werkstoff-know-how, verbunden mit der Möglichkeit einer umfassenden Werkstoffcharakterisierung. Um optimierte Lösungen anbieten zu können, beschäftigen sich die Wissenschaftler neben der Strahltechnik auch mit alternativen Techniken. Dies führt zu so genannten Hybridverfahren, bei denen die Vorteile der Lasertechnik mit den besonderen Eigenschaften anderer Verfahren zu einer kostengünstigen Lösung kombiniert werden.

Durch die enge Zusammenarbeit mit Anlagen- und Systemanbietern können den Kunden Problemlösungen aus einer Hand angeboten werden. Die Ausstattung des Instituts erlaubt es, Kundenanfragen mit modernster Anlagentechnik zu bearbeiten. Darüber hinaus ist es möglich, Pilotanlagen zu installieren und die erarbeiteten Problemlösungen an Null-Serien zu erproben. Wir bieten folgende Dienstleistungen an:
- Beratungen und Machbarkeitsstudien,
- Durchführung von FuE-Arbeiten,
- Verfahrenserprobungen, Systementwicklungen,
- Aufbau und Betrieb von Pilotanlagen,
- Werkstoff- und Bauteilprüfung,
- Schadensfallanalysen sowie die
- Ausbildung von Wissenschaftlern, Ingenieuren, Anlagenbedienern und Laboranten. ∎

The "Fraunhofer Institut für Werkstoff- und Strahltechnik /IWS" (Institute for Material and Beam Technology) carries out applied research and development in the fields of laser and surface technology. It disposes of special competencies in laser beam joining, cutting and ablation as well as in surface treatment and spray coating techniques.

One special distinctiveness of the institute is it's experience in beam and coating technology combined with a founded expertise in material technology and linked with the possibility to provide comprehensive materials analyses. In order to offer optimised solutions, scientists are also concerned with alternative technologies besides the beam technology. This leads to so-called hybrid processes in which the advantages of laser technology are pooled with particular characteristics of other procedures to result in a cost-effective outcome.

Through close co-operation with machine tool and system providers, our clients can be offered one-stop solutions. The facilities of the institute enable us to work out customer enquiries with the most modern system technology. Furthermore, it is possible to install pilot plants and to test the achieved problem solutions in pre-production series.

We offer the following services:
- Consulting and feasibility studies
- Execution of R&D work
- Processing tests, system developments
- Assembly and operation of pilot plants
- Material and component testing
- Failure analysis as well as
- Education and training of scientists, engineers, system operators, laboratory technicians. ∎

Lasergeneriertes Spritzgusswerkzeug.
Laser generated injection-molding tool.

Fraunhofer Institut Werkstoff- und Strahltechnik

Fraunhofer-Institut für Werkstoff- und Strahltechnik (IWS) Dresden

Institutsleiter/Head of Institute:
Prof. Dr.-Ing. habil. Eckhard Beyer

Gründungsjahr/Year of Foundation:
1992

Mitarbeiter/Employees:
156 (Jahr 2000)/156 (year 2000)

Umsatz/Turnover:
10 Mio.Euro (Jahr 2000)/10 million Euro (year 2000)

Geschäftstätigkeit/Business Activity:
- anwendungsorientierte Forschung und Entwicklung auf den Gebieten der Laser- und Oberflächentechnik
- Angebot von Dienstleistungs- und Werkverträgen, bei Bedarf strikte Vertraulichkeit garantiert
- Application-oriented research and development in the fields of: Laser and surface technology
- Provision of services and works' contracts, carried out in strictly guaranteed confidentiality if requested

Schwerpunkte/Focal Points:
- Laserstrahlfügen, -trennen und -abtragen,
- Oberflächenbehandlung, Spritztechnik
- Aufbringen von dünnen Schichten zur Vergütung von Oberflächen
- laser beam joining, cutting and ablation
- surface treatment, spraying techniques
- thin-film coating for the refinement of surfaces

Anschrift/Address:
Winterbergstraße 28
D-01277 Dresden
Telefon +49 (351) 25 83 324
Telefax +49 (351) 25 83 300
E-Mail info@iws.fhg.de
Internet www.iws.fhg.de

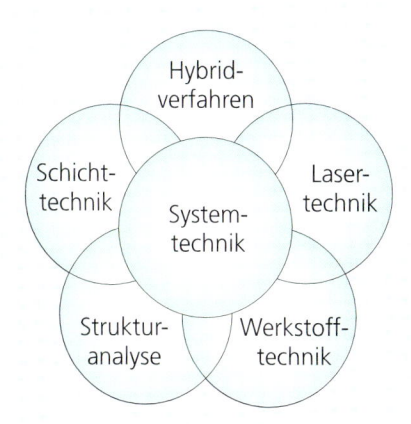

Handwerk

Dresdner Handwerk im neuen Jahrtausend

Dresden's skilled trades in the new millennium

Noch nie zuvor fanden in Wirtschaft und Gesellschaft so tiefgreifende und rasche Veränderungen statt wie heute. Das Handwerk ist ein Wirtschaftsbereich, dessen Anfänge bis in das 5. Jahrhundert vor Christus zurückreichen. Als immer entscheidende wirtschaftliche Basis stellt es sich seit Jahrhunderten den Herausforderungen der Zeit. Handwerk zeichnet sich seit eh und je durch Dynamik und Flexibilität aus. Fachliche Kompetenz, Verbindung von Tradition und Moderne, überschaubare Strukturen, Engagement und Schöpferkraft prägen die Existenz des Handwerks.

Drei Beispiele sollen belegen, dass das Handwerk im neuen Jahrtausend vor immensen Herausforderungen und maßgeblichen Veränderungen steht.

Erstens fordert die Zukunft eine Informations- und Wissensgesellschaft mit spezifischen Fachkenntnissen und der Bereitschaft zu kontinuierlichem, lebenslangen Lernen. Der Mittelstand ist in seiner ganzen Flexibilität gefordert, um mit seinen Strukturen der Schnelllebigkeit der Zeit besser gewachsen zu sein als weltweit agierende Großkonzerne. Industrielle Arbeitsplätze werden von Hochtechnologien abgelöst, der Arbeitsmarkt verschiebt sich in Richtung mittelständischer Industrie und Handwerk.

Zweitens wandelt sich unsere Gesellschaft immer mehr in Richtung Dienstleistungsgesellschaft. Dabei handelt es sich um qualitativ anspruchsvolle, häufig konsumorientierte Dienste, aber auch um hochwertige Unternehmerdienste. Hier erwartet das Handwerk neue Wirkungsfelder, die neues Denken erfordern. Angebote von komplexen Dienstleistungen beziehungsweise die Bündelung von Produkten mit den dazugehörigen Dienstleistungen erfordern innovatives Denken. Sie erfordern die Bereitschaft, über den eigenen Tellerrand hinauszusehen und die Bereitschaft zu überbetrieblichen Kooperationen.

Drittens steht in diesem Jahrtausend ein gemeinsames Europa mit einer neuen Währung, neuen Märkten, neuer Konkurrenz, neuen Kooperationsmöglichkeiten und weiteren Herausforderungen

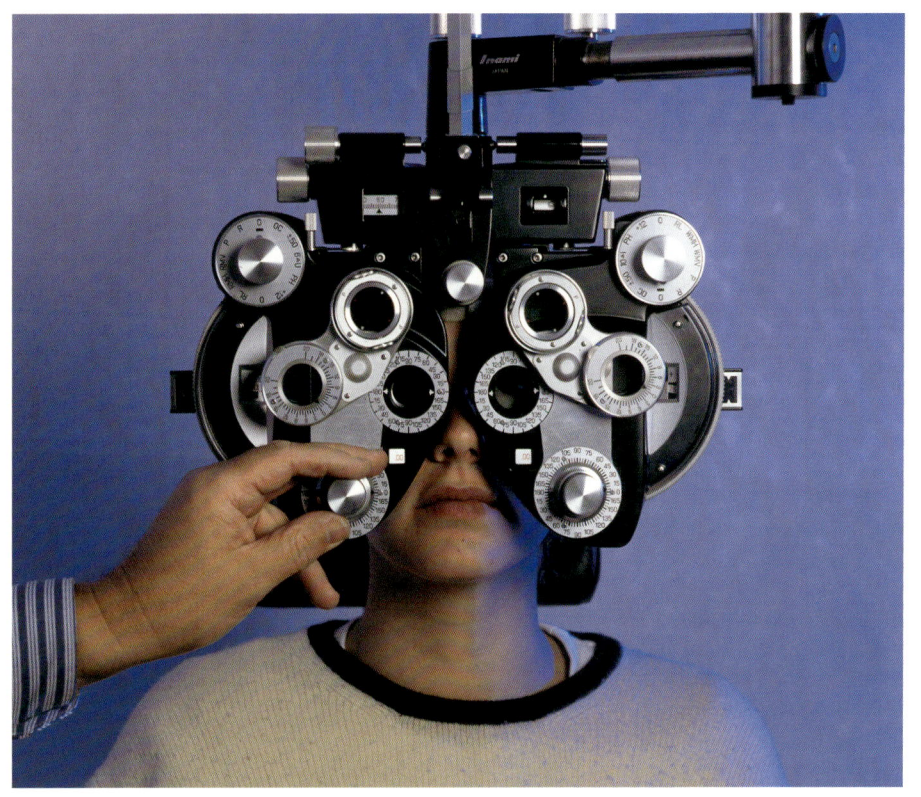

Modernste Technik und Technologien haben auch im Handwerk, wie hier beim Optiker, Einzug gehalten.

The most modern techniques and technologies have also entered the skilled trades sector, like here at the optician.

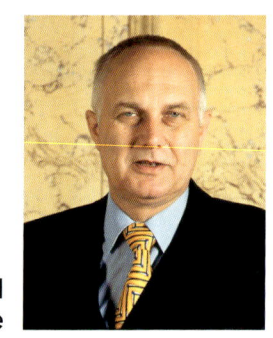

Bernd Rendle

Der Autor wurde 1941 in Dresden geboren. Er ist von Beruf Raumausstattermeister und betreibt seit 1972 seine private Firma in Dresden. Im Mai 1997 wurde er zum Präsidenten der Handwerkskammer Dresden gewählt. Er ist Vorstandsmitglied des Sächsischen Handwerkstages und weiterer hochrangiger Gremien.
Sein besonderes Engagement gilt seit Jahren dem Nachwuchs. Er bildete in seinem Unternehmen selber zahlreiche Lehrlinge aus.

The author was born in 1941 in Dresden. His profession is that of an interior decorator and he operates his own private business in Dresden since 1972. In May 1997, he was elected president of the Chamber of Handicrafts Dresden. He is a member of the board of the Handicrafts Commission of Saxony and of other high-ranking bodies.
He has been particularly engaged in promoting up and coming young people. He has also trained himself numerous apprentices in his company.

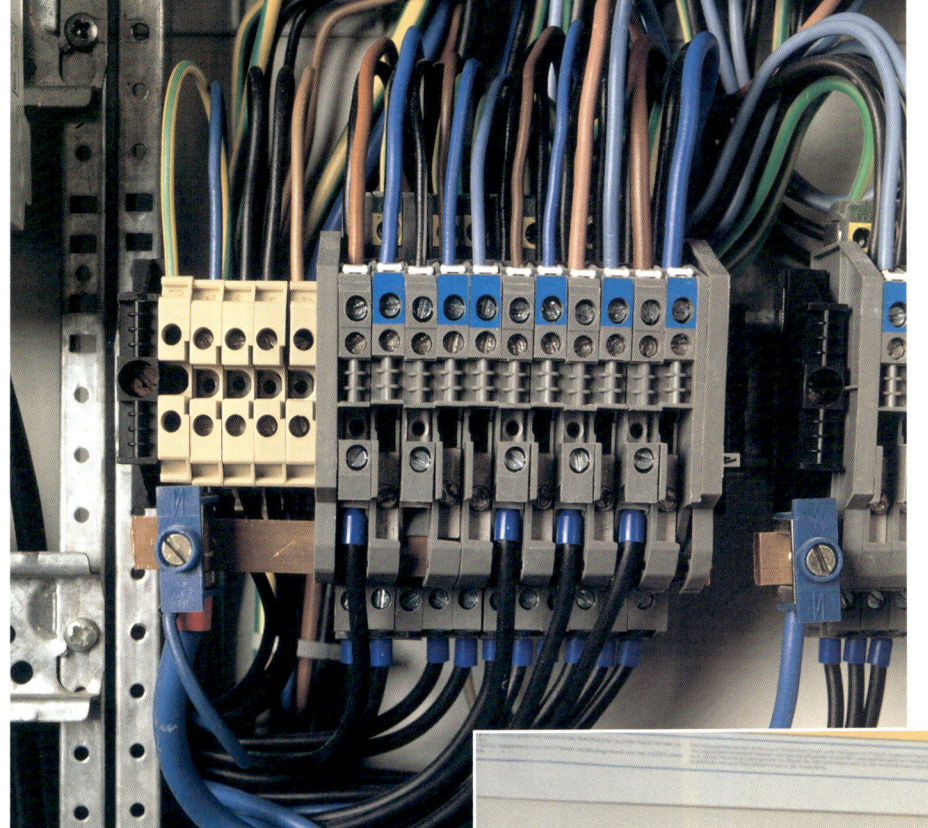

Skilled Trades

Zahlreiche Unternehmen haben Veränderungen vollzogen, die den traditionellen Begriff „Handwerksbetrieb" mit neuem Inhalt füllen.

Numerous companies have accomplished such changes that give the traditional term „Handicrafts Company" a new meaning.

Never before there have been such rapid and intensive changes in the economic sector and in society as today. The skilled trade is a sector of the economy that has roots reaching as far back as into the 5th Century B.C. It confronts the challenges of time always as a decisive economic foundation. Dynamism and flexibility distinguish the handicrafts since ancient times. Expert competence, the combination of tradition and modernism, clear structures, engagement and creativity characterise the existence of skilled trades.

Three examples shall serve to proof that the skilled trades is confronted with tremendous challenges and decisive changes in the new millennium. First of all, the future demands an information and knowledge-based society with specific expertise and the readiness to constant and lifelong learning. The middle-sized business sector is challenged to concentrate all its flexibility to be better prepared in its structures for these fast-moving times than multinational corporations active worldwide. Industrial workplaces are replaced by high technologies; the labour market is shifting towards the middle-sized industry and skilled trades sector.

Secondly, our society is changing more and more into a service providing society. This includes services of high claim in quality that are often consumer oriented, but also high-quality business-to-business services. In this area, the skilled trades are expecting new fields of activities that require new attitudes. The provision of complex services and the grouping of products with their corresponding services demand innovative ideas. They required the readiness to extend one's view beyond the own horizon and to be prepared for co-operation outside the companies.

Handwerk

Nicht nur im Kfz-Handel will der Kunde umworben sein und fordert komplexe Dienstleistungen.
Not only in automobile trade the customer wants to be courted and demands complex services.

vor der Tür. Da das Handwerk in der Regel, was seine Produktionsstandorte angeht, wenig flexibel ist, muss es den Wettbewerb vom heimischen Standort aus führen. Der Wettbewerbsdruck wird zunehmend über die Preisschiene erfolgen. Bestehen kann das deutsche Handwerk nur mit angemessenen Wettbewerbsstrategien, die weit über eine simple Kostensenkung hinausgehen. Erforderlich sind zum Beispiel Produkterneuerungen in Zusammenarbeit mit anderen Unternehmen und Innovationen im Dienstleistungsbereich.

Ist das Handwerk diesen Anforderungen gewachsen?

Der unternehmerische Mittelstand ist das Rückgrat der deutschen Wirtschaft. In mehr als 800.000 Betrieben arbeiten rund 6,5 Millionen Menschen. Die Unternehmen schätzen ihre wirtschaftliche Zukunft zur Zeit sehr vorsichtig ein, sehen sich selber aber für den Wettbewerb gut gerüstet. Dennoch belegt die Praxis, dass für die Zukunft erhebliche Reserven erschlossen werden müssen. Traditionelle Tugenden wie Fleiß, Erfahrung und Verlässlichkeit paaren sich im Handwerk noch nicht immer mit innovativen Einstellungen wie Offenheit, Kreativität und Mut.

Es stimmt bedenklich, wenn die Bereitschaft zu Investitionen nur noch bei rund 40 Prozent der ostdeutschen Handwerksbetriebe vorhanden ist. Strukturelle Veränderungen zur Zukunftssicherung, Geschäftsausweitung ins Ausland, Bildung von Netzwerken, Zusammenarbeit mit Forschungs- und Entwicklungseinrichtungen sind die Chancen für die Zukunft. Auch im Hinblick auf die Nutzung zeitgemäßer Führungsinstrumente und Unternehmensstrukturen gibt es im Mittelstand vielfach Nachholbedarf.

Ein hoher Qualitätsstandard liegt auf der fachlichen Qualifikation im Handwerk. Die Meisterprüfung schafft eine wesentliche Voraussetzung für die Wettbewerbsfähigkeit junger Betriebe auf den Märkten. Handwerkliche Unternehmen erweisen sich in wirtschaftlich schwierigen Zeiten auf der Grundlage der hohen fachlichen und betriebswirtschaftlichen Qualifikation ihrer Inhaber – gemessen an anderen Wirtschaftsbereichen – als stabiler. Diese Tatsache veranlasst auch immer mehr Kreditinstitute, den Meisterabschluss als eine Prämisse für die Kreditwürdigkeit von Unternehmen im handwerklichen Bereich heranzuziehen. Die Erfahrung zeigt, dass die Handwerksausbildung aufgrund der Vermittlung der erforderlichen Kenntnisse für eine Unternehmensgründung auch Anreize für die Existenzgründung gibt. Der Meisterbrief motiviert zur Selbständigkeit. Etwa 60 Prozent von jährlich rund 40.000 Jung-

Skilled Trades

Etwa 60 Prozent von den jährlich rund 40.000 Jungmeistern, die ihre Ausbildung abschließen, haben die Absicht, sich selbstständig machen.

Around 60 percent of yearly approx. 40,000 young masters that finish their training have the intention to become self-employed.

simple cost reductions. For example, product innovations in co-operation with other companies are necessary and innovations in the service sector.

Are the skilled trades ready to meet these challenges?

The entrepreneurial middle-sized business sector is the backbone of the German economy. In more than 800,000 companies, around 6.5 million people are employed. At present, companies see their economic future with very cautious estimations, but regard themselves as being well equipped for competition.

Nevertheless, practical experience has shown that for the future considerable reserves must be opened up. Traditional values like diligence, experience and reliability are still not easily linked

Third, in this new millennium a common Europe is awaiting us with a new currency, new markets, new competition, new possibilities of co-operation and other challenges. Since the handicrafts sector usually is not very flexible regarding its production locations, it must compete from its home base. The pressure of competition will increasingly be dealt with on the level of pricing. The German skilled trades will only be able to survive with adequate strategies of competition that go far beyond

in handicrafts with innovative attitudes like openness, creativity and courage. It is alarming if only around 40 percent of East German handicrafts companies are prepared to invest. The chances for the future lie in structural change for securing the future prospects, expansion of businesses to foreign countries, the building of networks, co-operation with research and development institutions. Also, with regard to the use of timely management instruments and company structures there is often a lot of catching up to do in the middle-sized business sector. A high quality standard is required in expert qualifications within the skilled trades. The master's diploma creates an essential prerequisite for the ability to compete of young companies in

Handwerk

Herausragende Qualität ist auch im Handwerk die entscheidende Voraussetzung für ein Bestehen am Markt.
Excellent quality is a decisive prerequisite for survival on the market also in skilled trades.

meistern wollen sich selbstständig machen. In der anderen Hälfte liegt ein Reservoir an potenziellen Existenzgründern.

Eine qualitative Verbesserung der Meisterausbildung, vor allem in Form ihrer Flexibilisierung wird dazu beitragen, die Absolventen noch besser und zielgerichteter auf ihre Selbständigkeit vorzubereiten. Neben dem Großen Befähigungsnachweis wird das Handwerk in Zukunft verstärkt fachspezifische und betriebswirtschaftliche Weiterbildungsmöglichkeiten anbieten, die es den Handwerksmeistern gestatten, ihre Betriebe nach den modernsten Gesichtspunkten zu führen. Ein gutes Beispiel in dieser Richtung ist, die bereits existierende – und mit großem Interesse genutzte – Fortbildung zum „Betriebswirt des Handwerks".

Hightech-Betriebe sind noch nicht die Regel im Handwerk. Zahlreiche Unternehmen haben jedoch in den letzten zehn Jahren Entwicklungen vollzogen, die den traditionellen Begriff „Handwerksbetrieb" mit neuem Inhalt füllen. Das Handwerk ist auf dem richtigen Weg. Dazu einige Beispiele:

Höchste Qualitätsansprüche

Herausragende Qualität ist die entscheidende Voraussetzung für ein Bestehen am Markt. Insbesondere Unternehmen, die als Zulieferer für Industriebetriebe arbeiten, garantieren die verschiedensten Qualitätsnormen – vom betrieblichen Qualitätsmanagement bis zur Zertifizierung.

Facility Management

Die komplexe Dienstleistung rund um die Immobilie ist ein attraktiver Wachstumsmarkt. Handwerksbetriebe verschiedenster Gewerbe kooperieren und gewährleisten ein ausgeklügeltes Management. Umfangreiche Tätigkeitsfelder können abgedeckt werden, kleine und mittlere Unternehmen haben die Chance, an Großaufträgen zu arbeiten.

Hightech

Modernste Technik und Technologien haben auch im Handwerk Einzug gehalten. Fernüberwachung von Anlagen, Herstellung von Präzisionswerkzeugen, Diagnosetechnik am Kraftfahrzeug und Installieren von Netzwerken sind Tätigkeiten im Handwerk.

Ausländische Märkte

Das Handwerk will aus der Globalisierung wirtschaftlichen Nutzen ziehen. Kooperationen mit ausländischen Firmen, Gründung von Firmenniederlassungen im Ausland, Export eigener Produkte sind erste Schritte auf ausländischen Märkten.

Internet

Dialog mit Kunden und Geschäftspartnern, weltweite Information und Kommunikation, E-Commerce prägen mehr und mehr den Alltag handwerklicher Betriebe.

Neue Berufe

Die Veränderung traditioneller Berufsbilder und die Schaffung neuer Berufe im Handwerk orientieren sich an der Entwicklung von Wissenschaft und Technik. Zum Beispiel gewährleistet der Handwerksberuf Informationselektroniker die technische Realisierung und Instandhaltung moderner Informations- und Kommunikationsmittel.

Das Handwerk macht sich Gedanken um seine Zukunft, gleiches erwarten die handwerklichen Unternehmen auch von der Bundesregierung, der Landesregierung und den kommunalen Behörden und Verwaltungen. Sie alle sollten sich bei ihrer Wirtschaftspolitik von der großen Bedeutung des unternehmerischen Mittelstandes für Arbeitsplätze und Investitionen in Deutschland leiten lassen. ■

Skilled Trades

the markets. Handicraft companies have proved more stable in times of economic difficulties – compared to other economic sectors – because of the high expert and economic qualification of their proprietors. This fact also give rise to more and more credit institutes to demand the accomplishment of the master's exam as a premise for the credibility of companies in the skilled trades sector. Experience has shown that training in handicrafts also gives motivation for company start-ups because of the acquisition of necessary knowledge for a company foundation. The master's diploma encourages self-employment. Very year, around 60 percent of approx. 40,000 young masters want to work for themselves. The other half contains a reservoir of potential company founders.

Through an improvement of the quality of the master's training, especially in terms of flexibility, will contribute to the graduates' additional and more targeted preparation towards their independence. Apart from the "Great Capacitating Certificate", the skilled trades sector will offer in future increasingly subject-specific and economic continual education possibilities that allow masters of handicrafts to manage their companies according to the most modern perspectives. A good example in this connection is the already existing further education course leading to "Economist of Handicrafts", which is being used with great interest.

High-tech companies are not that customary yet within the skilled trades. Numerous companies have, however, undergone such developments that give the term "Handicrafts Company" a new meaning. The skilled trades sector is on the right way. Here are some examples to portray this:

Highest Demands of Quality

Excellent quality is the decisive prerequisite for survival on the market. Particularly companies that work as supplier to industrial corporations warrant the most varied quality standards – ranging from in-house quality assurance management to pre-qualification certificate.

Facility Management

The complex services around the real estate business are an attractive growth market. Handicrafts companies of the most diverse trades co-operate and ensure an elaborated management. It is possible to cover the most extensive fields of activities, small and middle-size enterprises have the chance to participate in large orders.

High-tech

The most modern techniques and technologies have also entered the skilled trades sector. Remote surveillance of plants, production of precision tools, diagnostic technology at vehicles and the installation of networks are now among the activities of the skilled trade.

Foreign Markets

The skilled trades sector want to take advantage of globalisation. Co-operations with foreign companies, branch foundations of companies abroad, export of self-produced goods are the first steps on the foreign markets.

Internet

Dialog with customers and business partners, worldwide information and communication, e-commerce characterise more and more the daily work routine of skilled trade companies.

New Professions

According to the development of science and technology, the change of traditional professional careers and the creation of new professions within handicrafts will be oriented. For example, the skilled trade profession of information electronic technician ensures the technical realization and maintenance of modern means of information and communications.

The skilled trades sector is thinking about its future and they expect similar considerations from the part of the federal government and the communal authorities and administrations. They all should be guided in their economic policies by the great importance of the mid-sized entrepreneurial sector for workplaces and investments in Germany. ■

Der Beruf Maler und Lackierer erfordert neben handwerklichem Geschick künstlerische Begabung.
The profession of painter and decorator requires apart from skills in this trade also artistic talent.

Company Profile

Hochwertige Veredlung für Flugzeuge & Industriegüter

High-quality Refinement for aeroplanes and industrial goods

Nehlsen Flugzeug-Galvanik Dresden GmbH & Co. KG

Geschäftsführer/Manager:
Bernd Schmidt

Gründungsjahr/Year of Foundation:
1998

Mitarbeiter/Employees:
70 (einschl. Auszubildende/including trainees)

Jahresumsatz für 2000/Turnover:
ca./approx. 10 Mio. DM

Geschäftstätigkeit/Business Activity:
Betrieb einer Galvanik, insbesondere für Flugzeugteile
- Verkupfern, Vernickeln, Verchromen, Vercadmen, Verzinken, Verzinnen, Versilbern
- Chemisch Vernickeln, Phosphatieren, Brünieren, Gelbchromatieren (Al)
- anod. Oxidieren (Eloxal), Hartanodisieren, Chromsäureanodisieren
- galv. Aluminium alternativ zu Cadmium
- Vakuumkomponenten-Reinigung

Operation of galvanizing plants particularly for aeroplane parts
- Copper plating, nickel-plating, chromium-plating, cadmium-coating, zinc-coating, tin-plating, silver-plating
- Cold-galvanizing, phosphatizing, black finishing, yellow chromium-plating (A1)
- Electrolytic oxidation (Eloxal), hard anodising, chromic acid anodising
- Galvanized aluminium alternatively to cadmium
- vacuum component cleaning

Anschrift/Address:
Grenzstraße 2 (Halle 221)
D-01109 Dresden
Telefon +49 (351) 88 31 400
Telefax +49 (351) 88 31 404
E-Mail galvanik@nehlsen-dresden.de
Internet www.nehlsen-flugzeuggalvanik.de

Eloxalautomat für Bauteile bis 6 m Länge.
Eloxal automat for components up to 6 m length.

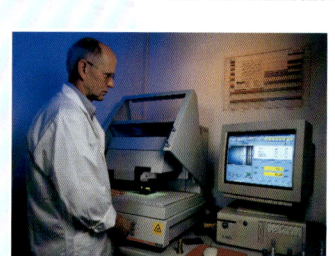

Schichtdickenprüfung mit dem Röntgenfloureszenz-Messgerät.
Coat thickness testing with x-ray flourescence measuring equipment.

Reinigungsautomat für Nasschemische Reinigung von Vakuumteilen.
Cleaning automat for chemical wet-cleaning von vacuum parts.

Aus der am Flughafen Dresden-Klotzsche ansässigen Flugzeugindustrie ist die Nehlsen Flugzeug-Galvanik entstanden und seit 40 Jahren mit dem Oberflächenschutz dieses Industriezweiges befasst.
Seit 1993 gehört der Betrieb zur Nehlsen-Gruppe und ist ab 1998 als GmbH & Co. KG firmiert.
Unsere Tätigkeitsschwerpunkte liegen in der Luftfahrtindustrie, zunehmend aber auch auf den Sektoren Maschinenbau/Elektrotechnik, Halbleiterindustrie, Wehrtechnik und Waggonbau. Für all diese Industriezweige veredelt die Nehlsen Flugzeug-Galvanik Teile aus unterschiedlichen Grundwerkstoffen, indem – gemäß Luftfahrtnorm bzw. Kundenwunsch – metallische Schichten abgeschieden oder oxidische Schichten erzeugt werden.
Die Nehlsen Flugzeug-Galvanik ist damit ohne Zweifel einer der führenden Anbieter hochwertiger, funktioneller Beschichtungen für die verschiedensten technischen Anwendungszwecke. Im Freistaat Sachsen ist Nehlsen der einzige luftfahrtzertifizierte Betrieb im Bereich der elektro-chemischen Oberflächenbeschichtung.
Ein hoher Qualitätsstandard hat bei uns Tradition und ist uns als Partner der Luftfahrtindustrie (QSF-B) nach DIN EN ISO 9000 durch Zertifikat bestätigt worden. Das EURAS-Gütezeichen QUALANOD und die Zulassung der Deutschen Bahn AG sind ebenfalls Ausdruck unseres hohen Qualitätsanspruches.
Im Oktober 1997 wurde eine technisch einzigartige Reinigungsanlage für Hochvakuumkomponenten der Halbleiterindustrie in Betrieb genommen. Als Dienstleister und Partner dieses Industriezweiges werden innovative Reinigungskonzepte mittels mechanischer, chemischer oder in Kombination chemisch-mechanischer Verfahren angeboten.
Als Industriepartner ist die Nehlsen Flugzeug-Galvanik Dresden GmbH & Co. KG an mehreren Forschungsprojekten der TU Dresden beteiligt. ■

The Nehlsen Flugzeug-Galvanik emerged from the aviation industry located at the airport Dresden-Klotzsche, which is active in the field of surface protection of this industrial branch. Since 1993, the company belongs to the Nehlsen Group and is registered as GmbH & Co. KG (German limited partnership) since 1998.
The main focus of our activities is on the aviation industry, but also increasingly on the sectors of machine construction and electro technology, semiconductor industry, arms technology and wagon construction. Nehlsen Flugzeug-Galvanik refines parts for all these industrial branches made of different basic materials by means of separating metallic coats or producing oxidic coatings, according to aviation standards or customer-specific orders.
Undoubtedly, Nehlsen Flugzeug-Galvanik is thus one of the leading providers of high quality, functional coatings for the most varied technical purposes of application. Nehlsen is the only aviation certified company in the field of electro-chemical surface coating in the Free State of Saxony.
We maintain a tradition of high quality standards and this has been endorsed to us, being a partner of the aviation industry (QSF-B), by the Certification according to DIN EN ISO 9000. Further proof of our high claim in quality is the EURAS mark of quality QUALANOD and the admission of the Deutsche Bahn AG (German Railways).
In October 1997, a technically unique cleaning plant for high-vacuum components of the semi-conductor industry started operations. As service provider and partner of this industrial branch, innovative cleaning concepts with mechanical, chemical or in combined chemical-mechanical procedures are on offer.
Nehlsen Flugzeug-Galvanik Dresden GmbH & Co. KG participates in several research projects as an industrial partner to the Technical University of Dresden. ■

Company Profile

MSD – maßgeschneiderter Stahl- und Maschinenbau

MSD – tailor-made steel and machine construction

Kamelienhaus im Schlosspark Pillnitz, eine MSD-Konstruktion.
The Kamelienhaus in the park of the Castle Pillnitz, a glass and steel construction by MSD.

Maschinen- und Stahlbau Dresden (MSD) ist ein mittelständisches Unternehmen, das Tradition und zukunftorientierte Technologien unter seinem Dach vereint. Als Firma Hünich & Löwe 1946 gegründet, wirkte das Unternehmen bereits beim Wiederaufbau Dresdens mit. Nach und nach entwickelte sich ein umfangreiches Produktionsprofil. Mittlerer bis schwerer Stahlbau wurde mit Maschinenbaukomponenten ergänzt. Anlagen für die Industrie, den Verkehrswegebau, die Deutsche Reichsbahn bzw. Bahn, die Bahnindustrie, die Bauwirtschaft und viele andere Partner forderten die heute 180 Mitarbeiter stets heraus. 1991 übernahm Martin Herrenknecht, ein international anerkannter Hersteller für Tunnelvortriebsmaschinen, die Firma.

Von der Konstruktion über die Fertigung bis hin zur Montage bietet Maschinen- und Stahlbau Dresden kundenspezifische Lösungen im Stahlbrückenbau, Stahlwasserbau, Ingenieurstahlbau, der Bahntechnik sowie dem Bau von Komponenten für Tunnelvortriebsmaschinen. Der „Große Eignungsnachweis" mit den Ergänzungen für Krantragwerke, Straßen- und Eisenbahnbrücken sowie die Zertifizierung nach DIN EN 729-2 sind Ausdruck dafür, dass MSD in der Lage ist, hohe Qualitätsanforderungen zu erfüllen. ∎

Maschinen- und Stahlbau Dresden (MSD) is a mid-sized company that combines tradition and future-oriented technologies under one roof. Founded as Messrs. Hünich & Löwe in 1946, the company was active in the re-construction of Dresden after the war. By and by, an extensive production profile was developed. Middle to heavy steel construction was complemented with machine component production. The now 180 staff members were constantly confronted with challenges like plants for industry, construction of transport routes, the German Railways, the railway industry, the building sector and many other partners. In 1991, Martin Herrenknecht, an internationally renowned producer of tunnel-driving machines, took over the company. Ranging from construction across to production up to assembly, Maschinen- und Stahlbau Dresden provides customer-specific solutions in steel bridge construction, steel hydraulic construction, steel construction engineering, railway engineering and the production of components for tunnel-driving machines. The pre-qualification "Großer Eignungsnachweis" with additions for crane girders, road and railway bridges as well as the certification according to DIN EN 729-2 are proof hat MSD is capable of meeting high quality standards. ∎

MSD Maschinen- und Stahlbau Dresden NL der Herrenknecht AG

Vorstandsvorsitzender/Chairman of the Board:
Dr. E. h. Martin Herrenknecht

Niederlassungsleiter/Branch Manager:
Dipl.-Ing. Jürgen Bialek

Gründungsjahr/Year of Foundation: 1946

Mitarbeiter/Employees: 180

Umsatz/Turnover:
30,5 Mio DM (1999)

Geschäftstätigkeit/Business Activity:
Konstruktion, Produktion und Montage von
Construction, production and assembly of
- Stahlbrücken/Steel bridges
- Stahlhallen/Steel halls
- Bürogebäuden/Office buildings
- Wartungs- und Montagebühnen/Maintenance and assembly ramps
- Bahntechnik (Schiebebühnen, Hebebockanlagen, Drehscheiben)/Railway engineering (traversers, lifting equipment, turntables)
- Tunnelvortriebstechnik/Tunnel-driving techniques
- Stahlwasserbau/Steel hydraulic structures
- Stahlsonderkonstruktionen/Speciality steel constructions

Anschrift/Address:
Hofmühlenstraße 5–15
D-01187 Dresden
Telefon +49 (351) 42 34-0
Telefax +49 (351) 42 34-103
E-Mail info.msd@herrenknecht.de
Internet www.msd-dresden.de

Fußgängerbrücke in Halle über die ICE-Strecke Halle-Erfurt.
Pedestrian bridge in Halle across the ICE route Halle-Erfurt.

Flughafen

Flughafen Dresden – Tor zur Welt

Dresden Airport – Gate to the world

Dresden ist als sächsische Landeshauptstadt das politische Zentrum des bevölkerungsreichsten der neuen Bundesländer. Gleichzeitig ist die Metropole an der Elbe Mittelpunkt einer bedeutenden Wirtschaftsregion. Diesem Umfeld entsprechend hat der Flughafen Dresden die Aufgabe, einen sich kräftig entwickelnden Ballungsraum mit der Welt zu verbinden.

In den vergangenen Jahren gelang es durch den Ausbau des Liniennetzes, regelmäßige Verbindungen in alle wichtigen Wirtschaftszentren Europas anzubieten. Das Passagier- und Frachtaufkommen konnte erheblich gesteigert werden. Kontinuierliche Investitionen in die Infrastruktur des Flughafens sicherten, dass die Abfertigungsanlagen, die Verkehrstechnik und -technologien die Anforderungen der wachsenden Verkehrsleistungen bewältigen konnten.

Das Einzugsgebiet des Flughafens Dresden greift über die Grenzen der Stadt Dresden hinaus und umfasst eine Bevölkerung von ca. 4 Millionen Einwohnern. Dazu gehören neben den sächsischen Regierungsbezirken Dresden und Chemnitz auch Gebiete im Süden des Landes Brandenburg. Mit Chemnitz findet sich dabei ein zweiter Ballungsraum mit großem ökonomischen Potenzial.

Auch für Passagiere und Luftfracht aus den an Deutschland grenzenden Gebieten Polens und der Tschechischen Republik ist der Flughafen Dresden ein attraktiver Verkehrsdienstleister.

Flugziele und Kapazitäten

Im Jahr 1999 erreichte der Flughafen Dresden mit über 1,75 Millionen Fluggästen das bisher beste Ergebnis seiner 65jährigen Geschichte. Dieser Fluggastrekord, mit einer Steigerung von 3,5 Prozent gegenüber dem Vorjahr, beruht hauptsächlich auf der sehr guten Entwicklung im Touristikflugverkehr. Dennoch stellten Linienfluggäste mit rund einer Million Passagieren im Jahr 1999 etwa zwei Drittel des gesamten Aufkommens. In diesem hohen Anteil von Linienfluggästen spiegelt sich die Bedeutung Dresdens als politisches und wirtschaftliches Zentrum deutlich wieder.

An der Tatsache, dass am Flughafen Dresden im Jahr 1990 insgesamt nur zirka 200.0000 Passagiere

Volkmar Stein

Der Autor wurde 1943 in Stettin geboren. Nach dem Abitur in Frankfurt/Main studierte er bis 1973 Bauingenieurwesen und Luftfahrttechnik an der TH Darmstadt. Bis 1977 war er als Wissenschaftlicher Mitarbeiter in der Abteilung Planung und Bau der Arbeitsgemeinschaft Deutscher Verkehrsflughäfen tätig, anschließend bis 1992 bei der Flughafen München GmbH als Abteilungsleiter Ingenieurbau.
Seit 1992 war Volkmar Stein Geschäftsführer der Flughafen Dresden GmbH und ist jetzt Vorstand der Mitteldeutschen Flughafen AG.

The author was born in 1943 in Stettin. After attaining his A-levels in Frankfurt/Main, he studied civil engineering until 1973 and aviation technology at the TH Darmstadt. Until 1977, he worked in the department of planning and construction of the Arbeitsgemeinschaft Deutscher Verkehrsflughäfen, afterwards until 1992 at the Airport Munich GmbH as head of department of civil engineering.
Since 1992, Volkmar Stein has been Managing Director of Flughafen Dresden GmbH and is now Executive Board Member of Mitteldeutsche Flughafen AG.

1,75 Millionen Fluggäste wurden 1999 auf dem Flughafen Dresden gezählt.
1.75 million passengers were counted in 1999 on the Airport Dresden.

abgefertigt wurden, lässt sich ablesen, welchen Weg der Flughafen in der vergangenen Dekade zurückgelegt hat.

Inzwischen bestehen von Dresden aus regelmäßige Verbindungen in alle wichtigen Wirtschaftszentren Europas. Im Sommerflugplan 2000 wurden beispielsweise pro Woche von 29 Airlines 336 Flugverbindungen zu 51 Direktflugzielen angeboten. Mit dem neuen Flughafen Dresden Terminal, das

Airport

Flughafen Dresden Terminal, Modellfoto, Innenansicht, 1999.

Airport Dresden Terminal, photograph of model, inner view, 1999.

As the regional capital of Saxony, Dresden is the political centre of the most densely populated province in East Germany recently unified. At the same time, the metropolitan city on the river Elbe is the focal point of an important economic region. Corresponding to the environment, the task of the Dresden Airport is to unite a constantly developing congested urban area with the world.

It has been possible in the past years to offer regular flights connecting Dresden with all-important economic centres of Europe through the extension of the network of routes. The amount of passenger and freight transport has been increased considerably. Continuous investments into the airport's infrastructure ensured that the dispatch plants, the transport techniques and technologies were capable of managing the mounting transport services.

The catchment area of the Dresden Airport goes far beyond the city limits of Dresden and comprises a population of approx. 4 million inhabitants. This includes apart from the Saxon governmental districts of Dresden and Chemnitz also areas in the South of the province of Brandenburg. In Chemnitz can be found in this sense a second congested urban area of great economic potential.

Also, for passengers and freight from the bordering regions of Poland and the Czech Republic, the Dresden Airport is an attractive provider of transport services.

Flight Destinations and Capacities

In 1999, the Dresden Airport achieved the hitherto best result of its 65-year history with over 1.75 million passengers. This record of flight passengers with an increase of 3.5 percent compared to the previous year is due mainly to the excellent development of tourism air transport. However, passengers of scheduled air traffic provided with around one million passengers about two thirds of the total result in 1999. This high share of scheduled flight passengers clearly mirrors the importance of Dresden as a political and economic centre. The fact that only 200,000 passengers approx. were checked in at the Dresden Airport in 1990 shows clearly the development of the airport in the past decade.

Meanwhile there are regular flights from Dresden into all important economic centres of Europe. The summer flight plan 2000 for example provides 336 flight connections to 51 direct destinations by 29 airlines per week. Another giant step into the future offers the new Airport Dresden Terminal that will start operating as per March 2001. The new construction of the terminal is the core piece of a long-term concept, with which the Dresden Airport meets its significance as essential location factor and gate to the world for the City of Dresden and the State of Saxony also after the millennium change.

Apart from passenger transport, also the air cargo and airmail transport are important factors. The Airport Dresden is closely connected to the logistics of various transport organisations and transport bodies. After completion of the freight transfer centre in January 1996, the airport disposes of a capacity of approx. 10,000 tons per year for the handling of freight and airmail.

The Airport and Economic Location

The Free State of Saxony and its regional capital can look back on a rich industrial tradition as well as an encouraging economic development in past years. Between 1990 and 1996, considerable amounts have been invested in the modernisation of the economic infrastructure. As a result, it was possible to maintain the traditionally broad service provision of the enterprises in Dresden, to more than multiply their number in this period and to confer international importance to individual branches in Dresden through the settlement of renowned companies. Luckily, it was achieved to take up the old traditions of the regional capital in high-tech industries such as microelectronics and computer technology and to expand in these fields through important investments.

The Dresden Airport is involved in these developments in many ways. This links us to the investments made at the airport: since the beginning of

Flughafen

Das neue Flughafen Dresden Terminal – Ansicht von den Flugbetriebsflächen aus.
The new Aiport Dresden Terminal – View from the areas of operational control.

im März 2001 in Betrieb gehen wird, erfolgt ein weiterer großer Schritt in die Zukunft. Der Neubau des Terminals ist Kernstück eines langfristigen Konzeptes, mit dem der Flughafen Dresden auch nach der Jahrtausendwende seiner Bedeutung als wesentlicher Standortfaktor und Tor zur Welt für die Stadt Dresden und das Land Sachsen gerecht werden wird.

Neben dem Fluggastverkehr ist das Luftfracht- und Luftpostaufkommen ein weiterer bedeutender Faktor. Der Flughafen Dresden ist durch enge Beziehungen in die Logistik unterschiedlicher Verkehrsträger und Transportunternehmen eingebunden. Nach der Fertigstellung des Frachtumschlagzentrums im Januar 1996 verfügt der Flughafen für die Abfertigung von Fracht und Luftpost über eine Kapazität von ca. 10.000 t pro Jahr.

Der Flughafen als Wirtschaftsstandort

Der Freistaat Sachsen und seine Landeshauptstadt können sowohl auf eine reiche industrielle Tradition wie auch eine ermutigende wirtschaftliche Entwicklung in den vergangenen Jahren verweisen. Zwischen 1990 und 1996 wurden in Dresden bedeutende Summen in den Ausbau der wirtschaftlichen Infrastruktur investiert. Im Ergebnis dessen gelang es, das traditionell breite Leistungsspektrum der Dresdner Unternehmen zu erhalten, ihre Zahl in diesem Zeitraum weit mehr als zu verdoppeln und durch die Niederlassung renommierter Firmen einzelnen Dresdner Branchen zu internationaler Bedeutung zu verhelfen.

Erfreulicherweise war es dabei möglich, besonders die Traditionen der Landeshauptstadt in den Hightech-Industrien wie Mikroelektronik und Informationstechnik aufzugreifen und durch bedeutende Investitionen auszubauen.

Der Flughafen Dresden ist in diese Entwicklungen vielfältig einbezogen. In diesem Zusammenhang müssen auch die Investitionen am Flughafen gesehen werden – seit Anfang der 90er Jahre wurden hier immerhin rund 850 Millionen Mark verbaut. Die Nähe zum Flughafen und zu dessen Verknüpfungen mit dem erdgebundenen Verkehrsnetz ist ein wichtiges Entscheidungskriterium bei der Ansiedlung besonders international operierender Unternehmen und solcher mit engen inhaltlichen Bindungen an den Luftverkehr. So entstand in den vergangenen Jahren eine Wirtschaftsregion in der Nachbarschaft des Flughafens, die dem wirtschaftlichen Potential des Dresdner Nordens eine neue Qualität verlieh.

Am Flughafen Dresden selbst haben sich fast 90 Unternehmen angesiedelt. Sie beschäftigten 1999 insgesamt 1416 Mitarbeiter, gut elf Prozent mehr als noch 1998. Die Mehrzahl dieser Unternehmen ist mit Serviceleistungen im und um den Luftverkehr befasst.

Mit der Ansiedlung der von Firmen wie den Mikroelektronik-Unternehmen Infineon und AMD, der IMA Materialforschung und Anwendungstechnik GmbH oder auch der erfreulichen Entwicklung des Flugzeugbaus in den zur EADS (European Aeronautic Defence and Space Company) gehörenden Elbe-Flugzeugwerken sind im Umfeld des Flughafens wirtschaftliche Potenziale entstanden, die den Standort Dresden prägen.

Der Flughafen als Tourismus-Drehscheibe

Die Reiselust der Sachsen ist sprichwörtlich. Schätzungsweise drei Viertel von ihnen unternehmen jährlich eine Urlaubsreise von wenigstens fünf Tagen Länge. Dabei ist das Flugzeug nach dem PKW bereits jetzt zweitwichtigstes Verkehrsmittel. In den nächsten Jahren kann damit gerechnet werden, dass das Ferienflugsegment eine weitere Steigerung erfährt. Schon jetzt zählt der Flughafen Dresden jährlich über 600.000 Ferienfluggäste.

Nicht nur für den Flughafen, sondern auch für die sächsische Landeshauptstadt ist der Tourismus ein wesentlicher Wirtschaftsfaktor. Mehr als 10 Prozent des städtischen Steueraufkommens werden in diesem Bereich erbracht. Pro Jahr kommen ca. 6 Millionen Besucher nach Dresden, es werden rund als 2 Millionen Übernachtungen gezählt. Die touristische Infrastruktur der Stadt ist in den vergangenen Jahren erheblich ausgebaut worden. Heute erwarten beispielsweise 60 Hotels mit ca. 10.000 Betten die Besucher der Stadt. Der Flughafen Dresden bringt mit seinem kontinuierlich erweiterten Abfertigungspotenzial eine wichtige Komponente in den Wirtschaftsbereich Tourismus ein.

Neues Terminal– kurze Wege

Der Flughafen Dresden verzeichnet seit der Gründung der Flughafen Dresden GmbH im Jahr 1990 ein stetiges, in den Anfangsjahren sogar überdimensionales Wachstum in Bezug auf Flugzeugbewegungen, Passagierzahlen und Frachtumschlag.

Airport

the nineties, the considerable amount of around 850 million DM has been used in constructions. The nearness to the airport and its interrelations with the earth-bound transport network is an important criteria in deciding for the settlement of particularly internationally operating companies and such that have a close connection to air transport because of the nature of their business. In this manner, the past years an economic region has emerged in the vicinity of the airport that has given a new quality to the economic potential of the North of Dresden. Almost 90 companies have settled at the Airport Dresden itself. In 1999, they employed a total of 1,416 staff members just over eleven percent more than in 1998. The majority of these companies deal in service provisions in and around air transport. In the environment of the airport economic potentials have emerged that distinguish the Dresden location with the settlement of companies from the field of microelectronics Infineon and AMD, the IMA Materialforschung und Anwendungstechnik GmbH (Materials Research and Application Technology) or also the pleasant development of aeroplane construction in the Elbe-Flugzeugwerke that are part of EADS (European Aeronautic Defence and Space Company).

The Airport as a Turning wheel for Tourism

The desire to travel of the Saxons is proverbial. An estimation of three quarters of them takes a holiday trip for at least five days each year. The aeroplane has already become the second most important means of transport after the car in this respect. In the coming years one can expect that holiday air travel will increase further. Already the Dresden Airport counts more than 600,000 holiday passengers a year.
Not only for the airport, but also for the Saxon regional capital tourism is an essential economic factor. More than 10 percent of the municipal tax income is reached in this area. Each year, approx. 6 million visitors come to Dresden, more than 2 million overnight stays are accounted for. The tourism infrastructure of the city has been expanded considerably in the past years. Today, for example, 60 hotels with approx. 10,000 beds await the visitors to the city. The Dresden Airport contributes an important component to the economic sector of tourism with its continuously expanding dispatch potential.

New Potential – Short Roads

The Dresden Airport shows since the foundation of the Flughafen Dresden GmbH in 1990 a continuous growth in relation to flight movements, passenger numbers and freight transfer that was oversized even in the initial years. This can be attributed above all to the rising importance of the economic region around Dresden apart from increases in the tourism business. In parallel to this development, planned and timely investments ensure a permanent adjustment of the airport infrastructure to the increasing requirements.

Aim of these efforts is an airport of short roads. This is achieved through direct linkage of air transport with the road systems and railways as well as with a compact, technically up-to-date infrastructure when coping with passengers and aeroplanes. With the realization of the Airport-2000-Concept, the expansion of the Airport-Dresden-Terminal and the new transport connections with cars and city railways a renewed, clear improvement of the effectiveness and attractiveness of the airport is accomplished.

In a dynamic process of adjustment, a complex system of dispatch facilities, transport connections and parking possibilities is being created. Centrepiece of the programme is the new building of the Airport Dresden Terminal with a yearly dispatch capacity of around 3,5 million passengers. This corresponds to the amount of passengers to be expected in Dresden on a mid-term scale. The new terminal will combine the tasks of the two existing terminals – arrivals and departures in one. At the same time, the new terminal offers space for events, restaurants of various categories, recreational

Frachtflugzeug Beluga über der Baustelle des neuen Flughafen Dresden Terminals.
Cargo plane Beluga above the construction site of the new Airport Dresden Terminal.

Flughafen

Dies ist neben den Steigerungen im Touristik-Geschäft vor allem auch der wachsenden Bedeutung der Wirtschaftsregion rund um Dresden zu verdanken. Parallel zu diesen Entwicklungen sorgen planvolle und rechtzeitige Investitionen für eine kontinuierliche Anpassung der Flughafen-Anlagen an die steigenden Anforderungen.

Ziel dieser Anstrengungen ist ein Flughafen der kurzen Wege. Dies erfolgt durch die direkten Verknüpfungen des Luftverkehrs mit der Straße und der Schiene sowie einer kompakten, technisch auf dem neuesten Stand befindlichen Infrastruktur bei der Abfertigung von Passagieren und Flugzeugen. Mit der Verwirklichung des Airport-2000-Konzepts, dem Ausbau des Flughafen-Dresden-Terminals und der neuen Verkehrsanbindungen von Auto und S-Bahn wird eine erneute, deutliche Verbesserung der Leistungsfähigkeit und Attraktivität des Flughafens erreicht

In einem dynamischen Anpassungsprozess entsteht ein komplexes System aus Abfertigungseinrichtungen, Verkehrsanbindungen und Parkmöglichkeiten.

Kernstück des Programms ist der Neubau des Flughafen Dresden Terminals mit einer jährlichen Abfertigungskapazität von rund 3,5 Millionen Passagieren. Dies entspricht dem mittelfristig in Dresden zu erwartenden Fluggastaufkommen.

Das neue Terminal wird die Aufgaben der beiden bisher bestehenden Terminals – Ankunft und Abflug – in sich vereinigen. Gleichzeitig bietet das neue Terminal Platz für Veranstaltungen, Gastronomie unterschiedlicher Kategorien, Erlebnisbereiche inclusive einer 2.000 Quadratmeter umfassenden Aussichtsplattform, Verkaufsflächen und Geschäftsräume. Das neue multifunktionale Fluggastgebäude ist damit auf dem Weg zu einem Kommunikationszentrum der Landeshauptstadt. Der Baustart erfolgte 1998, im März 2001 wird das neue Flughafen Dresden Terminal mit dem Sommerflugplan in Betrieb gehen.

Das multifunktionale Fluggastgebäude entsteht durch den Umbau eines ehemaligen Flugzeughangars und zeichnet sich durch eine außergewöhnliche Architektur aus. Seine einmalige Charakteristik erhält das Gebäude durch die Aufnahme der stählernen Grundstrukturen des Industriebaus – des alten Flugzeughangars – und durch die optisch markanten Gliederungen in ein Mittel- und zwei Seitenschiffe.

Verglaste Fassaden und Dachflächen ermöglichen die optimale Nutzung des Tageslichtes und schaffen eine offene, helle und freundliche Atmosphäre. Einen besonderen Reiz verleihen dem Terminal die Sichtverbindung zu den Abstellflächen der Flugzeuge, den Rollbahnen und zur Start- und Landebahn.

Der Flughafen erhält eine technisch auf dem neuesten Stand befindliche Infrastruktur.
The airport receives a new infrastructure that is on the latest state-of-the-art.

Das umfangreiche Raum- und Flächenangebot des Flugzeughangars, aus dem das neue Terminal 2000 entsteht, ermöglicht es, Großzügigkeit und durchdachte Funktionalität zu elegant zu verbinden.

Das neue Terminal hat eine Grundfläche von 170 x 150 Metern und misst in der Höhe 25 Meter. Auf zwei Ebenen und den Galerien werden Passagiere und Besucher des Flughafens moderne Abfertigungseinrichtungen, zahlreiche Geschäfte und eine attraktive Gastronomie vorfinden. Das Mittelschiff des Gebäudes wird geprägt durch den repräsentativen öffentlichen Bereich mit Serviceeinrichtungen. Die Seitenschiffe werden in den einzelnen Ebenen mit Warteräumen, Büros und operativen Diensten ausgestattet. Eine Neuheit für Dresden sind die Fluggastbrücken, die dem Passagier den Übergang zum bzw. vom Flugzeug schnell, bequem und wettergeschützt ermöglichen.

Verkehrsanbindungen

Eine direkte Autobahnanbindung über das Dreieck Dresden zur A 4 und zur A 13 verbessert bereits seit August 1998 die Erreichbarkeit des Airports entscheidend. Damit wird auch der künftige Zentralbereich des Flughafens über eine neue Zufahrt erschlossen. Die Gesamtgestaltung des neuen Zentralbereiches für den Flughafen Dresden ist auf das Umfeld gestalterisch und funktional abgestimmt.

Der Zentralbereich wird durch das neue Terminal, das gegenüberliegende Parkhaus und den vierspurigen Vorfahrtbereich für Individualverkehr, Busse und Taxen geprägt. Vor Regen schützt eine großzügige Überdachung. Für Parker stehen zirka 1500 Pkw-Stellflächen im neuen Parkhaus zur Verfügung. Zur besseren Orientierung und Kapazitätssteuerung erhält das Parkhaus ein modernes Parkierungssystem.

In einem Tunnel direkt unter der Vorfahrt in der Minus-Eins-Ebene liegt der Bahnhof für den Flughafen-Shuttle (S-Bahn-Anschluss). Die Schnellbahn verbindet den Flughafen über den Hauptbahnhof mit der Stadtmitte und anderen zentralen Punkten Dresdens.

Moderne Technik kommt auch auf dem Vorfeld zum Einsatz. Auf der Ost- und Nordseite des Terminals werden – wie oben schon erwähnt – Andocksysteme für Fluggastbrücken installiert. Ein Rollführungssystem weist den Flugzeugen den Weg von den Rollbahnen bis zur Parkposition am Terminal. Eine vollautomatische Sortieranlage für das Gepäck der abfliegenden Passagiere garantiert schnelle Ladezeiten und eine präzise Zuordnung der Gepäckstücke zum jeweiligen Flug.

Die bessere Integration des Flughafens in das städtische Nahverkehrsnetz durch den S-Bahn-Anschluss, die bereits im August 1998 in Betrieb genommene Direktanbindung an die Autobahnen, der Neubau des Parkhauses sowie das Potential des neuen Terminals tragen als Paket wesentlich zu einer größeren Attraktivität des Dresdner Flughafens bei. Die neue Infrastruktur ist Garant dafür, dass der Flughafen auch weiterhin seine Aufgaben als Dresdens Tor zur Welt und als Motor für die Ansiedlung international renommierter und moderner Wirtschaftsunternehmen erfüllen wird. ■

Airport

areas including a viewing platform comprising 2.000 m², sales areas and office space. The new multifunctional passenger building is thus on its way to become a communication centre for the regional capital. Constructions were started in 1998; in March 2001, the new Airport Dresden Terminal will start operation with the summer flight plan.

The multifunctional passenger building is being constructed through the conversion of a former airplane hangar and is characterise d by its striking architecture. The building receives its unique style through the adoption of the steel foundation structures of the industrial building – the old airplane hangar – and through the optically marked division into middle and two side bays. Glass façades and roofs enable the ideal use of daylight and create an open, bright and pleasant atmosphere. One particular attraction of the terminal is provided by the view to the garages of the airplanes, the runways and the starting and landing ways. The extensive room and areas that the airplane hangar offer for the creation of the new Terminal 2000 enables one to link generosity with well thought-out functionality elegantly. The new terminal as a ground area of 170 x 150 metres and is 25 metres in height. On two levels and the galleries, passengers and visitors of the airport will find modern dispatch facilities, numerous shops and attractive restaurants. The middle bay of the building will be distinguished by the representative public area with service facilities. The side bays will be equipped on each single level with waiting halls, offices and operative services. One novelty in Dresden are the passenger bridges that will allow passengers to cross to or from the airplane rapidly, comfortable and protected from the weather.

Transport Connections

A direct motorway connection across the Dresden triangular to the A 4 and to the A 13 is already improving since 1998 the accessibility of the airport decisively. This also opens the way to the future central area of the airport by means of a new access road. The complete design of the new central area of the Airport Dresden has been adjusted in terms of shape and functional to its environment.

The central area of the new terminal is characterised by the opposite car park and the four-way major road with right of way for individual traffic, busses and taxis. A generous roof protects one from rain. There are around 1.500 car spaces for parkers in the new car park. For the purpose of better orientation and better control of capacities, the car park receives a modern parking system. In a tunnel, directly beneath the major road on the minus-one-level, lies the train station of the airport shuttle (city railway connection). The fast train connects the airport across the main train station with the city centre and other central points of Dresden.

Modern technology has also been employed on the apron. On the East and North sides of the terminal docking systems for passenger, bridges will be installed – as mentioned above. Guiding roller system shows the airplanes their way from the runways to their park position at the terminal. A fully automatic sorting plant for the luggage of departing passengers ensures fast loading times and fast allocation of each piece of luggage to its corresponding flight.

A considerably greater attractiveness of the Dresden Airport will be achieved in one package, as a result of the better integration of the airport into the local transport network of the city through the city-railway-line, the direct link to the motorways already operating since August 1998, the new building of the car park as well as the potential of the new terminal. The new infrastructure is a guarantee for the airport to continue to fulfil its task as Dresden's gate to the world and as a driving force for the settlement of internationally renowned and modern economic enterprises. ■

Schon jetzt zählt der Flughafen Dresden jährlich über 600.000 Ferienfluggäste.
The Airport Dresden is already now counting over 600,000 passengers each year.

Company Profile

MBM Metallbau Dresden GmbH

Geschäftsführer/Managing Director:
Gunter Schreiber

Gründungsjahr/Year of Foundation:
1895

Mitarbeiter/Employees:
110

Umsatz/Turnover:
ca./approx. 25 Mio. DM

Geschäftstätigkeit/Business Activity:
- Fassaden
- Glaskuppeln und -dächer
- Stahlkonstruktionen
- Leichtmetallfenster und -türen
- denkmalgeschützte Stahl- und Glaskonstruktionen
- Forschungs- und Schaugewächshäuser
- Façades
- Glass roofs and domes
- Steel constructions
- Light-metal windows and doors
- Protected steel and glass monuments
- Research and display greenhouses

Referenzobjekte/Reference Objects:
- Bioinstrumentezentrum Jena
- Medienzentrum Leipzig
- Porsche-Werk Leipzig
- Flughafenneubauten Paderborn
- Landeszentralbank Halle
- Fachhochschule Koblenz/Remagen 2. BA
- Universität Mainz, Fachbereich Chemie
- Sparkassenversicherung Sachsen
- Forschungsgewächshausanlage Novartis Crop Protection/Schweiz
- Max-Planck-Institut Dresden
- Media Centre Leipzig
- Porsche Works Leipzig
- New airport constructions Paderborn
- Regional Central Bank Halle
- Technical University Koblenz/Remagen 2. BA
- University of Mainz, Faculty of Chemistry
- Savings Bank Insurance Saxony
- Research greenhouse plant Novartis Crop Protection/Switzerland
- Max-Planck-Institute Dresden

Anschrift/Address:
Niedersedlitzer Straße 60
D-01257 Dresden
Telefon +49 (351) 280 90
Telefax +49 (351) 280 91 03
E-Mail info@mbm-dresden.de
Internet www.mbm-dresden.de

Spezialist für komplizierte Metallbaukonstruktionen

Specialist for complicated metal constructions

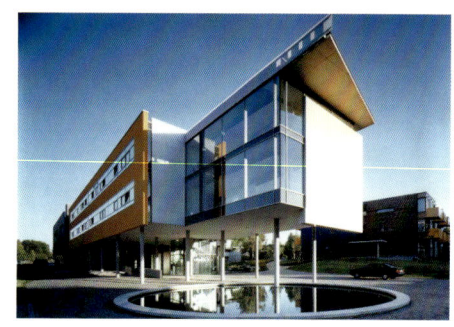

Max-Planck-Institut, Dresden.
Max-Planck-Institute, Dresden.

We have developed from a specialist company for greenhouse construction into a recognized specialist for complex metal constructions, being a metal construction company of Dresden with a tradition of more than 100 years. In order to be able to carry out demanding large projects in metal construction, we dispose of technically and in terms of staff highly equipped construction department, which plans individual solutions using CAD technology as well as of the most modern expertise and sufficient capacities.

Als Dresdner Metallbauunternehmen mit einer über 100jährigen Tradition haben wir uns von der Fachfirma für Gewächshausbau zu einem anerkannten Spezialisten für komplizierte Metallbaukonstruktionen entwickelt.
Wir verfügen über eine personell und technisch auf hohem Niveau ausgestattete Konstruktionsabteilung, in der unter Nutzung von CAD-Technik anspruchsvolle individuelle Lösungen geplant werden sowie über modernstes Know-how und ausreichende Kapazitäten, um anspruchsvolle Großaufträge im Metallbau übernehmen zu können.

Fachhochschule Koblenz – Teilansicht Lehrgebäude mit Glasgang, Treppenhaus und Aula/Mensa.
Technical University Koblenz – Part view of the building for class instructions with glass passage, staircase and assembly hall / Mensa.

It is our aim to confront the architectural and construction challenges of our time and to realize projects in first-rate skilful quality. In this, we also rely on our experiences from the co-operations with many renowned architectural offices. Especially in the past years of difficult economic situations in the construction industry, the company was able to improve its financial results continuously.
It is our aim that MBM would mean to our clients: Makes the Best Possible. ■

Medienzentrum Leipzig.
Media Centre, Leipzig.

Unser Ziel ist es, architektonische und bautechnische Herausforderungen unserer Zeit anzunehmen und handwerklich einwandfrei umzusetzen. Wir stützen uns dabei auch auf unsere Erfahrungen aus der Zusammenarbeit mit vielen namhaften Architekturbüros.
Das Unternehmen konnte gerade in Zeiten einer schwierigen Baukonjunktur in den letzten Jahren seine wirtschaftlichen Ergebnisse ständig verbessern.
Unser Ziel ist es, dass MBM für unsere Kunden heißt: Macht Besonderes Möglich. ■

Bioinstrumentezentrum Jena – Haupteingang zur Glashalle mit „Auge" links und Modul 1.
Centre of Bio-instruments Jena – Main entrance to the glass hall with "Eye" left and module 1.

Company Profile

Test Line – komplex, individuell, zukunftsweisend

Test Line – complex, individual, trend-setting

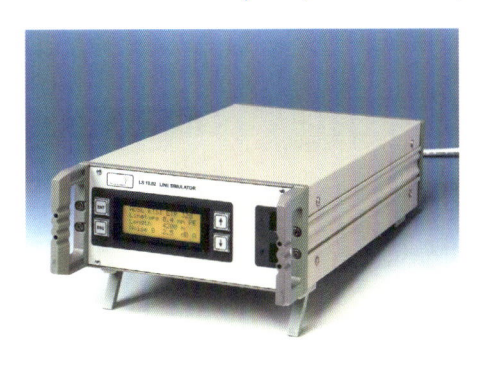

TEST LINE ELECTRONICS
Testkonzeptionen
Systemintegration
Automation
Projektierung

Test Line entwickelt Hard- und Software für Testanwendungen in vielfältigen Industriebranchen mit dem Schwerpunkt Telekommunikationsindustrie. Ebenso bietet das Unternehmen aber auch Lösungen für die Elektronikindustrie insgesamt, die Bauelementenindustrie, Sensorik oder die Automotive-Rebuilding-Industrie an.

Langjährige Erfahrung
Ein Team von Fachleuten mit langjähriger Erfahrung in Projektierung, Entwicklung und Fertigung von Hightech-Lösungen im Bereich der Prüftechnik und Testautomaten bildet die Basis zur Umsetzung von kundenoptimierten und branchenspezifischen Einzel- und Komplettlösungen im Test-Equipment-Sektor. Auf dem Gebiet der Erstellung von In-Circuit-Test-Adaptern und Programmen steht ein umfassendes Know-how zur Verfügung. Die Palette des Leistungsangebotes wird zusätzlich durch Projektierung und Realisierung von vollautomatischen Stand-alone-Testsystemen oder In-line-Lösungen abgerundet.

Hoher Qualitätsstandard
Zur Realisierung vielfältiger Testaufgaben und komplexer Systemlösungen steht ein umfangreiches Leistungspaket zur Verfügung. Die Forderung nach Einhaltung der Qualitätsstandards auf Basis ISO 9000 stellt an jeden Testsystem-Anbieter sehr hohe Ansprüche. Diesen gerecht zu werden, ist für uns eine Selbstverständlichkeit.

Umfassender Service
Die Test Line electronics GmbH garantiert Ihnen ebenfalls so wichtige Faktoren wie kurzfristige Projektrealisierung und umfassende Serviceleistung. Auf dieser Basis steht Ihnen ein zukunftsorientierter, zuverlässiger und leistungsstarker Partner zur Seite. ∎

Test Line develops hardware and software for testapplications in a wide range of industrial sectors, most notably the telecommunications industry. The company also offer solutions for the electronics industry as a whole, for the components industry, the sensor technology sector and for the automotive rebuilding industry.

Many years of experience
A team of experts, with many years of experience in the project management, developement an production of high-tech solutions in the field of testing technology and automatic testing systems, devices individual and complete solutions in the test equipment sector, tailored to provide customers with the best possible results and to meet the needs of specific sectors. The company has extensive expertise at its disposal in terms of the creation of in-circuit-test adapters and programms. To round off the range of services we plan and implement fully automatic stand-alone test systems or inline solutions.

High standard of quality
There is a comprehensive package of services aviable for implementing a wide array of different test procedures and system solutions. The need to conform to ISO 9000 quality standards places very high demands on every supplier of test systems. Needless to say, we meets those requirements.

Comprehensive service
Test Line electronics GmbH can also guarantee very important performance factors, such as short-term project completion and a comprehensive pallet of services. You will come to value Test Line electronics as a strong, reliable partner, whose products will set the pace. ∎

Test line electronics GmbH

Geschäftsführer/Manager:
Dipl.-Physiker Dietmar Kramer

Gründungsjahr/Year of Foundation:
1996

Mitarbeiter/Employees:
16

Geschäftstätigkeit/Business Activity:
Kundenspezifisches Test-Equipment
Customized Test-Applications

Anschrift/Address:
Gostritzer Straße 61–63
D-01217 Dresden
Telefon +49 (351) 87 18-381
Telefax +49 (351) 87 18-453
E-Mail   tle.dd@testline.de
Internet www.testline.de

Company Profile

Hightech-Messtechnik für das neue Jahrtausend

High-Tech Measuring Technology for the New Millennium

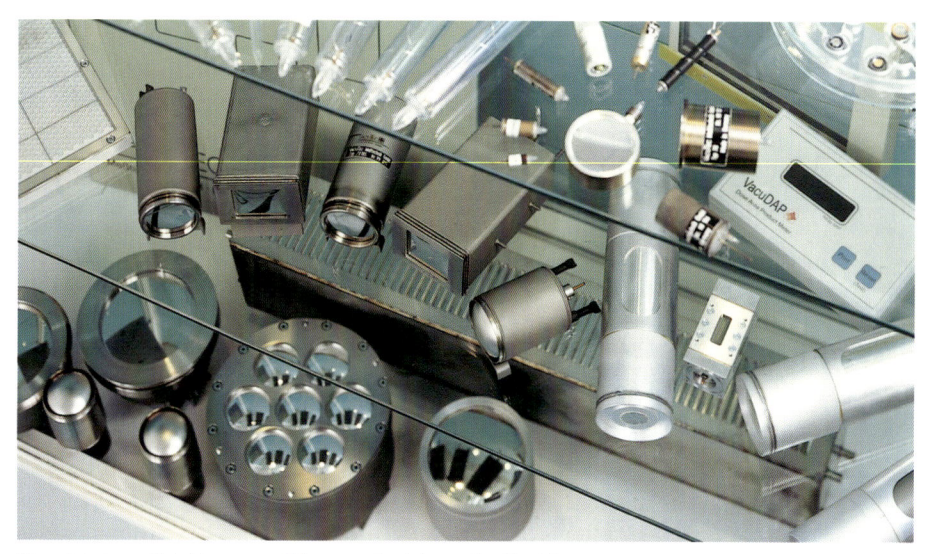

VacuTec Messtechnik GmbH

Geschäftsführender Gesellschafter/Managing Partner:
Dr. Christian Feige, Dipl.-Physiker

Gründungsjahr/Year of Foundation:
1956, Neuformierung 1992

Mitarbeiter/Employees:
37

Umsatz/Turnover:
5 Mio. DM

Geschäftstätigkeit/Business Activity:
Entwicklung und Fertigung von Sensoren zur Erfassung von Alpha-, Beta-, Gamma- und Röntgenstrahlen
Development and production of sensors for the detection of Alpha-, Beta-, Gamma- and X-radiation

Auslandsvertretungen/Foreign Branch
Argentinien
Brasilien
Japan
Chile
Taiwan
USA
Belgien
Frankreich
Großbritannien
Schweden
Iran

Anschrift/Address:
Dornblüthstraße 14
D-01277 Dresden
Telefon +49 (351) 317 24-0
Telefax +49 (351) 310 50 85
E-Mail vacutec@t-online.de
Internet www.vacutec-gmbh.de

Verschiedene Detektoren zur Messung ionisierender Strahlung.
Various detectors for the measuring of ionized radiation.

Der Mensch hat leider nur fünf Sinne. Um z. B. Radioaktivität festzustellen, benötigt er Hilfsmittel – Detektoren. VacuTec Messtechnik GmbH entwickelt und produziert sie bereits seit 1956. Ein Höchstmaß an ausgefeilter Technologie und Know how ist nötig, um die heute weltweit geforderten hohen Nachweisempfindlichikeiten zu erfüllen. Mit Hochvakuum-Technik, Chemie, Gasdosierung, Reinraumatmosphäre und nicht zuletzt mit seinen solide ausgebildeten Mitarbeitern, die nach dem Qualitätssicherungssystem nach ISO 9001 arbeiten, sichert das Unternehmen den Erfolg. 1992 neu formiert, ist VacuTec Messtechnik GmbH heute ein Weltmarktführer auf diesem Gebiet und alleiniger Hersteller allseitig geschweißter Ionisationskammern für die radiometrische Dickenmessung. Dies gilt auch für die absolute Neuheit in dieser Branche: die Ionisationskammer-Arrays mit dünnsten Edelstahl- Strahleneintrittsfenstern für die bewegungsfreie 100 %-Querprofilkontolle zu. Hierüber liegen für das Unternehmen bereits erteilte Patente vor.

Weitere Spitzenerzeugnisse sind Ionisationskammern für den medizinischen Bereich (Dreifelder-Messkammer für Belichtungsautomaten an Röntgenanlagen und Dosisflächenprodukt-Messgeräte zur Patientendosis-Messung). Gerade Letztere sind zur Minimierung der Strahlenbelastung im medizinischen Bereich von außerordentlicher Bedeutung. ∎

Unfortunately, the human being has only five senses. In order to perceive radioactivity, for example, he needs aids – detectors. VacuTec Messtechnik GmbH develops and produces these since 1956 already. The highest degree of sophisticated technology and know how is necessary in order to fulfil the worldwide demand of high detection sensitivity. With high-vacuum technology, chemistry, gas apportioning, clean room atmosphere and last not least with its thoroughly trained staff that work according to ISO 9001 quality assurance system, the company secures its success. Newly formed in 1992, VacuTec Messtechnik GmbH today is a world market leader on this field and sole manufacturer off all-welded ionized chambers for radiometric thickness measurement. This is also valid for the absolute innovation in this branch: the ionization chamber-arrays with the thinnest stainless steel radiation entrance windows for position-free 100 %-edge control. For this product, the company possesses already registered patents.

Further top products are the ionization chambers for the field of medicine (three-field measuring chamber for sensory x-ray exposure control units and dose area products measuring applications for patient dose measurement). Especially the latter are extremely important for minimising the radiation exposure in the field of medicine. ∎

Entwicklungsbesprechung vor Ort – Auswertung eines Designvorschlages.
On-site development discussions – Evaluation of a design proposal.

Company Profile

Wissenschaftlicher Rat für Zukunft der Regionen

Scientific Advice for the Future of the Regions

Eingang zum Institut.
Entrance to the institute.

Das Dresdner Institut für ökologische Raumentwicklung e. V. (IÖR) wurde am 1. Januar 1992 auf Empfehlung des Wissenschaftsrates gegründet. Als eine von der Bundesrepublik und dem Freistaat Sachsen gemeinsam finanzierte Forschungseinrichtung gehört das IÖR mit seinen insgesamt etwa 100 Mitarbeiterinnen und Mitarbeitern zur Wissenschaftsgemeinschaft Gottfried Wilhelm Leibniz e. V. Organe des Instituts sind das Kuratorium, der Vorstand und der Wissenschaftliche Beirat.

Das Institut erforscht Grundfragen der ökologischen Erneuerung altindustrialisierter Regionen, der Landes- und Regionalentwicklung und der Stadtökologie und untersucht darüber hinaus Grundfragen des Wohnungswesens. Die Haupt-arbeitsrichtung des Instituts ist durch das Themenfeld „Siedlungsentwicklung und Zusammenarbeit auf interkommunaler Ebene als Mittel zur Schaffung nachhaltiger Raumstrukturen" gekennzeichnet.

Das Institut kooperiert mit einer Vielzahl von Partnern in Wissenschaft, Politik und Verwaltung. Die Zusammenarbeit mit der Technischen Universität Dresden ist im Rahmen des Raumwissenschaftlichen Kompetenzzentrums Dresden besonders eng. Darüber hinaus bestehen enge Forschungskooperationen mit Partnern in Mittel-, Ost- und Südosteuropa sowie der Ohio State University in Columbus/Ohio. ■

The Dresdner Institut für ökologische Raumentwicklung e. V. /IÖR (Dresden Institut for ecological land development) was founded on 1st January 1992 on recommendation of the Scientific Council. The IÖR belongs with a total of around 100 employees to the society Wissenschaftsgemeinschaft Gottfried Wilhelm Leibniz e. V. as a research institution financed by both the federal government and the Free State of Saxony. The organs of the institute are the committee, the executive board and the scientific council.

The institute investigates fundamental issues of ecological regeneration of formerly industrialised regions, of land and regional development and of urban ecology, furthermore it investigates basic questions relating to housing. The main field of work of the institute is characterised by the subject: land-settlement development and co-operation on intercommunal level as a means of creating lasting spatial structures.

The institute co-operates with a number of partners of science, politics and administration. Especially close is the co-operation with the Technical University of Dresden with the framework of the Raumwissenschaftlichen Kompetenzzentrum Dresden (Scientific Spatial Competence Centre Dresden). Furthermore, there are close research co-operations with partners in Middle, East and South-East Europe as well as the Ohio State University in Columbus/Ohio. ■

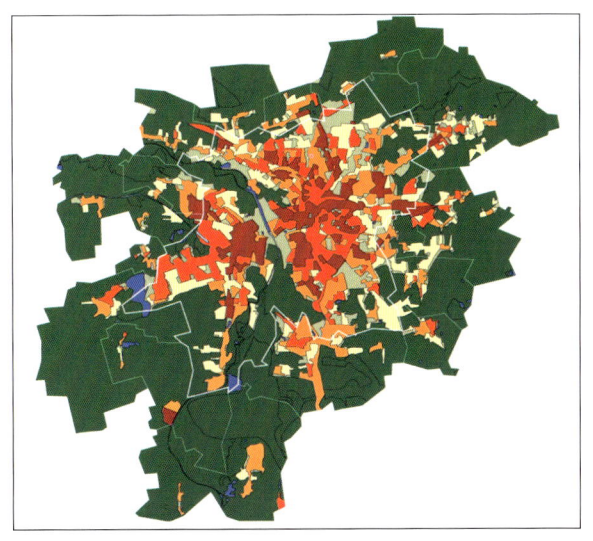

Computergrafiken und …
Computer graphics and …

Institut für ökologische Raumentwicklung e.V.

Vorstand und Direktor/Executive Board:
Prof. Dr. Bernhard Müller

Gründungsjahr/Year of Foundation:
1992

Mitarbeiter/Employees:
ca./approx. 100

Geschäftstätigkeit/Business Activity:
Anwendungsorientierte Grundlangenforschung in Fragen einer ökologischen Raumentwicklung
Forschungsschwerpunkte:
- Ressourcenschonende Flächennutzung
- Ressourceneffizientes Bauen und Wohnen
- Nachhaltiger Strukturwandel
- Europäische Integration

Application-oriented fundamental research in issues of ecological land development
Focal points of research:
- Resource-efficient use of space
- Resource-efficient construction and living
- Lasting structural change
- European integration

Anschrift/Address:
Weberplatz 1
D-01217 Dresden
Telefon   +49 (351) 46 79-0
Telefax   +49 (351) 46 79-212
E-Mail   Raumentwicklung@ioer.de
Internet www.ioer.de

… Luftbildaufnahmen bilden die Grundlage für Entscheidungen in der Raumplanung.
… Aerial photographs are the basis for decisions in spatial planning.

City-Management

Dresdens City – sehenswert, lebenswert, attraktiv

Dresden's City – worth seeing, worth living in, attractive

Als ich im Jahre 1995 im Spätherbst erstmals geschäftlich nach Dresden kam, war ich überrascht und fasziniert von dieser Stadt. Der Blick von der Augustusbrücke auf die Altstadt und der Gang über die Brühlsche Terrasse hat mich schnell meine Vorurteile (Ansammlung von Plattenbauten mit Semperoper und Zwinger) beiseite schieben lassen. Diese Stadt hat mehr. Das anschließende tiefere Eindringen in die Innenstadt hat zwar manch architektonische Geschmacksfrage zu Tage gebracht, aber die anschließende Fahrt durch die Stadtteile wie Striesen, Blasewitz, Loschwitz und Weißer Hirsch haben mich in meinem ersten Eindruck bestätigt. Eine solche Vielzahl von gut erhaltenen Villenvierteln aus der Zeit der Jahrhundertwende hatte ich nicht erwartet.

„In Chemnitz wird gearbeitet, in Leipzig wird gehandelt und in Dresden wird gelebt." Dies ist ein Ausspruch, den man von alteingesessenen Dresdnern des Öfteren mit einem Augenzwinkern hört. Der vermutlich aus der Jahrhundertwende stammende Satz zeigt, wie stolz die Dresdner auf ihre Stadt sind. Man hat den Eindruck, dass sich in Dresden im Gegensatz zu fast allen anderen Städten der früheren DDR eine bürgerliche Schicht erhalten hat.

40 Jahre Sozialismus haben in Dresden weniger Spuren hinterlassen als in fast allen anderen Städten der ehemaligen DDR.

Die Stadt ist weitläufig und geräumig. Einen Eindruck davon bekommt man schon, wenn man sich aus Richtung Autobahn der Stadt nähert und einen Blick auf den faszinierenden Elblauf und die Stadt in der Landschaft hat.

Auch verfügt die Stadt Dresden über ungewöhnlich viele Grünflächen – sei es das Elbufer, das

Taschenbergpalais und Cholerabrunnen.
Taschenberg Palace and Cholera Well.

Rückansicht Semperoper und Verwaltungsgebäude.
Rear view of the Semper opera and administration buildings.

Wolfgang Wirz

Der Autor wurde 1947 in Trier geboren. Nach dem Abitur begann er eine Ausbildung zum Handelsassistenten bei der Firma KARSTADT in Hamburg. Einer Tätigkeit als Assistent der Verkaufsleitung in der Hauptverwaltung in Essen schlossen sich mehrere Stationen als Geschäftsführer in folgenden Verkaufshäusern an: Wilhelmshaven, Mönchengladbach-Rheydt, Hamburg-Wandsbek und seit 1997 Dresden.

Seit 1997 ist Wolfgang Wirz Präsident des Landesverbandes der Mittel- und Großbetriebe des Einzelhandels in Sachsen und Mitglied des Präsidiums der Bundesarbeitsgemeinschaft der Mittel- und Großbetriebe des Einzelhandels und seit 1999 Vorsitzender des Vereins Citymanagement Dresden.

The author was born in Trier in 1947. After attaining his A-levels, he started training as a merchant's assistant at the department store KARSTADT in Hamburg. He then worked as assistant to the sales management in it's headquarters in Essen and afterwards occupied various positions for the same company as managing director in the department stores following of the following cities: Wilhelmshaven, Mönchengladbach-Rheydt, Hamburg-Wandsbek and since 1997 in Dresden.

Since 1997, Wolfgang Wirz is President of the Regional Association of middle-size and large Companies of the Retail Trade in Saxony and Member of the Executive Board of the Federal Working Committee of middle-size and large Companies of the Retail Trade and since 1999, Chairman of the Association for City Management Dresden.

City-Management

In 1995, when I came to Dresden on business for the first time in late autumn, I was fascinated and surprised by this city. The view from Augustus Bridge on the historic part of the city and walking across the Brühlsche Terrace removed my prejudgements about it very quickly (collection of slab-stone block constructions with Semperopera and Zwinger). This city offers a lot more. Afterwards, questions of architectural taste emerged while deeply penetrating into the inner city, but following a trip through the districts of Striesen, Blasewitz, Loschwitz and Weißer Hirsch, my first impression was confirmed. I did not expect such a great number of well-kept exclusive residential areas from the turn of century period.

"In Chemnitz one works, in Leipzig one trades and in Dresden one lives". This is a saying one can often hear mischievously from the old traditional citizens of Dresden. This saying, probably dating from the turn of century, shows how proud the citizens of Dresden are of their city. One has the impression that in Dresden contrary to almost all other cities of the former DDR, a bourgeois middle-class has been maintained.

40 years of socialism have left behind in Dresden less traces than in almost all other cities of the former DDR. The city is spacious and covers a wide area. This is the first impression one has, when getting closer to the city from the motorway, one has a view on the fascinating course of the river Elbe, and the city imbedded in its landscape.
Furthermore, the City of Dresden has unusual stretches of green areas – be it the shores of the Elbe river, excellent possibilities for walks and bicycle tours into the Sächsische Schweiz (Switzerland of Saxony) or the Dresdner Heide (Dresden Heath), which is a large uninterrupted area of woods directly adjoining to the city, a unique reservoir of fresh air or the large garden located in the middle of the city.

City in the Greens is an attribute that has been given to Dresden. The fact that distinguishes Dresden from other cities is that a relatively high share of inhabitants still lives in locations of the inner city. Of course, there is like anywhere else a tendency to move to the countryside, however, the great efforts of all participating parties to maintain the urban character of the inner city have had positive effects on the ability to live in it.

The vigorous destruction of the inner city in the last weeks of the war is the reason why Dresden is still a city in reconstruction. Fallow land in the inner city is only filled slowly with new constructions. The right method of reconstruction is being discussed vehemently. High prices for real estate,

Akademie der Künste.

Academy of Fine Arts.

architectural competitions, building restrictions and very hesitant procedures from the part of urban developers in the shaping of new structures for the inner city, do not make it easy for investors to decide for a settlement in the City of Dresden. However, ten years after the German reunification one can sometimes also be glad not to have taken a careless and hasty decision, which one perhaps would have regretted again today. At the forefront stands now the art of urban construction instead of urban construction. Municipal authorities and investors feel that their great responsibility lies in the reconstruction of the inner city. In this regard,

one is proud of the diversity in architectural styles that is meanwhile recognizable. Whereas the contours of the future Altmarkt (old market) are outlined already, the design of the Neumarkt (new market) is still intensely debated. Here, the supporters of a historic Neumarkt with the reconstruction of up to 300 historical buildings are opposed to the supporters of a combination of historical reconstructions with new buildings.

What may be accomplished with present construction art can be seen in the reconstruction of the Frauenkirche. Anyone who saw, like me, the

City-Management

hervorragende Möglichkeiten für Spaziergänge und Fahrradfahrten in Richtung Sächsische Schweiz bietet, oder die Dresdner Heide, ein großes zusammenhängendes Waldgebiet unmittelbar an die Stadt angrenzend, ein einzigartiges Frischluftreservat oder der Große Garten mitten in der Stadt liegend.

Stadt im Grünen ist ein Attribut, das man Dresden gegeben hat. Was Dresden von anderen Städten unterscheidet ist, dass ein relativ hoher Anteil seiner Bewohner noch in Innenstadtlagen wohnt. Zwar gibt es, wie andernorts auch, eine Tendenz zum Umzug aufs Land, doch wirken sich die großen Anstrengungen aller Beteiligten, die Urbanität der Innenstadt zu erhalten, positiv auf ihre Bewohnbarkeit aus.

Die starke Zerstörung der Innenstadt in den letzten Kriegswochen ist Grund dafür, dass Dresden nach wie vor eine Stadt im Aufbau ist. Brachflächen in der Innenstadt füllen sich nur langsam mit Bauten. Der richtige Weg zum Wiederaufbau wird heftig diskutiert. Hohe Grundstückspreise, Architektenwettbewerbe, Bauauflagen und ein sehr behutsames Vorgehen der Stadtentwickler bei der Neuausformung der Innenstadt machen es den Investoren nicht leicht, sich für eine Ansiedlung in der Dresdner City zu entscheiden. Allerdings kann man in Dresden zehn Jahre nach der Wiedervereinigung hier und da auch froh darüber sein, nicht frühzeitig und leichtfertig Entscheidungen gefällt zu haben, die man vielleicht heute schon bereut hätte. Stadtbau-Kunst statt Stadtbau steht im Vordergrund. Stadt und Investoren spüren ihre große Verantwortung bei dem Wiederaufbau der Innenstadt. Dabei ist man stolz auf die Vielfalt der Architektur, die sich mittlerweile schon erkennbar macht. Während sich die Konturen für den künftigen Altmarkt schon abzeichnen, wird um die Gestaltung des Neumarktes noch hart gerungen. Hier stehen sich die Befürworter eines historischen Neumarktes mit dem Wiederaufbau von bis zu 300 historischen Gebäuden und die Befürworter einer Verquickung zwischen historischem Wiederaufbau und Neubauten gegenüber. Was heutige Baukunst zu leisten vermag, kann man am Wiederaufbau der Frauenkirche erkennen. Wer, wie ich, Mitte der 90er Jahre die Restruine und den umgebenden Trümmerhaufen gesehen hat, konnte Zweifel haben, ob ein Wiederaufbau der Frauenkirche sinnvoll ist. Alle Zweifel sind inzwischen längst widerlegt. Mit welcher Überzeugung, Kraft und Begeisterung der Wiederaufbau betrieben wird, ist schon beispielhaft. Es macht einfach Freude, den Baufortschritt mitzuerleben und zu spüren, dass hier etwas ganz Großes entsteht.

Bei der Bebauung des Wiener Platzes vor dem Hauptbahnhof ist die Stadt mit dem Bau eines Tunnels und weiteren Baumaßnahmen in Vorleistung getreten. Den erwarteten Investoren, die die Grundstücke erwerben und die Vorleistungen der Stadt wieder ausgleichen, bietet sich hier Bauland in bester Citylage.

Anders als beispielsweise in Leipzig hat man in Dresden frühzeitig erkannt, dass ein überdimensioniertes Wachstum von Verkaufsflächen an nicht integrierten Standorten den Innenstädten erheblichen Schaden zufügt. Gleichwohl befindet sich der innerstädtische Einzelhandel in Dresden in einem ständigen Abwehrkampf gegen geplante großflächige Einzelhandelsansiedlungen am Standrand und außerhalb der Stadt im Einzugsgebiet. Die innerstädtischen Einzelhändler sind bemüht, das Angebot in der City weiter zu verbessern. Das Defizit an kleinen, möglichst

Prager Straße.
Prague Street.

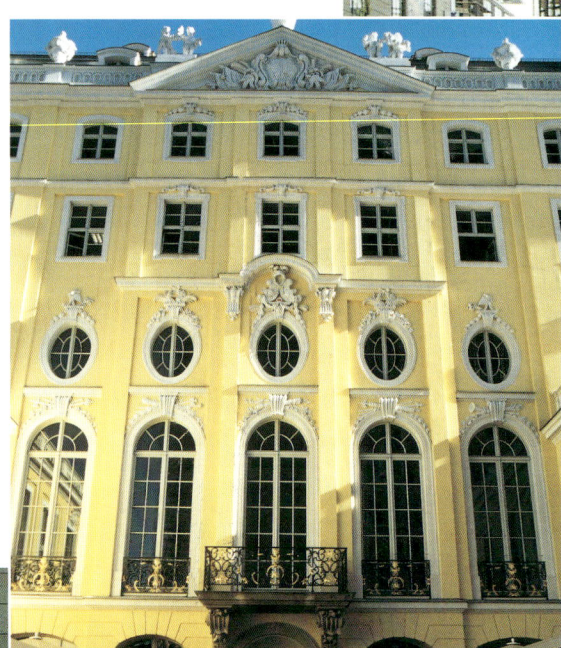

Cosel-Palais.
Cosel Palace.

Prager Straße.
Prague Street.

106

City-Management

remaining ruins and the heap of rubble surrounding it in the mid-nineties, could have doubts whether the reconstruction of the Frauenkirche made any sense at all. All doubts have meanwhile been removed. The zeal, which is placed in the reconstruction in terms of conviction, strength and enthusiasm, is exemplary. It simply gives great pleasure to experience the progress of constructions and to feel that something really great is developing here. In building up the Wiener Platz (Viennese Square) in front of the main train station, the municipal authorities provided advance services with the construction of a tunnel and other building measures. Expected investors that purchase real estate and settle the advance services of the municipal authorities again have land available here for building that is situated in the best city location.

Contrary to Leipzig for example, in Dresden it was recognised early that a disproportionate growth of sales areas in not integrated locations would damage the inner cities considerably. Nonetheless, the inner city retail trade in Dresden is continuously counteracting plans for large spaces of retail settlements on the city's outskirts and outside the city in its catchment area. The inner city retail shops take great effort to improve the provision within the city further. The deficit in small specialist shops, possibly managed by their owners, and also in restaurant businesses is being removed slowly, however, too slowly for the citizens of Dresden justifiably. Any further settlement of commercial enterprises is welcomed, because it helps improve the attractiveness of the inner city. The saying "Competition stimulates business" can be experienced here as a practical example. This is why the accusation of investors in non-integrated locations that the inner city trade only wants to see removed unwanted competition, is not applicable.

One proof for the possible and necessary extension of inner city trade is its value of centrality. The purchasing power of the citizens of Dresden relating to retail trade lies at approx. 4.4 billion DM a year. This sum corresponds roughly to the total turnover of the Dresden retail trade as a whole and the statistical value of centrality amounts thus to 1.0. For an upper centre with a surrounding area

UFA-Kino.

UFA Cinema.

City-Management

inhabergeführten Fachgeschäften und auch gastronomischen Betrieben wird langsam beseitigt, jedoch in Schritten, die den Dresdnern verständlicherweise nicht schnell genug gehen. Jede weitere Ansiedlung von Handelsbetrieben wird begrüßt, weil sie die Attraktivität der Innenstadt verbessern hilft. „Konkurrenz belebt das Geschäft" kann hier am praktischen Beispiel erlebt werden. Deshalb läuft der Vorwurf der Investoren an nichtintegrierten Standorten, der innerstädtische Handel wolle sich nur missliebige Konkurrenz vom Halse schaffen, ins Leere.

Ein Beleg für den möglichen und nötigen Ausbau des innerstädtischen Handels ist der Zentralitätswert. Die einzelhandelsrelevante Kaufkraft der Dresdner liegt bei ca. 4,4 Milliarden DM im Jahr.

Altmarkt.
Old Market.

Baustelle Altmarktgalerie (ECE).
Building site Old Market Gallery (ECE).

Diese Summe entspricht in etwa dem Gesamtumsatz des Dresdner Einzelhandels, somit beträgt die Zentralitätskennziffer 1,0.
Für ein Oberzentrum mit einem nicht zu unterschätzenden Umland ist dieser Zentralitätswert zu niedrig. Der Wert zeigt an, dass die Kaufkraftzuflüsse aus dem Umland noch nicht stark genug ausgeprägt sind. Ein Grund hierfür ist sicherlich auch der noch nicht perfekte Branchenmix in Dresdens City, was jedoch mit Riesenschritten behoben wird. Zu schaffen macht sicher auch die noch nicht befriedigende Verkehrssituation in Dresdens City. Während die Zahl der Besucher mit PKW deutlich ansteigt, haben Verantwortliche in der Stadtverwaltung Anfang der 90er Jahre versucht, den ÖPNV deutlich zu bevorteilen. Erst in jüngster Zeit gibt es Anzeichen zu integriertem Verkehrskonzept für alle Mobilitätsgruppen.
Bei der Erschließung des Umlandes ist die Verbesserung der Verkehrsinfrastruktur für PKWs mindestens genauso wichtig wie das Erreichen neuer Kundengruppen durch zusätzliche S-Bahn-Strecken.

Dresden als Standort einer Technischen Universität mit über 25.000 Studenten sowie dem Sitz der früheren Firma Robotron war prädestiniert für den Ausbau des Bereichs Mikroelektronik. Dies ist in beispielhafter Weise durch die

Karstadt Dresden in der Prager Straße.
Karstadt Dresden in Prague Street.

City-Management

that should not be underestimated this value of centrality is too low. The value shows that the influx of purchasing power from the surrounding area is not strongly developed yet. One reason for this is surely also the not yet perfected mixture of branches in the City of Dresden, a fact that is being resolved in giant steps however. Another factor surely is also the not yet satisfactorily transport situation in the City of Dresden. Whereas the number of visitors with passenger cars is increasing markedly, responsible persons in the municipal authorities have tried at the beginning of the 90ies to grant preferential advantages to the ÖPNV (local public passenger transport). Only in recent times, there are signs of an integrated transport concept for all mobile groups. In the development of the surrounding areas, the improvement of transport infrastructure for passenger cars is at least just as important as reaching new groups of customers through additional lines of the city railway.

Dresden was predestined for the expansion of the field of microelectronics, being a location with a technical university with over 25,000 students as well as the seat of the former Robotron Company. This has been accomplished in exemplary manner through the settlement of Siemens Infineon and AMD as well as various supplier companies. A further highlight is the construction of a glass manufacturing hall for the Volkswagen Company. Interestingly, in this case we are actually dealing with the return of a factory operated in the inner city. Buyers of luxury vehicles can observe the final assembly of their car on site and receive the vehicle in connection with cultural events here in Dresden.

Far more than 6 million people visit Dresden each year. However, the share of tourist from overseas is increasing disproportionately. Apart from the known tourist attractions and cultural places, there are in Dresden also cultural and artistic events in society rooms and also in enterprises. Several supraregional events lure visitors each year from the extended surrounding areas. This includes the Dixie Festival in May, the City Festival in August and the Striezel Market in the season of Advent. In the year 1996, the tax group City Marketing was founded as an instrument for the integral city development and marketing of the city in the co-operations between private and public sectors. At the beginning of 1997, four working groups inner city and centre management, retail trade, tourism, congresses, exhibitions and economic sector and regions took up their activities. In a secluded meeting, the guideline portrayed below for positioning the City of Dresden was worked out.

Since summer 1999, the Association of City Management Dresden has replaced the working group inner city and centre management. This association – a co-operation between private and public bodies – has the purpose to promote the development of the regional capital Dresden, particularly of the city centre in the areas between main train station up to the streets Hauptstraße and Königsstraße. It is intended to contribute to the improvement of the exploitation of the city centre of the regional capital Dresden, particularly in it's tasks in the areas of trade and service provisions, tourism, working and

Einmaliges Projekt – Wiederaufbau der Frauenkirche.
Unique project: Reconstruction of the Frauenkirche.

Coselpalais und Frauenkirche.
Cosel Palace and Frauenkirche.

Altmarkt mit Kreuzkirche.
Old Market with Kreuzkirche.

City-Management

Ansiedlung von Siemens Infineon und AMD plus diverser Zuliefererbetriebe gelungen.

Ein weiterer Höhepunkt ist die Errichtung einer Gläsernen Manufaktur der Firma Volkswagen. Hierbei handelt es sich interessanterweise um die Rückkehr eines Fabrikationsbetriebes in die Innenstadt. Käufer eines Luxusfahrzeuges können die Endmontage ihres Wagens vor Ort beobachten und das Fahrzeug verbunden mit kulturellen Ereignissen hier in Dresden in Empfang nehmen.

Weit über 6 Millionen Besucher zählt Dresden jährlich. Dabei steigt der Anteil der Überseetouristen überproportional. Neben den bekannten touristischen Attraktionen und Kulturstätten gibt es in Dresden auch Kunst- und Kulturveranstaltungen in gesellschaftlichen Räumen und auch Unternehmen

Mehrere überregionale Veranstaltungen locken alljährlich Besucher aus dem weiten Umland an. Dazu zählen das Dixiefestival im Mai, das Stadtfest im August und der Striezelmarkt in der Adventszeit. Als ein Instrument der ganzheitlichen Stadtentwicklung und Vermarktung der Stadt im Zusammenwirken des privaten und öffentlichen Sektors wurde im Jahre 1996 eine Steuergruppe Stadtmarketing gegründet. Vier Arbeitskreise Innenstadt und Zentrenmanagement/Einzelhandel/Tourismus, Kongresse, Ausstellungen und Wirtschaft und Region nahmen ihre Arbeit Anfang 1997 auf. In einer Klausurtagung wurde das nachfolgend abgebildete Leitbild für die Stadt Dresden erarbeitet.

Leitbild für die Stadt Dresden

Hochtechnologie- und Wissenschaftsstandort	Kunst- und Kulturstadt	Tourismus	Stadt in der Landschaft
1 Dresden wird ein führender Standort der Mikroelektronik in Forschung, Entwicklung und Produktion.	1 Dresden profiliert sich zur Kunst- und Kulturmetropole von europäischen Rang.	1 Dresden bietet eine einzigartige Kombination von Kunst, Kultur, Wirtschaft und Wissenschaft.	1 Dresden verbindet Urbanität und Landschaft zu einem lebenswerten Stadtraum. Natur und Naherholung beginnen mitte in der Stadt.
2 Dresden zieht weitere Zukunftstechnologien an. Wir verstärken die breite Basis der Dresdner Hochschul- und Forschungslandschaft.	2 Dresden verbindet große kulturelle Vergangenheit mit kühnen zeitgenössischen Projekten.	2 Dresden entwickelt sich zur Tourismusmetropole und zur Tagungs- und Kongreßstadt von internationalem Rang.	2 Dresden setzt mit moderner Architektur und Städtebau neue Akzente – stehts dem hohen Niveau der Vergangenheit verpflichtet.
3 Dresden schafft günstige Rahmenbedingungen für Unternehmensgründungen, insbesondere im technologieorientierten Dienstleistungsbereich und stärkt das breite Spektrum der mittelständigen Wirtschaft.	3 Dresden wächst als Veranstaltungsort von bedeutenden nationalen und internationalen Ereignissen in den Bereichen Kultur und Sport.	3 Dresden nimmt Besucher offen auf und ist im besonderem Maße gastfreundlich.	3 Dresden gibt der Entwicklung der Innnenstadt zu einem attraktiven Dienstleistungs- und Einkaufszentrum höchste Priorität.
4 Dresden baut seine Position als Tor zum Osten weiter aus.	4 Dresden erhält seine unverwechelbare Attraktivität durch die Verbindung von Hochkultur und vielfältiger Stadtteilkultur.		4 Dresden unterstützt durch eine leistungsfähige Verkehrsinfrastruktur die Funktion der City sowie die Entwicklung des Oberzentrums und hilft den Besuchern bei der Orientierung in der Stadt.
5 Dresden bietet an neuen Berufsbildern ausgerichtete Aus- und Fortbildungen.			5 Dresden gewährleistet Sicherheit und Sauberkeit im öffentlichen Raum durch staatliche Maßnahmen und bürgerschaftliches Engagement.
6 Dresdens Verwaltung arbeitet bürgerfreundlich und dienstleistungsorientiert.			

Seit Sommer 1999 wurde der Arbeitskreis Innenstadt und Zentrenmanagement durch den Verein City-Management Dresden abgelöst. Dieser Verein – eine Kooperation privater und öffentlicher Kräfte – hat den Zweck, die Entwicklung der Landeshauptstadt Dresden, insbesondere des Stadtzentrums im Bereich zwischen Hauptbahnhof bis zur Haupt- und Königsstraße, zu fördern. Er soll dazu beitragen, dass das Stadtzentrum der Landeshauptstadt Dresden, insbesondere seine Aufgaben in den Bereichen Handel und Dienstleistungen, Tourismus, Arbeiten und Wohnen, Kultur, Bildung, Wissenschaft, Sport und Freizeit, besser wahrnimmt. Der Verein City-Management Dresden e. V. hat inzwischen einen Citymanager engagiert, der hauptamtlich die Aufgaben wahrnimmt.

Die Stadt Dresden verfügt über ein gewaltiges Wachstumspotenzial. Es gilt, die richtigen Weichen zu stellen für die zukünftige Entwicklung. Der weitere Ausbau der Innenstadt – das Herz jeder Stadt – und die Gewährleistung der ausreichenden Zuwegung – den Hauptschlagadern – steht auf der Prioritätenliste für das Citymanagement ganz weit oben. Eine Stadt lebt nur, wenn die City pulsiert, und daran arbeiten wir mit Hochdruck.

Große Hoffnungen setzt man in Dresden auf die Erweiterung der EU. Die bisherige Randlage verwandelt sich nach der Aufnahme unserer Nachbarländer in eine Mittellage.

Dresden als Tor des Ostens ist eine gern gebrauchte Metapher. Hierüber wird aber nicht nur geredet, sondern auch gehandelt. Besonders an Wochenenden begrüßen wir in Dresden viele Besucher aus Tschechien und Polen. Der Autobahnausbau nach Görlitz und die im Bau befindliche Autobahn nach Prag werden die gegenseitigen Besuche noch fördern.

Dresden war und ist sehenswert, lebenswert und attraktiv.

Aber faszinierend sind die Zukunftsaussichten und die Gestaltungsmöglichkeiten, die diese Stadt noch bietet und an denen wir mitwirken dürfen. ■

Landtag.

Regional Parliament.

City-Management

Guideline for Positioning the City of Dresden

Location of high-technology and science	City of fine arts and culture	Tourism	City in a beautiful landscape
1 Dresden will be a leading location for microelectronics in research, development and production.	1 Dresden achieves the profile of an art and cultural metropolitan city of European ranking.	1 Dresden provides a unique combination of art, culture, economy and science.	1 Dresden links urban aspects with landscape resulting in an urban space worth living in. Nature and nearby spaces of relaxation start in the middle of town.
2 Dresden attracts further future technologies We strengthen the broad base of Dresden's university and research landscape.	2 Dresden combines great cultural past with courageous contemporary projects.	2 Dresden develops into metropolitan city for tourism and into a meeting and conference city of international ranking.	2 Dresden sets new trends with modern architecture and town development – always committed to the high standard of the past.
3 Dresden accomplishes favourable frame conditions for company foundations, particularly in the technology-oriented service sector and builds up the broad spectrum of the middle-sized businesses.	3 Dresden grows as a venue for important national and international events in the fields of culture and sports.	3 Dresden is open for visitors and is extremely hospitable in a particular way.	3 Dresden gives the highest priority to the development of the inner city into an attractive service and shoppingcentre.
4 Dresden extends it's position as gateway to the East further.	4 Dresden receives it's indisputable attractiveness through the fusion of high culture with varied district cultures.		4 Dresden supports the function of the city as well as development of the upper centre through an efficient transport infrastructure and helps visitors in their orientation across the city.
5 Dresden offers training and further education that is oriented towards new professional careers.			5 Dresden ensures safety and cleanliness in public spaces through official measures and civil engagement.
6 Dresden's administration works service-oriented and in support of it's citizens.			

housing, culture, education, science, sports and leisure time. The association Verein City-Management Dresden e. V. has now employed a city manager that carries out these tasks on a full-time basis.

The City of Dresden disposes of a tremendous growth potential. It is now important to lay down the appropriate course for future developments. On first place of the list of priorities of the City Management stand the further extension of the inner city – the heart of each city – and the guarantee of an adequate access – the main arteries. A town only lives if the city is pulsating and we are working on it with relentless pressure.

Great expectations have been placed on the extension of the EU in Dresden. The present marginal position will be changed into a middle position after the admission of our neighbouring countries. The expression 'Dresden as Gate to the East' is used frequently. But this is something not only being talked about, but also acted upon. Especially on weekends, we welcome in Dresden many visitors from Czech Republic and Poland. The extension of the motorway to Görlitz and the motorway to Prague, which is under construction, will enhance the mutual visits even further.

Dresden was and is still worth seeing, worth living in and attractive.

Indeed, fascinating are the future perspectives and the possibilities of design that this city still has on offer and that we all are invited to shape. ■

Prager Straße.

Prague Street.

Company Profile

Europas Kompetenzzentrum für multimediale Lösungen

Europe's Competence Centre for Multimedia Solutions

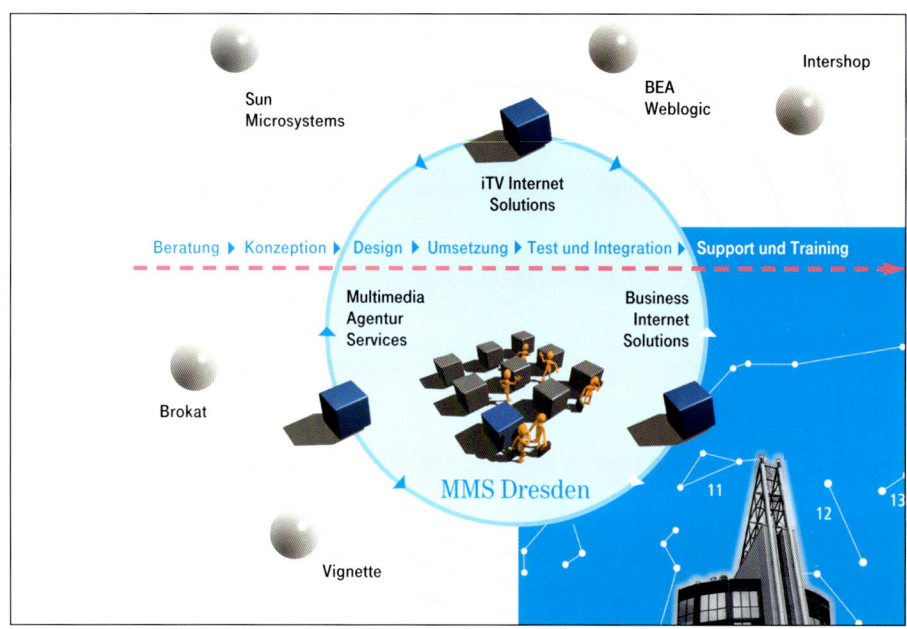

Multimedia Software GmbH Dresden
Deutsche Telekom Gruppe

Multimedia Software GmbH Dresden

Geschäftsführer/Managing Directors:
Dr. Joachim Niemeier
Dr. Klaus Radermacher

Gesellschafter/Corporate member:
Deutsche Telekom AG

Gründungsjahr/Year of Foundation:
1995

Mitarbeiter/Employees:
214

Gesamtleistung/Overall Performance:
17,31 Mio. Euro

Anschrift/Address:
Riesaer Straße 5
D-01129 Dresden
Hotline +49 (800) 667 83 26
Telefax +49 (351) 85 05-555
E-Mail mms-dresden@telekom.de
Internet www.mms-dresden.de

Multimediale Software-Kompetenz der MMS Dresden.
Multimedia software competence of MMS Dresden.

Multimediale Software-Lösungen sind der Schlüssel für die Zukunft. Aber nur dann, wenn Einzelkomponenten in ein Gesamtkonzept integriert sind. Schluss mit Insellösungen und Teilleistungen. Die Multimedia Software GmbH Dresden bietet Ihnen multimediale Software-Kompetenz auf der ganzen Linie. Vom Design bis zur Implementierung. Mit innovativen Tools und ausgereifter Technologie. Mit Beratung und dem nötigen Biss für schnelle Umsetzung.

Wir gehören zu den Top-Five Multimediaunternehmen in Europa. Als Software-Schmiede der Deutschen Telekom arbeiten wir an völlig neuen Systemkonzepten und entwickeln zukunftsweisende Lösungen für Kunden wie ABB, Daimler Chrysler, die Kirch-Mediengruppe und das ZDF.

Die intelligente Verknüpfung von Diensten, Daten, Kommunikation und Information ist keine Vision mehr. Ob iTV Internet Solutions bei der Verschmelzung interaktiver Dienste mit dem digitalem Fernsehen, ob Multimedia Agentur Services zur Gestaltung innovativer Websites oder Business Internet Solutions für den sicheren Weg ins E-Business: Wir bieten Ihnen konkrete Lösungen und neue Möglichkeiten. ∎

Multimedia software solutions are the key for the future. Sure, but only if single components are integrated within a comprehensive concept. Enough of isolated solutions and partly performed services. Multimedia Software GmbH Dresden provides you with multimedia software competence in the whole field. Ranging from the design up until implementation. With innovative tools and advanced technology. With consulting and the necessary drive for a rapid realization.

We are one of the top five multimedia companies in Europe. Being a software development workshop of Deutsche Telekom, we are working on completely new system concepts and develop pioneering solutions for clients like ABB, Daimler Chrysler, the Kirch Media Group and ZDF Television.

The intelligent linkage of services, data, communication and information is not a vision any longer. Whether iTV Internet Solutions in the merger of interactive services with digital TV, or be it Multimedia Agency Services for the design of innovative websites or Business Internet Solutions for a safe way into e-Commerce: We offer you concrete solutions and new possibilities. ∎

Unternehmenssitz der Multimedia Software GmbH Dresden.
The business seat of Multimedia Software GmbH Dresden.

Company Profile

Werkstoff-Forschung von den Grundlagen bis zum Produkt

Materials Research from Fundamental Research up to the Finished Product

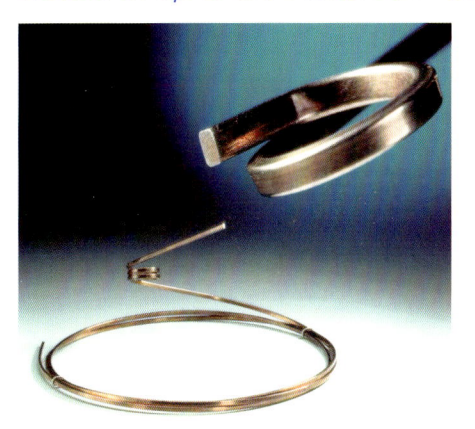

Institut für Festkörper- und Werkstoffforschung Dresden

Vorstand/Executive Board:
Prof. Dr. Helmut Eschrig,
Wissenschaftlicher Direktor/
Administrative Director

Peter Joehnk,
Kaufmännischer Direktor/Commercial Director

Gründungsjahr/Year of Foundation:
1992

Mitarbeiter/Employees:
ca./approx. 400

Anschrift/Address:
Helmholtzstraße 20
D-01069 Dresden
Telefon +49 (351) 46 59 380
Telefax +49 (351) 46 59 500
E-Mail c.langer@ifw-dresden.de
Internet www.ifw-dresden.de

Ergebnisse der Forschung und Entwicklung aus dem IFW werden zeitnah in der Wirtschaft genutzt.
Findings of research and development from the IFW are applied timely in the economic sector.

Das IFW Dresden betreibt Forschung und Entwicklung auf dem Gebiet der Festkörper und Werkstoffe. Das Forschungsprogramm umfasst fünf Forschungsgebiete, in denen Aspekte der physikalischen, chemischen und Werkstoffforschung sowie technologische Fragestellungen disziplinübergreifend behandelt werden. Daneben gehört es zu den Aufgaben des Instituts, die Fortbildung des wissenschaftlichen und technischen Nachwuchses zu fördern und die gewonnenen Erkenntnisse für die Wirtschaft nutzbar zu machen.

Das IFW Dresden ist Mitglied der Wissenschaftsgemeinschaft Gottfried Wilhelm Leibniz. Es wird von der Bundesrepublik Deutschland und dem Freistaat Sachsen zu gleichen Teilen gefördert. Ein beträchtlicher Teil der Sach- und Personalkosten wird von Projektmitteln bestritten, die im Wettbewerb mit anderen Forschungseinrichtungen eingeworben werden.

IFW Dresden is active in research and development on the field of solid state and materials. The research programme comprises five research areas in which aspects of physical, chemical and materials research as well as technological issues are treated in interdisciplinary manner. Furthermore, the task of the institute includes the promotion of continuing education of scientific and technical young professional people and to render applicable the gained findings for the economy.

The IFW Dresden is a member of the scientific society Wissenschaftsgemeinschaft Gottfried Wilhelm Leibniz. The Government of the Federal Republic of Germany and the Free State of Saxony supports it in equal parts. A considerable part of the costs for physical resources and personnel is financed with project funds that are acquired in competitions with other research institutions.

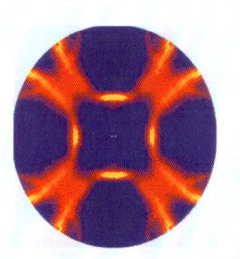

Fermi-Fläche eines Supraleiters.
Fermi-surface of a superconductor.

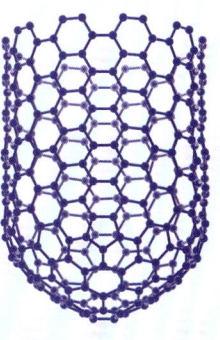

Kohlenstoff-nanoröhre.
Carbon nano tube.

Company Profile

materni-visions: Raum für Ideen

materni-visions: Space for New Ideas

materni | visions

Geschäftsführer/Managing Director:
Dave Bosworth

Gründungsjahr/Year of Foundation:
1998

Mitarbeiter/Employees:
8

Geschäftstätigkeit/Business Activity:
Telekommunikation/Telecommunications

Anschrift/Address:
Maternistraße 17
D-01067 Dresden
Telefon +49 (351) 45 25 20
Telefax +49 (351) 45 25 299
Internet www.materni.de

Unser Team.
Our team.

Dave Bosworth, Geschäftsführer.
Dave Bosworth, Managing Director.

Die materni-visions entwickelt in Dresden ein Zentrum für Telekommunikation. In der Maternistraße 17 entstehen unter einem Dach ein Call Center, Internet Service Provider und andere Telekommunikationsdienste der Zukunft. Die visionäre Vorstellung der materni-visions über die digitale Welt der Telekommunikation findet u. a. Platz in einem digitalen Kino, das in Deutschland seinesgleichen suchen wird.

Die Möglichkeiten der Telekommunikation sind heute für private Nutzer und Geschäftsanwendungen vielfältig. Diese Möglichkeiten zu verbinden und Synergien innerhalb der Infrastruktur zu nutzen, ist erklärtes Ziel der materni-visions. materni-visions stellt für verschiedene Telekommunikationsunternehmen Technik zu Verfügung, wie zum Beispiel für ein Call Center bis zu 90 Arbeitsplätze, Switches und Router. Um die Basis der einzelnen Unternehmungen zu stärken und potenzielle Mitarbeiter auszubilden, wird materni-visions ergänzend ein Trainings- oder Schulungszentrum für Telekommunikation aufbauen. „Ideen brauchen Raum. Den stellen wir zur Verfügung. Ebenso wie die Infrastruktur, die Visionen in Produkte umsetzt", sagt Dave Bosworth, materni-visions Geschäftsführer.

Die Investitionen in die Technik sind auf den wachsenden Markt ausgerichtet. Die Technologien sind immer auf dem letzten Stand. State of the art technology ist ein erklärtes Ziel der materni-visions. Nur so ist es einem Call Center der „vierten Generation" mit Internet-basierten Services und einem Management Reporting System möglich, Kunden die notwendigen Dienste anzubieten.

Nach dem Ausbau der Infrastruktur wird als erstes Projekt das Call Center an den Start gehen, dessen Aufgaben über die reine Telefonie weit hinaus gehen. Die Anforderungen steigen weiter: durch E-Mail-Management, Internet-Telefonie, Outsourcing, Videostreaming, Voice over IP usw. Das Unternehmen in der Maternistraße verfügt bereits heute über alle technischen Möglichkeiten eines „Hochleistungs-Centers" für in- und outbound Kommunikation. Ein weiteres Standbein des Call Centers soll die Zusammenarbeit mit anderen Call Centern darstellen. Freie Kapazitäten lassen sich als „Back-up-Lösung" nutzen: Bei Überlast einer Serviceline werden eingehende Anrufe automatisch nach Dresden geleitet. ■

Materni-visions is developing in Dresden a new centre of telecommunications. In the buildings of Maternistrasse 17 a call center, an Internet service provider and other telecommunications services of the future are being created under one roof. The visionary ideas of materni-visions about the digital world of telecommunications find space for example in a digital cinema that will not easily find comparison in Germany.

The possibilities of telecommunications today are diverse both for private and business users. It is materni-visions' declared aim to combine these possibilities and to use synergies within the infrastructure. materni-visions provides technologies for various telecommunications companies, like for example for a call center up to 90 workplaces, switches and routers. In order to support the foundations of individual companies and to train potential staff, materni-visions will establish in addition a training and education centre for telecommunications. "Ideas need space. We provide it. As well as the infrastructure that converts visions into products", says Dave Bosworth, Managing Director of materni-visions.

Investments in technology are oriented towards the growing market. Technologies are always on the most up-to-date level. State-of-the-art technology is a declared aim of materni-visions. This is the only way that a call center of the "fourth generation" with Internet-based services and a management reporting system is capable of offering the necessary services to it's clients.

After building-up the infrastructure, the first project will be the call center, which will have tasks going far beyond those of pure telephony. Demands will increase further: through e-mail management, Internet-telephony, outsourcing, video streaming voice over IP etc. The company in Maternistrasse disposes even today already of all the technical possibilities of a "High-tech center" for in- and outbound communication. A further branch of the call center will be the co-operation with other call centres. Free capacities may be used as "back-up solution": on overload of a service line, incoming calls are automatically routed to Dresden. ■

Company Profile

Forschung an den Grenzen des Wissens

Research on the Borders of Science

Der Neubau des Instituts.
The new building of the institute.

Durch die Gründung des Max-Planck-Instituts für Molekulare Zellbiologie und Genetik in Dresden stellt sich die Max-Planck-Gesellschaft einer neuen Herausforderung biologischer Forschung: molekularer Zellbiologie im post-genomischen Zeitalter.

Ein besonderes Anliegen ist es, die angrenzenden Staaten des ehemaligen Ostblocks stärker in die internationale Forschungslandschaft zu integrieren. Die Förderung begabter junger Wissenschaftler und die Schaffung eines speziellen Ausbildungsprogramms ist deshalb ein vorrangiges Ziel. Dresden ist ein idealer Standort, eine geschichtsträchtige Stadt, reich an Architektur und Kultur und jene Landeshauptstadt, die den angrenzenden zentral- und osteuropäischen Staaten am nähesten liegt. Der Reiz Dresdens wird es auch erleichtern, hochkarätige internationale Wissenschaftler anzuziehen und damit ein Garant für den internationalen Charakter und einen hochqualifizierten Mitarbeiterstab sein. In Dresden wird eine neue Forschungslandschaft aufgebaut. Zwischen den Ingenieurwissenschaften, der Biologie und der Medizin sollen zusammen mit der Technischen Universität Dresden Brücken geschlagen werden. Diese Entwicklung von Forschung und Lehre wird von der Stadt Dresden und dem Freistaat Sachsen tatkräftig unterstützt. Das neue Institut ist auch an der Ansiedlung mehrerer Biotech-Gründerfirmen beteiligt, um die Vision „BIOPOLIS Dresden" zu realisieren.
Damit das Institut nicht nur aus wissenschaftlicher Sicht Beachtung findet, haben vielbeachtete finnische und deutsche Architekten einen eindrucksvollen Neubau entworfen und bauen lassen, der zu Beginn des Jahres 2001 bezogen wurde. ■

Through the foundation of the Max Planck Institute of Molecular Cell Biology and Genetics in Dresden, the Max Planck Society is confronting a new challenge in biological research: molecular cell biology in the post-genomic age.

Our special interest is to integrate the bordering states of the former Eastern Block increasingly in the international research landscape. One task of priority is therefore the promotion of talented young scientists and the creation of a special training programme.

Dresden is a perfect location, a city of historic importance, rich in architecture and culture and the German regional capital situated closest to the neighbouring countries of Central and Eastern Europe. Dresden's appeal will also facilitate to attract high-calibre international scientists and thus be guarantee the international character and a highly qualified team of staff members. In Dresden, a new research landscape is being built up. Bridges are to be built between the sciences of engineering, biology and medicine together with the Technical University of Dresden. This development between research and teaching is actively supported by the City of Dresden and the Free State of Saxony. The new institute also participates in the settlement of various biotech start-ups in order to realize the vision "BIOPOLIS Dresden".

So that the institute would not only find recognition from a scientific point of view, renowned Finnish and German architects have designed and constructed an impressive new building, which was occupied in the beginning of the year 2001. ■

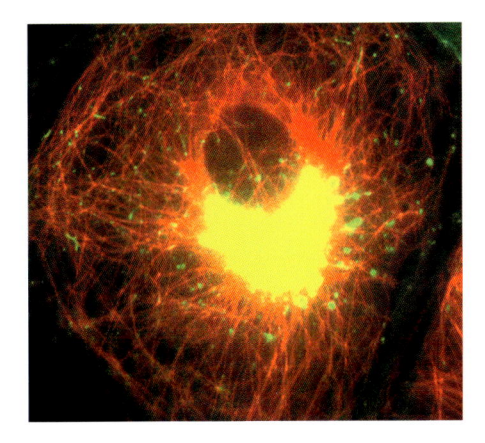

**Max-Planck-Institut
für Molekulare Zellbiologie und Genetik
Max-Planck-Institute
of Molecular Cell Biology and Genetics**

Gründungsdirektoren/Founding Directors:
Kai Simons (Geschäftsführender Dirketor/*Executive Director*)
Forschungsgebiet: Zellpolarität, insbesonders in epithelialen Zellen, die Struktur der Zellmembran sowie die Rolle von „lipid rafts" beim Membrantransport, der Signalübertragung und der Krankheitsentwicklung.
Research field: cell polarity, particularly in epithelial cells, structure of cell membrane as well as the role of lipid rafts in membrane trafficking, signal transmission and disease.

Tony Hyman
Forschungsgebiet: Verschiedene Aspekte der Zellteilung mit der Konzentration auf die Rolle der Mikrotubuli.
Research field: Various aspects of cell division while concentrating on the role of microtubules.

Marino Zerial
Forschungsgebiet: Untersuchung des Mechanismus, wie Membranvesikel andocken und verschmelzen, insbesonders die Rolle von Rab GTPasen bei diesem Prozess.
Research field: Investigation of mechanisms like vesicular membrane docking and merging, particularly the role of Rab GTPases in this process.

Wieland Huttner
Forschungsgebiet: Entwicklung der spezialisierten sekretorischen Organellen von Neuronen und neuroendokrinen Zellen.
Research field: Development of specialised secretory organelle structures in neuronal and neuron-endocrinal cells.

Gründungsjahr/Year of Foundation: 1998

Anschrift/Address:
Pfotenhauerstraße 108
D-01307 Dresden
Telefon   +49 (351) 210-20 30
Telefax   +49 (351) 210-20 00
E-Mail   claudia.lorenz@mpi-cbg.de
Internet www.mpi-cbg.de

Tourismus

Dresden wird eine der wichtigsten deutschen Tourismus-Destinationen

Dresden is becoming one of the most important German destinations for tourism

Dresden gehört wieder zu den bedeutendsten Tourismus-Destinationen in Deutschland. 2000 zählte die Stadt über 2,4 Millionen Übernachtungen. Der Anteil der ausländischen Besucher liegt derzeit bei etwa 16 Prozent. Im Jahr 2001 werden weitere Steigerungen erwartet.

Diese erfolgreichen Zahlen sind das Ergebnis von mehreren Faktoren. Der wohl wichtigste ist natürlich die Jahrhunderte währende Tradition von Dresden als Kunst- und Kulturstadt innerhalb einer einzigartigen Landschaft. „Dresden war eine wunderbare Stadt", erinnerte sich der Schriftsteller Erich Kästner, der hier 1899 geboren wurde. „Geschichte, Kunst und Natur schwebten über Stadt und Tal, wie ein von seiner eigenen Harmonie bezauberter Akkord." Der barocke Dresdner Zwinger, die Semperoper, die Gemäldesammlung „Alte Meister" (eines von 30 Museen der Stadt) und die barocke Hofkirche im historischen Zentrum von Dresden sind die wichtigsten Sehenswürdigkeiten, die sich kein Besucher entgehen lassen möchte. Sie umrahmen den Theaterplatz, der als einer der schönsten Plätze Deutschlands gilt.

Mehr als sieben Millionen Besucher bewundern jährlich die Schönheiten Dresdens wie hier das Residenzschloss.

More than seven million visitors marvel yearly at the beauty of Dresden like for example the Residenzschloss (Residence Castle).

Blick auf Dresdens Altstadt. Der Erlwein-Speicher (links) wird zum Kongress-Hotel umgebaut.
View on Dresden's Historic City Centre. The silo "Erlwein-Speicher (left) is reconstructed into a Congress Hotel.

Yvonne Kubitza

Die Autorin wurde 1962 in Heidelberg geboren. Hier studierte sie auch von 1982 bis 1984 Germanistik, Politische Wissenschaft und Kunstgeschichte und von 1985 bis 1991 Anglistik, Romanistik und Kunstgeschichte. 1986 absolvierte sie zwei Auslandssemester an der Universität Perugia, 1988 folgte ein halbjähriger Auslandsaufenthalt in Boston, Mass., USA. 1991 bis 1992 übernahm sie die Leitung Marketing- und Akquisitionsbereich beim Incentive-Veranstalter in Heidelberg, 1994 wurde sie Geschäftsführerin. 1997 als Geschäftsführerin der Kurverwaltung „Kongresse-Touristik-Kur" in Freudenstadt. Seit 1998 ist Yvonne Kubitza Geschäftsführerin der Dresden-Werbung und Tourismus GmbH, zudem ist sie Geschäftsführerin der touristischen Werbegemeinschaft der deutschen Großstädte Magic Cities.

The author was born in 1962 in Heidelberg. Here she completed from 1982 until 1984 her German studies, political science and art history and from 1985 until 1991 English and Roman studies and art history. In 1986, she passed two semesters of studies abroad at the University of Perugia, in 1988 she spent half a year abroad in Boston, Mass., USA. From 1991 until 1992, she took over the management of the marketing and acquisitions department of an incentive events promoter in Heidelberg, where she was appointed Managing Director in 1994. In 1997, she joined the administration for health cures "Kongresse-Touristik-Kur" in Freudenstadt as Managing Director. Since 1998, Yvonne Kubitza is Managing Director of Dresden-Werbung und Tourismus GmbH, while at the same time being Managing Director of the tourism advertising union for large German cities called Magic Cities.

Tourism

Dresden: barocke Flaniermeile – in der Königstraße in der historischen Dresdner Neustadt lässt es sich gut bummeln, Interessantes einkaufen und in vielen Lokalen gepflegt und rustikal speisen.

Dresden: The baroque promenade – in Königstraße in the historic new part of the City of Dresden one can take nice walks, do interesting shopping and eat elegantly and in a rustic style.

Once again, Dresden is among the significant destinations for tourism in Germany. In the year 2000, the city counted more than 2,4 million overnight stays. The share of foreign visitors lies presently at around 16 percent. In 2001, further noticeable increases are expected.

These successful figures are the result of several factors. Probably the most important one is, of course, the centuries old tradition of Dresden as a city of art and culture located in an unique landscape. "Dresden was a wonderful city", the writer Erich Kästner remembered, and who was born here in 1899. "History, art and nature lingered about the city and the valley, like a chord enchanted by its own harmony." The baroque Zwinger of Dresden, the Semperoper, the collection of paintings "Old Masters" (one of the 30 museums of the city) and the baroque-style Hofkirche, the church in the historical centre of Dresden, are the most important sightseeing attractions that no visitor wants to miss. These surround the Theatre-Square in frame-like setting, which is regarded as one of the most beautiful squares in Germany. The imposing renaissance castle of the Kings of Saxony and the baroque Frauenkirche are the most remarkable symbols of the city's reconstruction. In the year 2006, they are to be restored complete besides other buildings destroyed in 1945 and thus enhance the cityscape.

A trip with one of the boats of the largest and eldest wheel steam fleet of the world down to the Chinese baroque Summer Palace Pillnitz with its wide garden arrangements is an incomparable experience.

The Dresden of around 1900 has been newly discovered lately, of which, among others, also the technical monuments of the ground funicular, the aerial mountain tramway and the bridge called "Blaues Wunder" (blue wonder) provide evidence. The city's district Dresden-Neustadt with its neighbouring suburbs, one of the largest entirely undamaged quarters of the German business-floating boom, the garden-city Hellerau and the suburbs of villas Blasewitz, Loschwitz and Weißer Hirsch do not only remind one of the great era of Dresden, but also stand for living quality, which is being regained little by little. The Neustadt, the new part of the city, houses a lively alternative scene with numerous international restaurants, cocktail and trendy bars and cosy artists' pubs.

The rich cultural life of the city with the State Opera of Saxony (named after it's architect Semperoper), the State Theatre, State Musical, Philharmonics, numerous festivals and uncountable small theatre, cabarets and event houses cause Dresden to be very attractive also at night.

Dresden thus offers also ideal conditions for seminars and congresses. The existing possibilities for holding congresses will be extended in the next years even further by the establishment of a new

Tourismus

Sommerresidenz – schon August der Starke reiste am liebsten per Schiff nach Pillnitz, heute beliebtes Ausflugsziel mit schönem Park.
Summer residence – even August the Strong used to prefer travelling to Pillnitz by boat, today a popular destination for excursions with a beautiful park.

Das mächtige Renaissanceschloss der sächsischen Könige und die barocke Frauenkirche sind die bedeutendsten Symbole für den Wiederaufbau der Stadt. Im Jahr 2006 sollen sie neben anderen, 1945 zerstörten Bauten völlig wiederhergestellt sein und so das Stadtbild bereichern.

Eine Fahrt mit einem Schiff der größten und ältesten Raddampferflotte der Welt zum chinesischbarocken Sommerpalast Pillnitz mit seinen weiten Gartenanlagen, ist ein unvergleichliches Erlebnis.

In der letzten Zeit neu entdeckt ist das Dresden um 1900, von dem nicht nur die technischen Denkmäler Standseilbahn, Bergschwebebahn und die Brücke „Blaues Wunder" zeugen. Der Stadtteil Dresden-Neustadt mit den angrenzenden Vororten, eines der größten geschlossen erhaltenen Gründerzeitviertel Deutschlands, die Gartenstadt Hellerau und die Villenvororte Blasewitz, Loschwitz und Weißer Hirsch erinnern nicht nur an eine große Epoche Dresdens, sondern stehen auch für Lebensqualität, die Stück für Stück wiedergewonnen wird. In der Neustadt gibt es eine lebendige alternative Szene mit zahlreichen internationalen Restaurants, Cocktail- und Szenebars und gemütlichen Künstlerkneipen.

Das reiche Kulturleben der Stadt mit der Sächsischen Staatsoper (nach ihrem Architekten Semperoper genannt), Staatsschauspiel, Staatsoperette, Philharmonie, zahlreichen Festivals und unzähligen kleinen Theatern, Kabaretts und Veranstaltungsorten macht Dresden auch abends attraktiv.

Dresden bietet so auch ideale Voraussetzungen für Tagungen und Kongresse. Die bestehenden Kongressmöglichkeiten werden in den kommenden Jahren noch durch ein neues Kongresszentrum, unweit des historischen Zentrums direkt an der Elbe gelegen, erweitert.

Nicht zu vergessen: die wunderschöne Umgebung. Die Sächsische Weinstraße führt nicht nur durch die Porzellan- und Weinstadt Meißen, sondern auch mitten durch Dresden, das sogar eigene Weinberge besitzt. Die Sächsische Schweiz lockt mit ihren bizarren Sandsteinfelsen Naturliebhaber an. Im Erzgebirge kann man neben weiter Landschaft auch mittelalterliche Städte und historische Silberbergwerke entdecken. In der Oberlausitz haben die Sorben ihre eigene slawische Kultur bis heute bewahrt. Und das Goldene Prag ist von Dresden aus in einem Tagesausflug zu erreichen.

Der Tourismus in Dresden hat eine lange Tradition

Als sächsische Hauptstadt zog Dresden schon seit Ende des 15. Jahrhunderts Besucher aus allen Teilen Europas an. Waren diese Besuche zunächst überwiegend politisch und wirtschaftlich orientiert, so folgte im ausgehenden 18. und im 19. Jahrhundert eine Welle des Bildungstourismus.

Tourism

congress centre not far from the historical centre directly located at the river Elbe.

Furthermore, the beautiful surrounding landscape should not be forgotten. The Sächsische Weinstrasse does not only lead through the city of porcelain and wine Meißen, but also right through Dresden, which even has its own vineyards. The Sächsische Schweiz (Saxon Switzerland) attracts nature lovers with its bizarre sandstone rocks. In the Erzgebirge (Ore Mountains), one can discover besides wide impressive landscapes also medieval cities and historical silver mines. In the region of Oberlausitz, the Sorbs have maintained their own Slavonic culture up until today. And the Golden City of Prague can be reached within a day's excursion trip.

Tourism has a long-standing tradition in Dresden.

Being the Saxon capital city, Dresden attracted visitors from all parts of Europe as early as since the end of the 15th Century. While these visits at first were mainly politically and economically oriented, by the time of the close of the 18th and in the 19th century a wave of educational tourism followed. Charles Burney, Johann Wolfgang von Goethe, Christian Andersen and many others had been enthused by the art treasures of Dresden. More and more international guests travelled to Dresden. As the most beautiful promenade of Dresden, the Brühlsch Terrace received the nickname "Balcony of Europe" not in vain. After the collapse of tourism in 1945 and the complete destruction of the inner city of Dresden, the reconstruction only proceeded slowly. The political situation of the DDR and the limited freedom to travel connected with it took its effect. Only since 1985, one can speak again of a new beginning of international tourism to Dresden. The reason for this were the occasions of the reopening of the Semperoper and the inauguration of the Hotel Bellevue as a five-star hotel of foreign exchange.

Romantische Abendstimmung – der Blick von der Marienbrücke über Dresdens vieltürmige Altstadt inspirierte schon viele Maler und Dichter.
Romantic evening atmosphere – the view from the bridge Marienbrücke above the many towers of Dresden's historic city centre inspired many painters and poets.

Tourismus

Blick von Dölzschen auf Dresden.
A view from Dölzschen on Dresden.

Charles Burney, Johann Wolfgang von Goethe, Christian Andersen und viele andere ließen sich von Dresdens Kunstschätzen begeistern. Immer mehr internationale Gäste bereisten Dresden. Die Brühlsche Terrasse als Dresdens schönste Promenade erhielt nicht umsonst ihren Beinamen „Balkon Europas". Nach dem Zusammenbruch des Tourismus 1945 mit der völligen Zerstörung der Dresdner Innenstadt ging der Aufbau zunächst nur zögerlich vonstatten. Die politische Situation der DDR mit der damit verbundenen beschränkten Reisefreiheit tat ihr übriges.

Messe mit Flair – moderne Architektur in denkmalgeschützten Bauten von Hans Erlwein.
A fair with flair – modern architecture in buildings of protected monument status designed by Hans Erlwein.

Erst 1985 kann man wieder von einem Neubeginn des internationalen Tourismus nach Dresden sprechen. Anlass waren die Wiedereröffnung der Semperoper und die Neueröffnung des Hotels Bellevue als 5-Sterne-Devisen-Hotel.

Nach der Wende erlebte der Tourismus einen rasanten Aufschwung. Auf der einen Seite wurde erheblich in die Verbesserung der touristischen Infrastruktur investiert. 2000 gab es in Dresden bereits 139 Hotels, Pensionen und Jugendherbergen mit einem Angebot von über 15.000 Betten. Die Struktur entspricht fast genau der aktuellen Nachfrage: rund die Hälfte der Hotelbetten sind im 4 bis 5-Sterne-Segment zu finden. Parallel dazu wurde in Dresden durch die Gründung der Dresden-Werbung und Tourismus GmbH im Jahr 1992 auch ein Struktur für ein effektives Tourismusmarketing geschaffen.

Tourismus-Marketing als Beitrag zur Wirtschaftsförderung

Durch die besondere Situation des Wirtschaftsstandorts Dresden kommt dem Tourismus eine besondere Bedeutung im Branchenmix der sächsischen Landeshauptstadt zu.

Damit generierte der Tourismus in Dresden einen Nettoumsatz von knapp 500 Mio. Euro in der ersten und über 700 Mio. Euro in der zweiten Stufe und es flossen geschätzte 13 Mio. Euro an Steuergeldern in die Stadtkasse.

Die Struktur der DWT mit der Stadt Dresden als Hauptgesellschafter sowie dem Deutschen Hotel- und Gaststättenverband, dem Tourismusverein Dresden, dem Marketingclub Dresden und dem Dresden Convention Bureau als weiteren Anteilseignern ist Möglichkeit und Programm zugleich, wird die DWT so doch zur Schnittstelle aller bedeutenden am Tourismus Beteiligten. Auch mit den Kultureinrichtungen besteht ein enger Kontakt, der immer wieder zu gemeinsamen Marketing-Aktivitäten führt. In ihrem Marketing hat sich die DWT auf Schwerpunktmärkte konzentriert: Deutschland, USA, Japan, Österreich, Schweiz, Großbritannien, Italien, Frankreich und Skandinavien. Dabei arbeitet die DWT mit allen klassischen Marketing-Mitteln wie Verkaufsförderung, Presse- und Öffentlichkeitsarbeit und Werbung.

Die Zielsetzung ist klar:
In Zukunft wird Dresden zu den wichtigen internationalen Touristenmetropolen gehören. ∎

Tourism

Tourism as a Contribution to Economic Promotion

Through the special situation of the economic location Dresden, tourism acquires a particular importance in the mix of branches prevalent in the city.

The sector of tourism generated in Dresden a net turnover of just under 500 million Euros in the first phase and more than 700 million Euros in the second phase and an estimated 13 million Euros in tax moneys went into the city's treasury.

Die 1978 eröffnete Semperoper – eines der schönsten Opernhäuser der Welt.
The Semperoper opened in 1978 – one of the most beautiful opera houses of the world.

After the German re-unification, the tourism sector experienced a tremendous upsurge. On the one part, considerable investments were made into the improvement of the tourist infrastructure. In the year 2000, Dresden had already 139 hotels, pensions and youth hostels with a provision of more than 15,000 beds. The structure does almost exactly correspond to the actual demand: around half the hotel beds are found in the 4 to 5-star segment. At the same time in Dresden was also created the structure for effective tourism marketing with the founding of the Dresden-Werbung und Tourismus GmbH.

Dresden, die grüne Stadt. Parkanlagen bieten auch Touristen viele Ruheplätze.
Dresden, the green city. The parks provide many places for relaxation also for tourists.

The structure of the DWT company with the City of Dresden being it's main associate partner together with the German Hotel and Restaurant Association, the Tourism Association of Dresden, the Marketingclub Dresden and the Dresden Convention Bureau as further share owner, provides a possibility and equally the programme, making the DWT thus to be the intersection of all important participants in tourism. There is also a close contact with the cultural institutions, which repeatedly leads to mutual marketing activities. In it's marketing, DWT has been concentrating on the focal markets: Germany, USA, Japan, Austria, Switzerland, Great Britain, Italy, France and Scandinavia. In this DWT employs all means of classic marketing like sales promotion, press and public relations work and advertising.

The target is clear:
In future, Dresden will be among the most significant international cosmopolitan cities of tourism.

Company Profile

FARU® – ideenreich für effizienten Umweltschutz

FARU® – imaginative ideas for an efficient environmental protection

FARU® Forschungsstelle für Analytik, Recycling und Umwelttechnologie GmbH

Geschäftsführer/Manager:
Dr. Armin Dittmar

Gründungsjahr/Year of Foundation:
1993

Mitarbeiter/Employees:
20 (2 Auszubildende)/20 (2 apprentices)

Geschäftstätigkeit/Business Activity:
- Umweltanalytik, Altlastenerkundung und Umweltmonitoring
- Technologieentwicklung zum Kunststoff- und Gummirecycling
- Softwareentwicklung, Messtechnik
- *Environmental analysis, reconnaissance of abandoned polluted areas and environmental monitoring*
- *Technology development for the recycling of plastics and rubber*
- *Software development, measuring technology*

Anschrift/Address:
Leipziger Straße 117
D-01127 Dresden
Telefon   +49 (351) 841 02-0
Telefax   +49 (351) 841 02-99
E-Mail   faru-dresden@t-online.de
Internet   www.faru-dresden.de

Die FARU® wurde 1993 in Dresden gegründet. In drei Geschäftsbereichen vereint das Unternehmen mit Spezialisten aus verschiedenen naturwissenschaftlichen, technischen und wirtschaftswissenschaftlichen Fachrichtungen ein großes Potenzial hochqualifizierter Mitarbeiter. Der Bereich Analytik/Altlasten führt in seinem akkreditierten Umweltlabor umfangreiche stationäre und mobile Analytikleistungen für Wasser, Boden, Abfall sowie Altlasten durch und bietet Studien und Gutachten zur Bewertung der Umweltrelevanz an.

Projekte zur Entwicklung fachspezifischer Software für Umweltschutz, Management und betriebswirtschaftliche Aufgaben können von der Analyse der Problemstellung über die programmtechnische Umsetzung bis hin zum Service beim Auftraggeber im Geschäftsbereich Software/Messtechnik realisiert werden.

Durch praxisnahe Forschungsarbeit entstand ein patentiertes Verfahren zur Messung der Restsalzkonzentration auf Fahrbahnen vom fahrenden Fahrzeug aus mit dem Ziel der Optimierung der Streusalzmenge.

Innovative Technologien zur Herstellung wettbewerbsfähiger Produkte aus Altgummi, Altkunststoffen und deren Gemischen sind Gegenstand der Forschungstätigkeit im Bereich Recycling. Ergebnis dieser Arbeiten ist z. B. das international patentierte und 1997 mit dem sächsischen Erfinderpreis ausgezeichnete Verfahren zur Reaktivierung von Altgummi, mit dem dieser wieder in vulkanisierfähiges Material (REVULCON®) verwandelt werden kann. Die FARU® arbeitet weiterhin an der großtechnischen Umsetzung des an der TU Chemnitz entwickelten ELAPLASTEN-Verfahrens, für das sie die exklusive, weltweite Lizenz besitzt. ∎

FARU® verfügt über moderne Labors ...
FARU® disposes of modern laboratories ...

FARU® was founded in Dresden in 1993. The company combines in the business fields with experts from various faculties of natural science, technical and economic sciences a great potential of highly qualified staff members. The field of analysis/abandoned polluted areas carries out in its accredited environment laboratories extensive stationary and mobile analysis services for water, soil, waste and abandoned polluted areas and offers studies and expert reports for the evaluation of their environmental relevance.

Different projects for the development of specialist software for environmental protection, management and commercial tasks can be realized within the business field software/measuring techniques ranging from the analysis of complex issues across to the technical programme implementation right down to service provision at the contracting client. Through the research work near to practical experience, a patented method emerged for the measuring of residual salt concentration on roadways from a moving vehicle with the aim of optimising the amount of de-icing salt.

Innovative technologies for the manufacture of competitive products made of waste rubber and plastics and their mixtures are the object of research activities in the field of recycling. One example of the result of this work is for instance the internationally patented method – that was awarded with the Saxon Inventor Prize in 1997 – for reactivating waste rubber, which is capable of being transformed again into a material (REVULCON®) suitable for vulcanisation. The FARU® Company is also continuing work on a large project of technical realization of the ELAPLASTEN method, developed by the Technical University of Chemnitz, for which it possesses an exclusive, worldwide licence. ∎

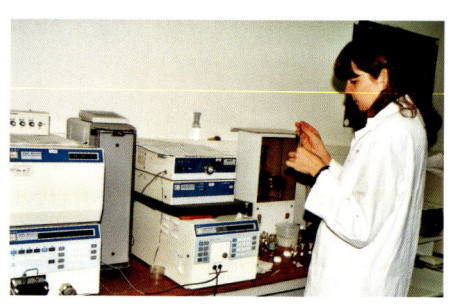

... und hoch qualifizierte Fachkräfte.
... and highly qualified experts.

Company Profile

DB Arbeit GmbH:
Unser Netzwerk verbindet!

DB Arbeit GmbH:
Our Network Connects!

Realistische Lösungsvorschläge bei Personalproblemen präsentieren, neue Wege gehen, mit innovativen Personalkonzepten der Zukunft begegnen – das sind die Stärken der DB Arbeit GmbH. Ihr Ziel: „Menschen von Arbeit in Arbeit vermitteln."

Die DB Arbeit GmbH bringt nicht nur frischen Wind in den konzerninternen Arbeitsmarkt, sie mischt jetzt auch verstärkt auf dem externen Arbeitsmarkt mit. Und sie bietet viel Neues: Heute vernetzen neunzehn Geschäftsstellen den bundesdeutschen Arbeitsmarkt. Der Großraum Dresden, die Lausitz und Sächsische Schweiz werden von Dresden, die Gebiete um Zwickau und Plauen von Chemnitz aus betreut. Die DB Arbeit GmbH verbessert damit die Vermittlungschancen ihrer Mitarbeiter wesentlich.

Die DB Arbeit GmbH ist das innovative Instrument zur Begleitung des sozialverträglichen Arbeitsplatzwandels des Bahnkonzerns. Konzentration auf die Kundenwünsche, umfassende Kenntnisse des internen und externen Arbeitsmarktes mit Blick auf unsere europäischen Nachbarn, tragfähige Lösungskonzepte für das Personalmanagement sowie leistungsmotivierte Mitarbeiter sind Voraussetzungen für den Umsetzungserfolg.

DB Arbeit GmbH: Qualifiziert, Flexibel, Mobil – Wir stehen für engagiertes Personalmarketing.

Unsere praxiserfahrenen Geschäftsstellenleiter und Personaldisponenten bieten allen Unternehmen einen individuellen Full-Service: Von der Vorvermittlung, Arbeitsvermittlung, Zeitarbeit, bedarfsgerechten Qualifizierung und mehrmonatigen Berufswegplanung für Mitarbeiter zur beruflichen Neuorientierung bis zur Personalmanagementberatung – alles ist machbar.

Die Performance der DB Arbeit GmbH am Markt zeigt einen steten Aufwärtstrend. Wir sehen diesen Erfolg vor allem in der Verstärkung der Marktinnovation und Kundennähe: Der direkte Draht zu unseren Kunden hat absolute Priorität. Partnerschaftliche Zusammenarbeit führen zu Auftragswachstum und damit zum gemeinsamen Geschäftserfolg. Die DB Arbeit GmbH wird diesen Weg konsequent fortsetzen. ∎

To present realistic proposals for solutions of personnel problems, to seek new avenues, to confront the future with innovative staffing concepts – these are the strengths of DB Arbeit GmbH. Its aim is: To arrange employment for people from work to work".

DB Arbeit GmbH does not only carry freshness into the internal company labour market, it is now also increasingly involved in the external labour market. And it offers many novelties: Today, nineteen branches link up the national German labour market. The Greater Dresden Area, the Lausitz and the Sächsische Schweiz are serviced from Dresden, the areas around Zwickau and Plauen from Chemnitz. DB Arbeit GmbH thus improves the chances of placement for their workers considerably.

DB Arbeit GmbH is the innovative instrument for accompanying the socially adequate change of workplaces within the group of the German Railways. Focussed concentration on customer requirements, comprehensive knowledge of the internal and external labour markets with a view to our European neighbours, acceptable concept solutions for personnel management as well as staff that is motivated for top performance are the prerequisites for the success of its realization.

DB Arbeit GmbH: Qualified, Flexible, Mobile, – We guarantee an engaged personnel marketing.

Our practically experienced branch managers and personnel disposal clerks offer an individual full-service provision to all companies: Ranging from pre-mediation, work placement, temporary work, qualifications fitting to demand and career planning of several months for staff's professional new orientation up to personnel management consulting – everything is possible.

DB Arbeit GmbH's performance on the market shows a continuous upsurge. We see this success above all as a result of the increase of market innovations and the nearness to our customers: Direct communication to our clients is of absolute priority. Partnership co-operations lead to a growth in order volumes and thus to a mutual business success. DB Arbeit GmbH will continue to follow this path with great commitment. ∎

DB Arbeit
Deutsche Bahn Gruppe

Geschäftsführer/Managing Director:
Heinrich Jürgen König
Dieter W. Noth

Personalmarketing/Personnel Marketing:
Ursula Ebert

Öffentlichkeitsarbeit/Public Relations:
Mathias C. Tank

Geschäftstätigkeit/Business Activity:
Vermarktung von Personalmarketing-Dienstleistungen, insbesondere Arbeitsvermittlung und Arbeitsüberlassung, Realisierung von Personalmarketing-Strategien und Konzepten
Provision of personnel marketing services particularly of employment agency and leasing, realization of personnel marketing strategies and concepts

Anschrift/Address:
Ruschestraße 104
D-10365 Berlin
Telefon +49 (30) 29 72 66 70
Telefax +49 (30) 29 72 61 02
E-Mail Ursula.Ebert@bku.db.de

Kontakte/Contacts:
Geschäftsstelle Dresden
Ammonstraße 8
D-01069 Dresden
Telefon +49 (351) 461 27 84
Telefax +49 (351) 461 27 80

Geschäftsstelle Chemnitz/Branch office Chemnitz
Bahnhofstraße 5
D-09111 Chemnitz
Telefon +49 (371) 493 32 41
Telefax +49 (371) 493 32 42

Industriegeschichte

Dresden, die Wiege vieler Innovationen – gestern, heute und in Zukunft

Dresden, the Cradle of many Innovations – yesterday, today and in future

Eine fast 800jährige wechselvolle Geschichte hat Dresden, die Landeshauptstadt des Freistaates Sachsen, geprägt. Nicht nur Künstler, sondern auch Ingenieure und Wissenschaftler haben die Stadt Dresden weltweit bekannt gemacht.

Die Verflechtung von Wissenschaft, Forschung, Entwicklung und Wirtschaft war für Dresden immer ein Schwerpunkt und wird auch zukünftig so bleiben. Dresden als Ort für die Entwicklung und Realisierung von Innovationen geht auf eine lange industrielle Tradition zurück. Innovationen und schöpferische Leistungen waren, sind und bleiben der Ausgangspunkt der Entwicklung zahlreicher bleibender Produkte und Verfahren.

Schon Anfang des 18. Jahrhunderts wurden in Dresden Pokale aus Kristallglas als ein Produkt der Dresdner Glashütte hergestellt, die um 1700 von Ehrenfried Walther Tschirnhaus, einem bedeutenden Gelehrten und Forscher, errichtet wurde. Die Qualität des Dresdner Kristallglases soll dem venezianischen ebenbürtig gewesen sein. Bereits 1697 stellte Tschirnhaus optische Linsen mit einem Durchmesser von mehr als einem Meter her.

Johann Friedrich Böttger fand 1708 in seinem Laboratorium auf der Brühlschen Terrasse statt Gold die Rezeptur für das weiße europäische Hartporzellan. Er begründete damit den weltweiten Ruf der sächsischen Porzellanmanufakturen, die noch heute als Synonym für einheimischen Kunstsinn und Handwerk gelten.

Im Jahr 1823 wurde die Schokoladenfabrik Jordan & Timaeus gegründet. Das war der Auftakt für die später weithin bedeutende Dresdner Genussmittelindustrie, die auch die Schweizer Milchschokolade, eine Dresdner Erfindung, hervorbrachte. Fünf Jahre zuvor, 1818, begann Adolf August Struve, Erfinder des künstlichen Mineralwassers, mit dem Aufbau seiner Mineralwasseranstalt in der Dresdner Seevorstadt. Eine Idee, die in ganz Europa Schule machte.

Seit dem Jahr 1839 war Friedrich Wilhelm Enzmann in Dresden einer der ersten industriellen Kamerahersteller der Welt. Weitere bedeutende Unternehmen der Fototechnik machten die Stadt zusammen mit herausragenden Fotografen zur Wiege der deutschen Fotoindustrie und zu einem Zentrum der Fotografie. In Dresden entstanden 1936 die ersten Kleinbild-Spiegelreflexkameras

Prof. Dr. rer. nat. Christian Wegerdt

Der Autor wurde 1935 in Dresden geboren. Von 1954 bis 1959 studierte er Eisenhüttenkunde in Berlin und Freiberg, promovierte 1964 am Institut für Metallkunde und Metallphysik der Bergakademie Freiberg, an der er 1990 zum Honorarprofessor berufen wurde. 1964 begann Christian Wegerdt seine Industrietätigkeit im Forschungsinstitut für Nichteisenmetalle Freiberg. Ab 1970 war er im Bergbau- und Hüttenkombinat Freiberg tätig, zuletzt als Direktor für Forschung und Technologie. 1990 wurde er Hauptgeschäftsführer des Instituts für Materialforschung und Anwendungstechnik und war von 1993 bis September 2000 als geschäftsführender Gesellschafter der daraus gebildeten IMA Materialforschung und Anwendungstechnik GmbH tätig. Christian Wegerdt ist seit 1992 Vorstandsvorsitzender des VERBAND INNOVATIVER UNTERNEHMEN E. V.

The author was born in 1935 in Dresden. From 1954 until 1959 he studied metallurgy of iron in Berlin and Freiberg, he attained his PhD in 1964 at the Institute of Metallurgy and Metal Physics of the Bergakademie Freiberg, where he was appointed honorary professor in 1990. In 1964, Christian Wegerdt started his activities at the Research Institute for Non-ferrous Metals Freiberg. From 1970 onwards, he worked in the Bergbau- und Hüttenkombinat Freiberg (mining and iron combinate), his last position there was that of Director of Research and Technology. In 1990, he became Main Managing Director of the Institute of Material Research and Application Technology and worked from 1993 until September 2000 as managing partner of the IMA Materialforschung und Anwendungstechnik GmbH that emerged from it. Christian Wegerdt has been Chairman of the Board of the VERBAND INNOVATIVER UNTERNEHMEN e. V. since 1992.

Originalgetreuer Nachbau der ersten deutschen Lokomotive „Saxonia".
True to the original reproduction of the first German locomotive "Saxonia".

Industrial History

Dresden, the regional capital of the Free State of Saxony, has been characterised by an almost 800-years long varied history. Not only artists, but also engineers and scientist have made the City of Dresden known worldwide.

The interrelation of science, research, development and economy has always been a focal point for Dresden and this will remain so also in future. Dresden as a place for the development and realisation of innovations can look back on a long industrial tradition. Innovations and creative achievements were and still are the starting point of the development of numerous lasting products and processes.

As early as in the beginning of the 18th Century, cups made of crystal glass were made in Dresden as a production of the glassworks Dresdener Glashütte, which had been founded by Ehrenfried Walther Tschirnhaus around 1700, a renowned scientist and researcher. The quality of the crystal glass of Dresden is said to have been equal to that of Venice.

Oben: Versuchsaufbau für Betriebsfestigkeitsuntersuchungen am Airbus A 340-600 in der IMA GmbH Dresden.
Links: Fertigung des düsenstrahlgetriebenen Verkehrsflugzeuges 152 im VEB Dresdner Flugzeugwerk im Jahr 1961.
Above: Test construction for the operational strength tests at the Airbus A 340-600 at IMA GmbH Dresden.
Left: Production of the jet-propelled transport plane 152 in the VEB Dresdener Flugzeugwerk in 1961.

Already in 1697, Tschirnhaus produced optical lenses of a diameter of more than one metre. Johann Friedrich Böttger found in 1708 in his laboratory on the Brühlsche Terrace instead of gold, the recipe for white European hard porcelain. Thus, he started the worldwide reputation of the Saxon porcelain manufactories, which are still today synonymous for indigenous artistic sense and handicraft.

In 1823, the chocolate factory Jordan & Timaeus was founded. This was the beginning of the later on widely renowned Dresden luxury food industry, which also brought about the Swiss milk chocolate, an invention made in Dresden. Five years before, in 1818, Adolf August Struve, inventor of the artificial mineral water, began constructing his mineral water plant in the suburb Seevorstadt of Dresden. An idea that found imitators all over Europe.

Since 1839, Friedrich Wilhelm Enzmann was one of the first industrial producers of cameras in the world in Dresden. Other important companies of photographic technology caused the city, together with excellent photographers, to be the cradle of the German photo industry and a centre of photography. In 1936, in Dresden the first candid reflex cameras of the world were produced. Also today, numerous innovative products of photography are produced in Dresden.

The first German locomotive comes from Dresden: The "Saxonia" was a work made by Professor Johann Andreas Schubert. In the year 1838, his locomotive embarked on first test journeys and in the following spring, Schubert himself drove the "Saxonia" to the inauguration of the first distance train line of Germany between Dresden and Leipzig. As early as 1837, Schubert also had designed the first steamboat on the Upper Elbe river, the "Königin Maria" (Queen Mary) and had it manufactured in Dresden. Even these innovations show the co-operation between science and the economic sector, since Schubert worked at one of the oldest technical education institutions of Germany, the predecessor of the Technical University of Dresden founded in 1828.

Karl August Lingner developed the first mouth water of the world "Odol" in 1893 in Dresden. Also other, today quite normal products are inventions made in Dresden: the toothpaste tube just as beer mats and filter cigarettes. As a symbol for the spirit of invention of Dresden are also the famous glass woman of the Dresden Hygiene Museum that already caused attention worldwide in 1930 and her "younger sister" – the virtual glass woman – that plays the violin in an 3-D-animation.

Thus, Dresden presented itself at the EXPO 2000 in Hanover with innovations and economic drive, with progressive initiatives and bold ideas.

From the beginnings of industrial manufacture during the baroque epoch, the branches typical for Dresden developed later in the 19th Century. In 1839, Friedrich Wilhelm Enzmann founded with

Industriegeschichte

Aqua Turbo Wasserkühler – Technik für die Umwelt aus dem Institut für Luft- und Kältetechnik Dresden.
The Aqua turbo Water cooler – Technology for the environment made by the Institute for Air Conditioning and Cooling Technology Dresden.

der Welt. Auch heute noch werden zahlreiche innovative Produkte der Fototechnik in Dresden produziert.

Die erste deutsche Lokomotive kommt aus Dresden: Die „Saxonia" war ein Werk von Professor Johann Andreas Schubert. Im Jahre 1838 unternahm seine Lokomotive erste Probefahrten und im darauf folgenden Frühjahr führte Schubert selbst die „Saxonia" zur Eröffnung der ersten Fernbahnlinie Deutschlands zwischen Dresden und Leipzig. Bereits 1837 hatte Schubert auch das erste Dampfschiff auf der Oberelbe, die „Königin Maria", entworfen und in Dresden herstellen lassen. Bereits diese Innovationen zeigen die Zusammenarbeit von Wissenschaft und Wirtschaft, denn Schubert war an einer der ältesten technischen Bildungseinrichtungen Deutschlands – der 1828 gegründeten Vorgängerin der Technischen Universität Dresden – tätig.

Das erste Mundwasser der Welt: „Odol" ist 1893 in Dresden von Karl August Lingner entwickelt worden. Auch andere, heute ganz alltägliche Produkte sind Dresdner Erfindungen: Die Zahnpastatube genauso wie Bierdeckel und Filterzigarette.

Symbolisch für den Dresdner Erfindergeist stehen auch die berühmte gläserne Frau aus dem Dresdner Hygiene Museum, die bereits 1930 für weltweites Aufsehen sorgte, und ihre „jüngere Schwester" – die virtuelle gläserne Frau –, die in einer 3-D-Animation Geige spielt. So präsentierte sich Dresden zur EXPO 2000 in Hannover mit Innovationen und Wirtschaftskraft, mit zukunftsweisenden Initiativen und kühnen Ideen.

Aus den Anfängen industrieller Fertigung während des Barocks entwickelten sich im 19. Jahrhundert die für Dresden später typischen Branchen. Im Jahre 1839 begründete Friedrich Wilhelm Enzmann mit seinen Kameras und Fotoplatten die optische Industrie in Dresden. Mit den Firmen Seidel & Naumann sowie Clemens Müller fasste die Näh- und Schreibmaschinenindustrie in der Stadt Fuß. Ebenso traditionsreich ist die Dresdner Nahrungs- und Genussmittelfertigung. Im Zusammenhang damit entstanden spezielle Zweige des Maschinenbaus, in denen Fertigungs- und Verpackungsmaschinen hergestellt wurden. Ludwig Gehe begründete die pharmazeutische Industrie in Dresden. Mit den Firmen Villeroy & Boch (Steingut) und der Glasfabrik Siemens entstanden die ersten Dresdner Großbetriebe.

Parallel zur wachsenden Konzentration und zunehmenden Internationalisierung in einigen der für Dresden wichtigen Industriezweigen bildeten sich am Anfang des 20. Jahrhunderts industrielle Innovationen und Reformbestrebungen heraus. Zahlreiche Innovationen dieser Zeit, die zu Weltneuheiten und traditionellen Markenartikeln führten, festigten den guten Ruf der Dresdner Schreibmaschinen, Fototechnik, elektrotechnischen Erzeugnisse und Verpackungsmaschinen. Obwohl z. B. im Jahr 1929 zehn Großbetriebe mit mehr als 1000 Beschäftigten existierten, wurde die außerordentliche Breite des Wirtschaftsprofils der Stadt ebenso von einer großen Zahl leistungsfähiger Klein- und Mittelbetriebe bestimmt.

1904 entwickelten Franz Joseph Koch und Karl August Sterzel in Dresden den ersten Ein-Megavolt-Prüftransformator Europas. Diese Tradition des Dresdner Elektromaschinenbaus, die in der Fabrik für Elektrotechnik Koch & Sterzel begründet wurde, wird heute im Sachsenwerk Dresden fortgesetzt.

Traditionell sind auch Innovationen in der Luftfahrt. So erfolgten Ende der fünfziger Jahre Entwicklung und Fertigung eines technisch innovativen düsenstrahlgetriebenen Verkehrsflugzeuges – der 152 – in den VEB Dresdner Flugzeugwerken, die 1961 ihre Produktion einstellen mussten.

Trotz der gesellschaftlichen Veränderungen nach 1945 wurden die meisten traditionellen Dresdner Industriezweige weitergeführt. Ausgangspunkt vieler Innovationen war bis 1989 die Technische Universität Dresden in Zusammenarbeit mit den großen Betrieben der Dresdner Industrietradition. Dazu zählten die Kombinate und Werke Starkstromanlagenbau, Transformatoren- und Röntgenwerk, Sachsenwerk (elektrische Maschinen), Elektromat, Schreibmaschinenwerk, Pentacon (Fototechnik), Mikromat, NAGEMA (Maschinen für die Nahrungs- und Genussmittelindustrie), Hochvakuum, Deutsche Möbelwerkstätten Hellerau, Messelektronik, Arzneimittelwerk sowie Luft- und Kältetechnik. Neben der elektrotechnischen Industrie waren in Dresden Ende der 80iger Jahre die Elektronik und die Mikroelektronik mit den Betrieben der Kombinate Carl-Zeiss Jena und Robotron strukturbestimmend.

Im Forschungsinstitut Manfred von Ardenne wurden in der DDR u. a. der Elektronenstrahl-Mehrkammerofen und der Plasmafeinstrahlbrenner entwickelt. Ardenne machte sich darüber hinaus in der Krebsforschung verdient, u. a. mit der Entwicklung der Krebs-Mehrschritt-Therapie.

In den zehn Jahren nach der Wiedervereinigung waren große Herausforderungen durch Wandel und Innovationen zu bewältigen. Kaum ein Unternehmen, eine Forschungseinrichtung, eine Familie, ein Ingenieur oder ein Wissenschaftler wurde von den gewaltigen gesellschaftlichen und wirtschaftlichen Umbrüchen verschont. Für Viele war es die Suche nach Neuem, was man nur ungenau oder noch gar nicht kannte. Nahezu drei Viertel aller Arbeitnehmer mussten ihren Arbeitsplatz wechseln, was einmalig in der Geschichte ist. Andererseits ergab sich durch diese

Gold- und Silberschmiede.
Gold and silver smiths.

Industrial History

his cameras and photo plates the optical industry in Dresden. With the companies Seidel & Naumann and Clemens Müller, the sewing and typewriter industry found a hold on the market. Just as rich in traditions is the Dresden food and luxury food production. In this relation special branches of machine construction emerged, which manufacture production and packaging machines. Ludwig Gehe founded the pharmaceutical industry in Dresden. With the companies Villeroy & Boch (stone goods) and the glass factory Siemens, the first large corporations of Dresden were created.

At the beginning of the 20th century, industrial innovations and reform attempts were made in some for Dresden very important industrial branches parallel to the growing concentration and increasing internationalisation. Numerous innovations of this time that led to world novelties

Folien-Sputteranlage FOSA 2150 zur Herstellung optischer Spezialfolien (Infrarot-Barriere) für die VSG-Autoverglasung der VON ARDENNE ANLAGENTECHNIK GmbH.
Foil-sputtering plant FOSA 2150 for the production of optical specialist foils (infrared barrier) for VSGcar glazing by VON-ARDENNE ANLAGENTECHNIK GmbH.

and traditional brand articles reinforced the good reputation of Dresden's typewriters, photographic technology, electro technical products and packaging machines. The extraordinary spectrum of the economic profile of the city was also shaped by a great number of efficient small and middle-size companies, although in 1929, for example, ten large corporations with more than 1,000 employees were active.

In 1904, Franz Joseph Koch and Karl August Sterzel developed in Dresden the first one-mega volt-test-transformer of Europe. This tradition of the Dresden electrical equipment construction, which was founded in the factory for electro technology Koch & Sterzel, is continued in the Sachsenwerk Dresden today.

Also of tradition are the innovations in the aviation industry. Thus, at the end of the fifties development and production of a technical innovative jet-propelled aircraft – the 152 – were carried out at the VEB Dresdner Flugzeugwerke, which was closed down in 1961.

Despite the social changes after 1945, most traditional industrial branches of Dresden were maintained. Starting point of many innovations were

until 1989 the Technical University of Dresden in co-operation with the large corporations of Dresden's industrial tradition. These included the combinates and works of high-voltage power plant construction, transformer and x-ray works, Sachsenwerk (electrical equipment), Elektromat, typewriter works, Pentacon (photographic technology), Mikromat, NAGEMA (machines for the food and luxury food industry), High-Vacuum, Deutsche Möbelwerkstätten Hellerau (German Furniture Works Hellerau), measuring electronics, pharmaceutical works as well as air conditioning and cooling technology. Apart from the electro technical industry, in the eighties, electronics and microelectronics with the companies of the combinates Carl-Zeiss Jena and Robotron were influential in determining the economic structure in Dresden.

At the research institute Manfred von Ardenne in the DDR, works developed include the electron beam multiple-chamber oven and the plasma fine-jet burner. Furthermore, Ardenne rendered outstanding services in cancer research, for example with the development of the multiple-step cancer therapy.

In the ten years after the unification, great challenges had to be coped with because of the change

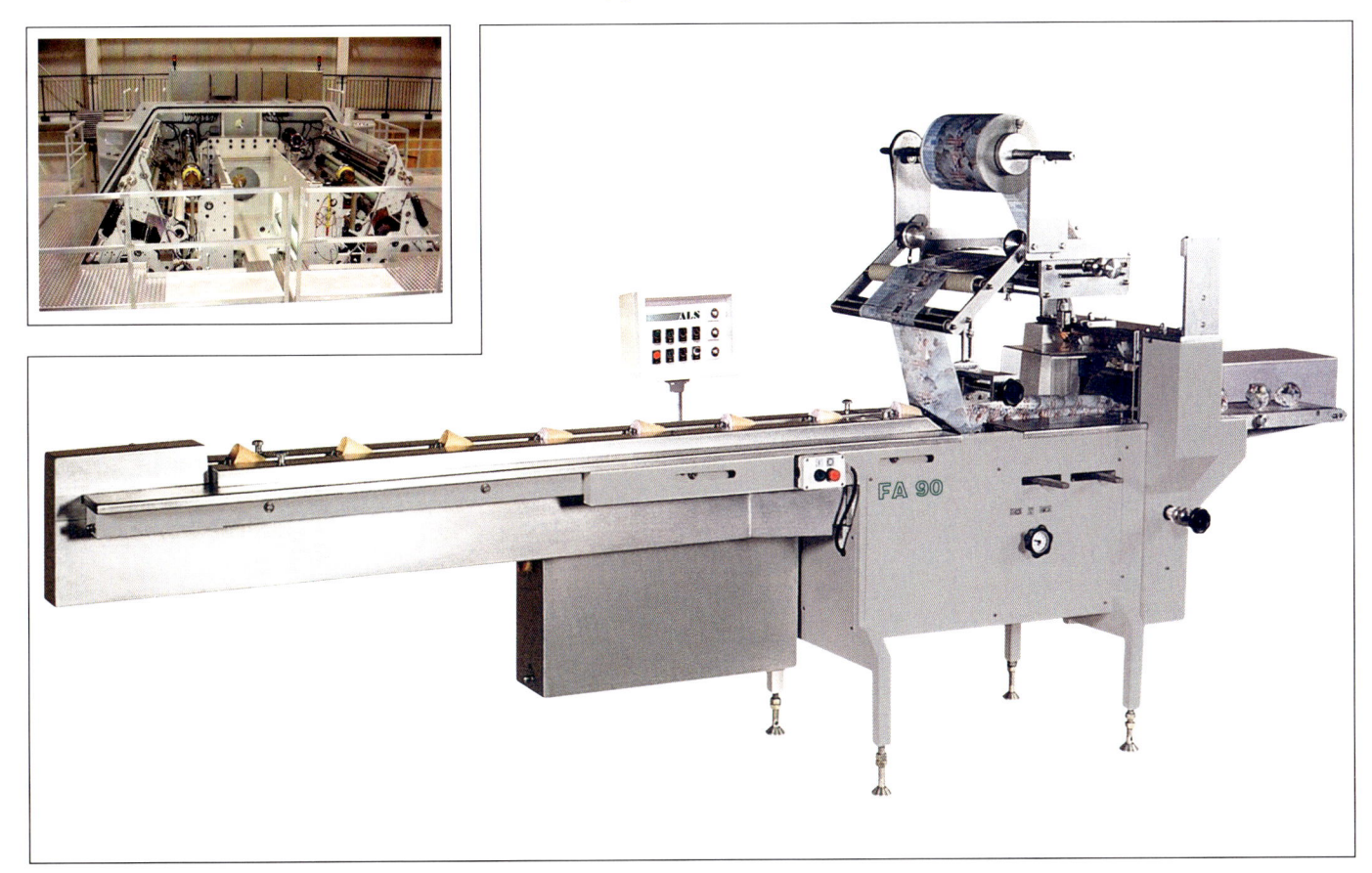

Verpackungsmaschine mit Beuteldichtheitsprüfsystem der IBN GmbH Dresden.
Packaging machine with bag leak test system made by IBN GmbH Dresden.

Industriegeschichte

Entwicklung auch für Dresden die Chance für neue zukunftsweisende industrielle und wissenschaftliche Strukturen sowie innovative Entwicklungen.

Einen entscheidenden Umbruch hat die Industrieforschung erfahren, die bis 1990 entsprechend der damaligen Wirtschaftsstrukturen – wie auch heute größtenteils in den alten Bundesländern – in den Kombinaten und Großbetrieben angesiedelt war. Diese, für die wirtschaftliche Entwicklung wesentlichen Innovationspotenziale, wurden auch in Dresden durch die Ausgliederung der Forschungs- und Entwicklungsbereiche aus den Kombinaten und Betrieben ohne Kapital und ohne Märkte sich selbst überlassen. Das führte durch die notwendige Bildung von privaten Einrichtungen und Unternehmen der externen Industrieforschung zu einem rasanten Abbau der Industrieforschungspotenziale auf etwa 20 Prozent im Jahr 1994. Der Rückgang der Industrieforschungspotenziale wurde auch mit Unterstützung des in Dresden ansässigen VERBAND INNOVATIVER UNTERNEHMEN E. V. gestoppt und hat sich seitdem auf geringem Niveau stabilisiert.

Die neugegründeten externen Industrieforschungseinrichtungen sind mit ihren Innovationspotenzialen für Dresden die Mittler zwischen Wissenschaft und Industrie sowohl im Bereich der Hochtechnologien als auch bei den traditionellen Dresdner Technologiebereichen. Sie sind die Träger des Know-how für den Wirtschaftsstandort Dresden, bilden die Keimzelle für viele wirtschaftsnahe Innovationen und haben sich zu Kristallisationspunkten für Unternehmensansiedlungen und für Unternehmensgründungen entwickelt. Außerdem sind diese privaten Industrieforschungseinrichtungen Innovationsmultiplikatoren

Blick auf Dresden.

Industrial History

and innovations. Almost no company, no research institution, no family, no engineer or scientist was left untouched by the tremendous social and economic transformations. For many this was the search for something new, something still vaguely known or even unknown altogether. Nearly three quarters of all employees had to change their workplaces, a unique situation in history. On the other hand, this development also brought about for Dresden the chance of the creation of new progressive industrial and scientific structures as well as innovative growth.

The sector of industrial research has experienced a significant change, which was organised corresponding to the former economic structures until 1990 – as also today mainly in the old West German provinces – and established in combinates and large corporations. These essential potentials of innovation important for economic development were left to themselves without capital and without markets through the outsourcing of research and development departments from combinates and companies. This led to an extreme reduction of the industrial research potential to around 20 percent in 1994, through the necessary creation of private institutions and companies of external industrial research. The reduction of the industrial research potential was also stopped by the support of the VERBAND INNOVATIVER UNTERNEHMEN E. V. (Association of Innovative Companies), located in Dresden and has since been on a stable low level. The newly founded external industrial research institutions act as mediators between science and industry both in the field of high technologies and in the traditional fields of technology of Dresden. They are the bearers of expertise for the economic location Dresden, form germ cells for

View on Dresden.

Industriegeschichte

sowohl für kleine und mittlere Unternehmen als auch für die Großindustrie.

Die IMA Materialforschung und Anwendungstechnik GmbH – hervorgegangen aus dem Institut für Leichtbau, einer Nachfolgeeinrichtung der Dresdner Flugzeugwerke – setzt heute die Tradition der Flugzeugprüfungen in Dresden fort. Die bisher größte Herausforderung für die Wissenschaftler und Techniker der IMA GmbH ist der Betriebsfestigkeitsversuch am Airbus A 340-600 – dem größten europäischen Verkehrsflugzeug. Diesen Prüfauftrag der EADS-Airbus GmbH erhielt die IABG mbH Ottobrunn gemeinsam mit der IMA Materialforschung und Anwendungstechnik GmbH aus Dresden im Herbst 1998 nach einem internationalen Auswahlverfahren gegen harte Konkurrenz. Ab 2001 wird die 90t schwere Teststruktur in der IMA-Versuchshalle am Dresdner Flughafen – in der bereits das Düsenstrahlflugzeug 152 geprüft wurde – einem 17 Monate dauernden dynamischen Belastungstest unterzogen.

Das ILK Institut für Luft- und Kältetechnik Dresden – eine Industrieforschungseinrichtung, die aus dem Forschungsbereich des Kombinates Luft- und Kältetechnik hervorgegangen ist – hat auf der Basis zahlreicher Innovationen ein Spitzenprodukt auf den Markt gebracht, das mit Wasser anstelle chemischer Kältemittel effektiv Kälte erzeugen kann. Der dazu notwendige Hightech-Turboverdichter entstand in Kooperation mit sächsischen Werkstoff- und Motorenspezialisten, denn die hochbelasteten Bauteile mussten alle neu entwickelt und erprobt werden. 1999 kam die erste Kälteanlage im Piloten-Trainingszentrum Luxemburg zum Einsatz, weitere folgten für die Universität Essen, die EXPO 2000 in Hannover, bei VW in der gläsernen Fabrik in Dresden und bei DaimlerChrysler in Düsseldorf. Damit hat dieses Dresdner Forschungsinstitut mit seinen 120 Mitarbeitern beispielhaft bewiesen, dass Innovationen Ausgangspunkt von wirtschaftlichem Wachstum und für die Schaffung neuer Arbeitsplätze sind.

Die Ideenschmiede des Kombinates Nagema findet nach der Wende in der Dresdner IBN Gesellschaft für industrielle Forschung und Technologie mbH ihre Fortsetzung. Die Ingenieure und Forscher der IBN haben mit ihren Innovationen die Dresdner Verpackungs- und Sondermaschinen wieder weltmarktfähig gemacht. Ein Beispiel ist das Beuteldichtheitsprüfsystem für Verpackungslinien. Durch die hohe Präzision der Maschine können Beutel mit geringstem Fehler erkannt und vom weiteren Prozess ausgeschlossen werden. Dieser Vorgang stellt ein äußerst schwieriges Verfahren dar, da neben dem Beutelmaterial auch die Menge des Füllstoffes Einfluss auf den Prüfprozess ausübt. Außerdem gewährleistet die große Flexibilität der Konstruktion eine schnelle Anpassung an vorhandene sowie neue Verpackungslinien.

Innovationen für die Zukunft zeigte das 1952 gegründete Institut für Holztechnologie Dresden (ihd) – ein Partner und Forschungsdienstleister für die mittelständische Holzindustrie und das Holzhandwerk – mit seinem weltweiten Projekt der

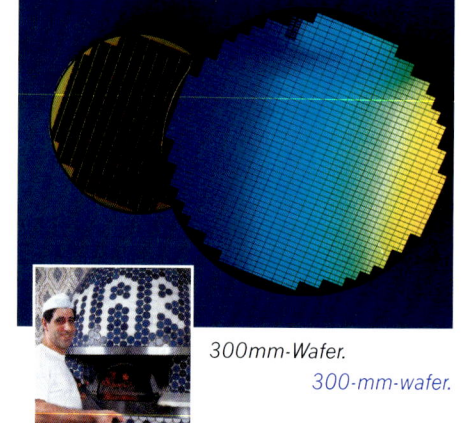

Variabel wohnen – Blick in den Wohnbereich mit geöffneten Trennwänden, EXPO 2000-Projekt des ihd Dresden.
Variable living – glance into the living quarters with open partition walls, EXPO 2000 project of ihd Dresden.

300mm-Wafer.
300-mm-wafer.

EXPO 2000 „Variabel Wohnen – Möbelvision 2020"
Mit vielfältigen innovativen Lösungen für die unterschiedlichsten Möbel und für die Wohnraumgestaltung hat das ihd mit Unterstützung vieler Partner aus Industrie und Handwerk eine Wohnung konzipiert, die das starke Bedürfnis der Menschen nach Veränderbarkeit und Variabilität berücksichtigt. Mittels verschiedenartiger variabler Trennwände kann die Wohnung entsprechend den Wünschen der Bewohner und den unterschiedlichen Situationen des Alltags angepasst werden.

Auf Basis ihrer industriewirksamen Innovationen hat sich die VON ARDENNE ANLAGENTECHNIK GMBH, 1991 von dem weltbekannten Dresdner Forschungsinstitut Manfred von Ardenne hervorgegangen, aus einer Industrieforschungseinrichtung zu einem umsatzstarken Unternehmen entwickelt, das den Ruf des Wirtschaftsstandorts Dresden heute in alle Welt trägt. Als Hightech-Ausrüster für kundenspezifische Vakuumprozesstechnik gehört dieses Unternehmen zu einem global agierenden elitären Kreis von Anbietern von Investitionsgütern für Photovoltaik, Displaytechnik, Großflächenbeschichtung von Architekturglas, Metall- und Kunststoffbänder, Keramikbeschichtung für Gasturbinenkomponenten, Nanotechnik, Mikrosystemtechnik und viele andere Applikationen, d. h. für hoch innovative Technikdisziplinen, die in der modernen Industriegesellschaft eine ständig steigende Rolle spielen. Eine aktuelle Innovation ist der Aufbau einer neuen Produktionsstätte zur Herstellung optischer Spezialfolien für die Autoverglasung gemeinsam mit dem amerikanischen Partner SOUTHWALL TECHNOLOGIES in einem Gewerbepark in der Nähe von Dresden. Die dafür benötigten Produktionsausrüstungen wurden komplett durch die VON ARDENNE ANLAGENTECHNIK GMBH entwickelt und bereitgestellt.

Dresden bietet die ideale Verbindung von Wirtschaft, Forschung und Wissenschaft: Neben der

Industrial History

many innovations practical to the economy and have evolved into centres of crystallization for company settlements and for company foundations. Furthermore, these private industrial research institutions are multipliers of innovation both for small and mid-sized companies and for the large industrial corporations.

The IMA Materialforschung und Anwendungstechnik GmbH – which emerged from the Institute for Light Constructions, a successor of the Dresden Aircraft Works – today continues the tradition of aircraft testing in Dresden. The hitherto greatest challenge for scientists and technicians of IMA GmbH is the operational strength test of the Airbus A 340-600 the largest transport plane of Europe. This testing contract of EADS-Airbus GmbH was assigned to IABG mbH Ottobrunn together with IMA Materialforschung und Anwendungstechnik GmbH of Dresden in autumn 1998 after an international selection procedure against strong competition. From 2001 on, the 90 t weighing test structure will be tested in the IMA test halls at the Dresden Airport – in which already the jet-propelled aircraft 152 was tested – in an 17 month long dynamic stress test.

The ILK Institut für Luft- und Kältetechnik Dresden – an industrial research institution, which emerged from the research department of the combinate for air conditioning and cooling technology – has launched a top product on the market on the basis of numerous innovations that is capable of producing cold with water instead of chemical cooling agents. The high-tech turbo-condenser was created in co-operation with materials and engine specialists of Saxony, because the highly stressed components all had to be newly developed and tested. In 1999, the first cooling plant was implemented in the pilot training centre Luxemburg, others followed at the University of Essen, the EXPO 2000 in Hanover, at VW in their glass factory in Dresden and at DaimlerChrysler in Düsseldorf. Thus, this research institute of Dresden with its 120 employees has proved exemplary that innovations are the starting point for economic growth and for the creation of new workplaces.

The workshop of ideas of the combinate Nagema found after the political change its continuation in the Dresden IBN Gesellschaft für industrielle Forschung und Technologie mbH (Society for Industrial Research and Technology). Engineers and researchers of IBN have rendered the Dresden packaging and specialist machines suitable for the world's markets again with their innovations. One example is the bag leak test-system for packaging lines. The high precision of this machine enables the detection of bags with minimal faults and their elimination of further processing. This process signifies an extremely difficult procedure, because apart from the bag material also the amount of the filling material influences the testing process. Furthermore, its great flexibility of the construction ensures a rapid adjustment to the existing as well as the new packaging lines.

The Institute für Holztechnologie Dresden/ihd (Institute of Timber Technology) founded in 1952 showed innovations for the future with its worldwide project at the EXPO 2000 "Variable Living – Furniture Vision 2020". With numerous innovative solutions for the most varied furniture and living room design, the ihd has conceptualised with the support of many partners of industry and skilled trades an apartment that takes account of the strong need of humans for changeability and variety. By means of different kinds of variable partition walls, the apartment may be adjusted according to the wishes of the resident and the most varied situations of daily life.

On the ground of its effective industrial innovations, the von Ardenne Anlagentechnik GmbH, which emerged in 1991 of the world renowned Dresden research institute Manfred-von-Ardenne, has evolved from an industrial research institute to a profitable company that carries the reputation of Dresden as an economic location into the whole world. This company is one among the elitist circle of globally active providers of investment goods, being a high-tech supplier of customer-specific vacuum process technology, especially for photovoltaic, display technology, large surface coating of architectural glass, metal and plastic bands, ceramic coating for gas turbine components, nano technology, micro system technology and many other applications, i. e. for highly innovative disciplines of technology that play a constantly increasing role in a modern industrial society. A current innovation is the building up of a new production hall for the manufacture of optical specialist foils for car glazing, together with its American partner Southwall Technologies in an industrial park near Dresden. The production equipment necessary for this project were developed and provided completely by von-Ardenne Anlagentechnik.

Dresden offers the ideal combination of economy, research and science: Apart from the technical University as well as higher institutes and polytechnics, numerous specialised companies and institutions of external industrial research, also numerous institutes including eight institutes of the Fraunhofer Society and three institutions of the Max-Planck Society speak for the innovative potential of the city. The institutional university

Hörsaal in der TU Dresden.

Lecturing hall in the TU Dresden.

Industriegeschichte

Deutsches Hygienemuseum Dresden.

Museum of Hygiene.

Technischen Universität sowie Hoch- und Fachschulen, den zahlreichen spezialisierten, privaten Unternehmen und Einrichtungen der externen Industrieforschung sprechen zahlreiche Institute, darunter acht Institute der Fraunhofer-Gesellschaft und drei Einrichtungen der Max-Planck-Gesellschaft, für das innovative Potenzial der Stadt. Die institutionellen universitären und außeruniversitären Forschungseinrichtungen haben sich auf hohem Niveau entwickelt und sind Ausgangspunkt einer Vielzahl von Innovationen insbesondere im Hightech-Bereich.

Mit der Infineon Technologies-Chipfabrik und dem Mikroprozessorenwerk Advanced Micro Devices (AMD), die sich insbesondere aufgrund der großen Innovationspotenziale und des ausgezeichneten Facharbeiterstammes in Dresden angesiedelt haben, sowie zahlreichen Zuliefer- und Service-Betrieben für diese großen, weltweit agierenden High-tech-Unternehmen entwickelt sich Dresden immer mehr zum modernsten Standort der Mikroelektronik in Europa. Das wird durch die Entwicklung der Herstellungs- und Bearbeitungstechnologie für die neue Generation von Wafern mit 300 mm Durchmesser nachdrücklich unterstrichen.

Das InnoRegio-Projekt „BioMeT – Innovationsnetzwerk Dresden" und das neue Max-Planck-Institut für „Molekulare Zellbiologie und Genetik" bedeuten noch mehr hochkarätige Forschung und Innovationen in Dresden. Damit wurde der Boden für künftige Ansiedlungen und neue innovative Unternehmen auf dem Gebiet der Biotechnologie – einem weiteren High-tech-Bereich – bereitet.

Eine wesentliche Grundlage für die künftige Sicherung des Innovationsstandortes Dresden sind eine große Anzahl hochmotivierter Arbeitskräfte mit Industrieerfahrung und Qualifikation für moderne Technologien, darunter über ein Viertel mit Hochschulabschluss. Daran wird sich auch in Zukunft nichts ändern, denn allein an der Technischen Universität studieren derzeit mehr als 24.000 junge Leute.

Innovationen von heute und in Zukunft werden kaum noch von Einzelpersonen geprägt, wie dies früher der Fall war. Aufgrund der Komplexität der Probleme und der starken Verflechtung der einzelnen wissenschaftlichen Fachgebiete werden Innovationen meist durch Team-Work bestimmt. Die Schnelllebigkeit der Zeit sowie die Schaffung und Sicherung von Arbeitsplätzen erfordern jedoch, dass die Innovationen kurzfristig in marktwirksame Produkte, Verfahren und Dienstleistungen umgesetzt werden.

Die Innovationen und Erfindungen in der modernen Industriegesellschaft entstehen vor allem dort, wo sich in interdisziplinärer Zusammenarbeit ein breites wissenschaftliches Potenzial und kreative Industrie finden. Dresden hat hier sehr gute Voraussetzungen und kann auf manches Beispiel innovativer Leistungen aus jüngster Vergangenheit verweisen: So entwickelt die TU Dresden 3D-Displays, stellen die Kamerawerke Noble eine einzigartige Panoramakamera her und werden in der Dresdner High-tech-Industrie Produkte gefertigt, die die Vision vom „Sächsischen Silicon Valley" greifbar machen.

Vielschichtige Innovationen waren und sind – wie die wenigen genannten Beispiele zeigen – die Basis der wirtschaftlichen Entwicklung in und um Dresden. Dresden ist mit seinen zahllosen Innovationen eine Stadt der Zukunft. Das wird auch vom Vertrauen der in Dresden angesiedelten Unternehmen wie Infineon Technologies, AMD, Volkswagen AG, Philip Morris, ABB, Heidelberger Zement, Gruner & Jahr oder die DaimlerChrysler Aerospace Airbus GmbH, um nur einige zu nennen, nachdrücklich unterstrichen. ■

Gewerbegebiet in Dresden-Gittersee.

Industrial area in Dresden-Gittersee.

Industrial History

Blick auf Schloss, Hofkirche und Semper-Oper (v. l. n. r).
View on castle, Hofkirche and opera (l. t. r.).

and extra-university research facilities have evolved on a high level and are the starting point of a number of innovations particularly in the high-tech area.

With the Infineon Technologies chip factory and the microprocessor work Advanced Micro Devices (AMD), which have settled in Dresden especially because of the great potential for innovations and the excellent expert staffing possibilities, as well as numerous supplier and service companies for these large worldwide active corporations, Dresden is developing more and more into the most modern location of microelectronics in Europe. This is highlighted particularly by the development of production and treatment technologies for the new generation of wafers of 300-mm diameter. The InnoRegio-Projekt "BioMeT – Innovationsnetzwerk Dresden" and the new Max-Planck Institute for "Molecular Cell Biology and Genetics" mean even more high-calibre research and innovations for Dresden. Thus, the conditions have been set for future settlements and new innovative companies on the field of biotechnology a further high-tech area.

An essential foundation for securing the innovation location Dresden in future is the great number of highly motivated employees with industrial experience and qualifications for modern technologies of which more than one quarter possess a university degree. This is not going to change even in future, since at the Technical University of Dresden alone presently more than 24,000 young people are studying.

Innovations of today and in future are hardly characterised by one individual person as it used to in the past. Because of the complexity of the problems and the strong interrelation between the single scientific subjects, innovations are mainly determined by teamwork. However, the fast-moving time as well as the creation and securing of workplaces require that innovations be applied on short-term in market effective products, procedures and services.

Innovations and inventions in a modern industrial society develop above all in such places where interdisciplinary co-operation finds a broad scientific potential and a creative industry. Dresden possesses the best prerequisites for this purpose and can boast of many examples of innovative achievements of the recent past: The TU Dresden, for example, develops 3D-displays, the camera factory Noble produces a unique panorama camera and products are made in the Dresden high-tech industry that enable the vision of "Saxon Silicon Valley" to take on concrete form. Innovations of multiple facets were and still are – as the few examples mentioned prove – the basis for economic development in and around Dresden. Dresden is with its numerous innovations a city of the future. This is also confirmed definitely by the confidence of the enterprises settled in Dresden like Infineon Technologies, AMD, Volkswagen AG, Philip Morris, ABB, Heidelberger Zement, Gruner & Jahr or the DaimlerChrysler Aerospace Airbus GmbH, just to name a few. ■

Postplatz.

Oben: Altmarkt um 1900. Unten: Altmarkt heute.
Above: Old Market around 1900, below: Old Market today.

The Postplatz square.

List of Companies

ALS Anlagentechnik und
SondermaschinenGmbH
Heidelberger Straße 12
D-01189 Dresden
Telefon +49 (351) 40 38-60
Telafax +49 (351) 40 38-688
Internet www.als-dresden.de   S. 83

American Microsystems GmbH
Bertolt-Brecht Allee 22
D-01309 Dresden
Telefon   +49 (351) 315 30 0
Telefax   +49 (351) 315 30 11
Internet   www.amis.com   S. 64

APOGEPHA Arzneimittel GmbH
Kyffhäuserstraße 27
D-01309 Dresden
Telefon +49 (0351) 33 63-3
Telefax +49 (0351) 33 63-440
Internet www.apogepha.de   S. 47

BIOCONSENS GmbH
biologische Wirkstoffe und Verfahren
Heidelberger Straße 12
D-01189 Dresden
Telefon +49 (351) 403 86-60
Telefax +49 (351) 403 86-66
Internet www.bioconsens.de   S. 83

DB Arbeit Deutsche Bahn Gruppe
Geschäftsstelle Dresden
Ammonstraße 8
D-01069 Dresden
Telefon +49 (351) 461 27 84
Telefax +49 (351) 461 27 80   S. 123

DELTEC electronic GmbH
Heidelberger Straße 18
D-01189 Dresden
Telefon +49 (351) 430 39-30
Telefax +49 (351) 430 39-33
Internet www.deltec.de   S. 45

Dresdner Bank AG Region Ost
Dresdner Bank AG in Dresden
Ostra-Allee 9
D-01067 Dresden
Telefon +49 (351) 489-0
Internet www.Dresdner-Bank.de   S. 34

DREWAG – Stadtwerke Dresden GmbH
Rosenstraße 32
D-01067 Dresden
Telefon +49 (351) 860-0
Telefax +49 (351) 860-45 45
Internet www.drewag.de   S. 28

FARU® Forschungsstelle für Analytik,
Recycling und Umwelttechnologie GmbH
Leipziger Straße 117
D-01127 Dresden
Telefon +49 (351) 841 02-0
Telefax +49 (351) 841 02-99
Internet www.faru-dresden.de   S. 122

Fraunhofer-Institut für
Integrierte Schaltungen
Angewandte Elektronik
Außenstelle Entwurfsautomatisierung
Zeunerstraße 38
D-01069 Dresden
Telefon   +49 (351) 46 40-701
Telefax   +49 (351) 46 40-703
Internet   www.eas.iis.fhg.de   S. 73

Fraunhofer-Institut
Keramische Technologien
und Sinterwerkstoffe IKTS
Winterbergstraße 28
D-01277 Dresden
Telefon +49 (351) 25 53-519
Telefax +49 (351) 25 53-600
E-Mail   info@ikts.fhg.de
Internet www.ikts.fhg.de   S. 35

Fraunhofer-Institut für Werkstoff-
und Strahltechnik (IWS) Dresden
Winterbergstraße 28
D-01277 Dresden
Telefon +49 (351) 25 83 324
Telefax +49 (351) 25 83 300
Internet www.iws.fhg.de   S. 85

Fraunhofer-Institut für
Elektronenstrahl- und Plasmatechnik (FEP)
Winterbergstraße 28
D-01277 Dresden
Telefon +49 (351) 25 86-0
Telefax +49 (351) 25 86-105
Internet www.fep.fhg.de   S. 72

Gesellschaft für Wissen- und Technologie-
transfer der TU Dresden GmbH
Chemnitzer Straße 48b
D-01187 Dresden
Telefon +49 (351) 463 17 20
Telefax +49 (351) 463 77 71   S. 75

Hochschule für
Technik und Wirtschaft Dresden (FH)
Friedrich-List-Platz 1
D-01069 Dresden
Telefon +49 (351) 462 31 02
Telefax +49 (351) 462 21 85
Internet www.htw-dresden.de   S. 60

IBN Gesellschaft für industrielle
Forschung und Technologie mbH
Heidelberger Straße 12
D-01189 Dresden
Telefon +49 (351) 40 38-60
Telefax +49 (351) 40 38-699
Internet www.ibn-dresden.de   S. 83

IFW Institut für Festkörper- und
Werkstofforschung Dresden
Helmholtzstraße 20
D-01069 Dresden
Telefon +49 (351) 46 59 380
Telefax +49 (351) 46 59 500
Internet www.ifw-dresden.de   S. 113

List of Companies

IMA Matrialforschung und
Anwendungstechnik GmbH
Hermann-Reichelt-Straße (am Flughafen)
D-01109 Dresden
Telefon +49 (351) 88 37-303
Telefax +49 (351) 880 43 13
Internet www.ima-dresden.de   S. 82

IMR In-Medias-Res
Gesellschaft für vernetzte Kommunikation mbH
Bismarkstraße 56
D-01257 Dresden
Internet www.in-medias-res.net   S. 84

Institut für ökologische Raumentwicklung e. V.
Weberplatz 1
D-01217 Dresden
Telefon +49 (351) 46 79-0
Telefax +49 (351) 46 79-212
Internet www.ioer.de   S. 103

Institut für Polymerforschung Dresden e. V.
Hohe Straße 6
D-01069 Dresden
Telefon +49 (351) 46 58-0
Telefax +49 (351) 46 58-284
Internet www.ipfdd.de   S. 74

IVG Holding AG
D-01109 Dresden
Telefon +49 (351) 88 557-0
Telefax +49 (351) 88 557-19
Internet www.micropolis.de   S. 31

KSW Microtec GmbH
Gostritzer Straße 63
D-01217 Dresden
Telefon +49 (351) 871 80-40
Telefax +49 (351) 871 84-11
Internet www.ksw-microtec.de   S. 65

materni visions
Maternistraße 17
D-01067 Dresden
Telefon +49 (351) 45 25 20
Telefax +49 (351) 45 25 299
Internet www.materni.de   S. 114

Max-Planck-Institut
für Molekulare Zellbiologie und Genetik
Pfotenhauerstraße 108
D-01307 Dresden
Telefon +49 (351) 311 78 98
Telefax +49 (351) 311 76 97
Internet www.mpi-cbg.de   S. 115

Max-Planck-Gesellschaft zur Förderung
der Wissenschaften e. V.
Max-Planck-Institut für Chemische Physik
fester Stoffe
Nöthnitzer Straße 40
D-01187 Dresden
Telefon +49 (351) 46 46-36 02
Telefax +49 (351) 46 46-10
Internet www.cpfs.mpg.de   S. 52

Max-Planck-Institut für
Physik komplexer Systeme
Nöthnitzer Straße 38
D-01187 Dresden
Telefon +49 (351) 871-0
Telefax +49 (351) 871-1999
Internet www.mpipks-dresden.mpg.de   S. 53

Metallbau Dresden GmbH
Niedersedlitzer Straße 60
D-01257 Dresden
Telefon +49 (351) 280 90
Telefax +49 (351) 280 91 03
Internet www.mbm-dresden.de   S. 100

MSD Maschinen- und Stahlbau Dresden NL
der Herrenknecht AG
Hofmühlenstraße 5–15
D-01187 Dresden
Telefon +49 (351) 42 34-0
Telefax +49 (351) 42 34-1 03
Internet www.msd-dresden.de   S. 93

Multimedia Software GmbH Dreden
Riesaer Straße 5
D-01129 Dresden
Hotline +49 (800) 667 83 26
Telefax +49 (351) 85 05-5 55
Internet www.mms-dresden.de   S. 112

Nehlsen Flugzeug-Galvanik
Dresden GmbH & Co. KG
Grenzstraße 2 (Halle 221)
D-01109 Dresden
Telefon +49 (351) 88 31 400
Telefax +49 (351) 88 31 404
Internet www.nehlsen-flugzeuggalvanik.de   S. 92

PACTEC Verpackungsmaschinen-
Fabrik Theegarten GmbH & Co. KG
Breitscheidstraße 46
D-01237 Dresden
Telefon +49 (351) 25 73-0
Telefax +49 (351) 25 73-329
Internet www.theegarten-pactec.de   S. 46

Polygraph KAMA GmbH
Kurt-Beyer-Straße 4
01237 Dresden
Telefon +49 (351) 270 36 0
Telefax +49 (351) 270 36 90
Internet www.polygraph-kama.de   S. 44

Test line electronics GmbH
Gostritzer Straße 61–63
D-01217 Dresden
Telefon +49 (351) 87 18-381
Telefax +49 (351) 87 18-453
Internet www.testline.de   S. 101

VacuTec Meßtechnik GmbH
Dornblüthstraße 14
D-01277 Dresden
Telefon +49 (351) 317 24-0
Telefax +49 (351) 310 50 85
Internet www.vacutec-gmbh.de   S. 102

Vakuumtechnik Dresden GmbH
Bismarckstraße 66
D-01257 Dresden
Telefon +49 (351) 28 05-0
Telefax +49 (351) 28 05 240
Internet www.vtd.de   S. 30

Impressum/Imprint

Wirtschafts- und Wissenschaftsstandort Dresden
Business- and Science Location Dresden

Verlag/Publishing House	EUROPÄISCHER WIRTSCHAFTS VERLAG GmbH
	Ein Unternehmen der MEDIEN GRUPPE KIRK HOLDING AG
	Groß-Gerauer Weg 1 in D-64295 Darmstadt
	Telefon (06151) 17 70-0
	Telefax (06151) 17 70-10
	LeoPro (06151) 17 70-48
	E-mail ewv@medien-gruppe.com
	Homepage www.medien-gruppe.com
Internet/Internet	www.ebn24.com
Herausgeber/Publisher	Christian Kirk ©
	in Zusammenarbeit mit der Stadt Dresden
Realisation/Production	Dieses Projekt wurde realisiert unter Mitarbeit der Autoren Dr. Kajo Schommer, Dr. Herbert Wagner, Rolf Wolgast, Dr. Werner Mankel, Dr. Peter Kücher, Dr. Bertram Dressel, Alfred Post, Werner Ulrich, Bernd Rendle, Volkmar Stein, Wolfgang Wirz, Yvonne Kubitza, Christoph Münch, Prof. Dr. rer. nat. Christian Wegerdt, Christiana Weber M. A. (Schlussredaktion) sowie in der Organisation Paul-Peter van Rossum, Danilo Erl, Judith Nießner, Immacolata Rametti, Monika Burger und Birgit Monßen
Gesamtherstellung/Collect-run Production	MEDIA TEAM Gesellschaft für Kommunikation mbH
Chefredaktion/Editor-in-Chief	Heinz-Dieter Krage
Produktionsleitung/Production Manager	Mirko Emde
Grafik & Satz/Graphics & Typesetting	Kerstin Rutscher, Steffi Sauermann-Schliebs, Martin Müller, Eva-Maria Prinz
Verantwortliche Übersetzerin/Responsible for translation	Asma Esmeralda Portales
Bildnachweis/Picture credits	Autoren der Artikel, portraitierte Unternehmen, Broschüre „Dresden – Europäische Stadt", Stadtplanungsamt Dresden, Czerny, Foto-Atelier Diebel, Doering/AMD, Rolf Grosser, Atelier Rolf Günther, Dresden, Frank Höhler, Marco Klinger, Michael Lange Fotodesign, BDG, Christoph Münch, Fotografie Jürgen von Oheimb, Dresden, Volkswagen AG, Friedrich Weimer – angewandte Fotografie, Foto-Studio-Wolff, Fotoagentur Zentralbild GmbH, Berlin
EBV, Computer to Plate	digitaltype GmbH, Darmstadt
Druck/Printers	Eduard Roether GmbH, Darmstadt
Papier/Paper	Rhein-Main-Papier GmbH & Co.KG, Bochum, Senden, Darmstadt. Papiersorte: Volley®Silk matt, 135 gr/m^2
Umsetzung für Internet/Internet implementation	IMR InMediasRes GmbH, Darmstadt
Vervielfältigung & Nachdruck/Reproduction & reprints	Alle Rechte vorbehalten. Kein Teil dieses Buches darf ohne schriftliche Genehmigung des Verlages vervielfältigt oder verarbeitet werden. Unter dieses Verbot fällt insbesondere die gewerbliche Vervielfältigung per Kopie, die Aufnahme ins Internet bzw. andere elektronische Datenbanken und die Vervielfältigung auf CD. Verstöße werden rechtlich verfolgt. Redaktionsschluss: 18. Mai 2001
ISBN/ISBN	3-932845-66-8, Ausgabe 2001/2002